LOVE
IN THE
DRIEST SEASON

Photograph by Jon Jones

LOVE
IN THE
DRIEST SEASON

A Family Memoir

NEELY TUCKER

CROWN PUBLISHERS
NEW YORK

Grateful acknowledgment is made to Oliver Mtukudzi for permission
to reprint song lyrics from *Mabasa* by Oliver Mtukudzi. Reprinted by
permission of Tuku Music, Ltd. on behalf of Oliver Mtukudzi.

Published by Crown Publishers, New York, New York.
Member of the Crown Publishing Group, a division of Random House, Inc.
www.crownpublishing.com

CROWN is a trademark and the Crown colophon is a registered trademark
of Random House, Inc.

Printed in the United States of America

Design by Lauren Dong

Library of Congress Cataloging-in-Publication Data

Tucker, Neely.
Love in the driest season : a family memoir / Neely Tucker.
1. Intercountry adoption—United States—Case studies.
2. Intercountry adoption—Zimbabwe—Case studies.   3. Abandoned
children—Zimbabwe—Case studies.   I. Title.
HV875.5 .T83 2003
362.73'4'096891—dc21   2002154095

ISBN 0-609-60976-9

First Edition

For Chipo, who lived.

And

In memory of
Tatenda Jeselant, Godfrey Muparutsa, Shingirai
Nyamayaro, Munashe Tsekete, Memory Chinyanga,
Joe Bhebhe, Frasia Chateuka, Ashley Mhlanga,
Caroline Razo, Collins Murehwa, Clara Mlambo,
Sandra Mahohoma, Rejoice Neshuro, Nyasha Dziva,
Abigail Mazviona, Tadiwanashe Mtero,
Sarah Chiwasa, Mable Kachembere, Ibrahim Hodzic,
Margaret Wanjiru Kangi Mungai,
and
Robert and Ferai,
who did not.

Nothing lives forever but / the love
that bears your name.

—CASSANDRA WILSON,
Solomon Sang

>>

Something happened to me inside the orphanages.

—JAMES NACHTWEY,
Inferno

CONTENTS

LOVE
IN THE
DRIEST SEASON

PROLOGUE

B Y NOON, the ants found the girl-child.

Left to die on the day she was born, she had been placed in the tall brown grass that covers the highlands of Zimbabwe in the dry season, when the sun burns for days on end and rain is a rumor that will not come true for many months. She had been abandoned in the thin shade of an acacia tree, according to the only theory of events police ever put forth. There were no clues as to exactly when she was left there, or why, or how, or by whom. She just appeared one day, like Moses in the bulrushes.

Patches of dried blood and placenta streaked her body. Her umbilical cord was still attached, a bloody stump dangling from the navel. A colorful yank of fabric, such as might be found in a store that sold such things by the yard, was wrapped around her torso.

Dozens of miles from any paved motorway, and nearly a mile from the nearest village of mud-and-thatch huts, she lay hidden in chest-high grass. The ragged clumps of acacia reached overhead. In the first glow of day, when night was fading but the sun had yet to climb above the horizon, it was a place of shadows and limited vision.

The ants came from everywhere.

They set upon the blood and the remnants of the placental

sac. Dozens, if not hundreds, poured over the fleshy stump of the umbilical cord. They began to eat her right ear.

The girl-child screamed.

The sun rose in the sky.

The hours passed.

There is a wind that moves through the high grass at that time of year. It makes a whisper of its own, a feathery undertone that rolls over the landscape and drifts through the trees. Some people from the village who were walking along the footpaths thought they heard a child's cries above the rustling, but no one stopped. There are many portents the ancestral spirits sometimes use to communicate with the living, and the mysterious, disembodied voice of a child on the upper reaches of the breeze carried an ominous sense of foreboding. The women kept walking, making for a concrete-block country store several miles away. They went there for sugar and salt and dry goods. Men went for the fat brown plastic jugs of traditional beer that smelled sour and left seeds between the teeth, but which carried a haze that melted the corners of the afternoon.

Late in the day, the sun fading away to the west, a woman named Constance paused on the path. She listened above the breeze. She waded into the grass, parting it with her hands, stopping, listening again. She moved to the clump of acacias. What she saw sent her stumbling backward, and then she turned and ran for the village. She found Herbert, the village elder, and dragged him back by the sleeve.

He moved into the grass, reached under the branches, and picked up the wailing infant. Then he sent a young man running for help.

"She was very dirty; there was dust all over her, her face. And the ants were running over her head, really biting into her ear," he would later say. "She was crying, crying. Eh-eh! Crying all the time. I picked the ants off her. We brushed the dust from her, though we could not get her clean."

In the time of AIDS in southern Africa, adrift on the tide of the deadliest disease to wash over humanity since the bubonic plague, the child who would change my life hung on to Herbert like a survivor from a shipwreck. She was one of an estimated ten million African orphans whose lives in the waning days of the twentieth century had been altered, if not devastated, by the AIDS epidemic. By the winter Herbert held her aloft in the late afternoon sunlight, Zimbabwe had become ground zero of a worldwide crisis. About one in four Zimbabweans between the ages of twenty-five and forty-four was thought to be HIV-positive, the highest rate in the world, along with next-door Botswana. The government and various United Nations agencies estimated that five hundred people were dying of the disease each week, a fatality every twenty minutes, twenty-four hours a day, seven days a week. Newspaper obituary columns were filled with memorials to young people who died after a short illness, a long illness, a sudden illness. The morgue in Harare, the Zimbabwean capital, began to stay open all night.

And still the bodies came.

No one knows exactly how many, for few of the dying ever knew or admitted to having the disease. Most, in fact, had never been tested. But the death toll was nearly some six hundred thousand since the disease was first recognized in the early 1980s. Zimbabwe's average life span plummeted from fifty-six years to thirty-eight, one of only five countries in the world to have a life expectancy of less than forty.

Young parents died in the tens of thousands, giving rise to a corresponding tide of orphans. There were perhaps 200,000 in 1994. Four years later, in a nation of 11 million, there was a flood of 543,000 children who had lost either their mother or both parents. This overwhelmed the traditional African social welfare net, the extended family. Zimbabwean uncles and aunts, grandparents, and cousins came forward in astounding numbers, but too many young parents had died. By the winter of 1998, children were being abandoned in record numbers across the country and the region. In Lusaka, the capital of neighboring Zambia, there had been an estimated thirty-five thousand street children in 1991. By 1998, there were more than seventy-five thousand and the number was climbing. In a remote province of Zimbabwe, Herbert was holding one of dozens of infants who had been flung into garbage bins, slipped into sewers, or left behind in open fields in a six-month period in that province alone. It was anyone's guess how many had been abandoned in the entire country.

The scale of death, and the depths of misery it entailed, defied the imagination even for someone like me, who had chronicled some of the world's deadliest conflicts for the better part of a decade. Before joining the *Washington Post*, I was a foreign correspondent for the *Detroit Free Press*, first assigned to a roving post based in Eastern Europe in 1993, then to sub-Saharan Africa in 1997, based in the Zimbabwean capital of Harare. I roamed more than fifty countries or territories in seven years, from Bosnia to Sierra Leone to Congo to Iraq to Rwanda to Nagorno-Karabakh to southern Lebanon to the Gaza Strip, a steady parade of greater- and lesser-known wars, riots, and rebellions. As the body counts multiplied, I tried to ignore the physical, mental, and emotional toll such work had begun to exact from me. My body had been riddled by typhus, food poisoning, and repeated viral infections; my hair turned completely white. The steady stream of violence had worn away my natural sense of compassion to the point where I could cover almost any horror but felt very little about anything at all. Sleep was either a blessed blank space or a disturbing hallway of nightmares. I woke up one morning to discover I had lost my religious faith, as if it were a suitcase left behind in a distant airport.

On the rare occasions I was home in Harare, my wife, Vita, and I began to volunteer at Chinyaradzo Children's Home, an orphanage set in an industrial slum on the south end of town. We could have no children of our own, a peculiar form of emptiness, and were touched by the fate of children who had no parents. In any event, we did what we could, and mostly that wasn't much. Thirty-five infants died in twenty-four months. Tatenda. Godfrey. Ferai. Robert. Caroline. Clara. A little girl with the sweetest name of Rejoice. They withered and died like flowers in the field. It is difficult to express the sorrow of such a thing. I witnessed all manner of death and human cruelty in my years as a foreign correspondent. I never learned to describe what it is like to see dead children in your dreams.

So in the final years of the century, with Zimbabwe falling into political and economic collapse, we began to devote a good deal of our time and resources to the orphanage as a means of becoming personally engaged in the despair sweeping the nation. Vita eventually got a $7,000 grant from the U.S. embassy, a fortune in local terms, in an effort to slow the mortality rate. We refurbished the kitchen and changing room, bought boxes of sanitary supplies, and brought in the nation's best pediatric cardiologist to train the staff, yet it was like plugging a dike with a finger. Zimbabwe was spending the equivalent of twelve cents per day to feed, clothe, house, treat, and educate each orphan, a hopelessly small sum against the ravages of malnutrition, diarrhea, dehydration, and AIDS.

In that miserable season, lost among the many in the orphanage, lay the girl-child Constance and Herbert discovered. She had fallen ill almost the day she was admitted. Her tiny stomach was bloated and distended, her arms and legs withered. She developed pneumonia. She could scarcely hold her milk. She had never smiled. Her weight dropped below four pounds, three ounces.

And still she wasted away.

There are moments in life, no more than two or three, when everything changes and you find yourself swept along in a series of events that are beyond your measure. And so it was that I picked up the girl-child one day in an orphanage at the epicenter of the world's AIDS crisis, in a country where foreign journalists, including myself, would shortly be declared to be enemies of the state. She regarded me with worried eyes and a whimper, and then she closed her left hand around my little finger.

Within ninety-six hours, she would come to mean everything to my wife and me, since she became, for as long as she should live, our only child.

1

PEOPLE LIKE US

HE BUREAUCRAT was not a happy man, and it didn't take long to understand that I was the source of his irritation. Richard Tambadini was a senior officer in Zimbabwe's Department of Immigration Control. In May 1997, in a drab office in a dreary government building known as Liquenda House, he looked over my papers. He was slow, careful of speech, and so disdainful he seldom looked up.

"You have sent your belongings here ahead of yourself," he said, sounding as if he were reading from an indictment. "You presume that we will give you a work permit. You think little black Zimbabwe needs big white American men like you."

He paused and looked out the window at downtown Harare. A car alarm was going off on the street below, the repeated bleating of its horn drifting above the sound of mid-morning traffic.

I shifted in my hard-back chair. This was becoming embarrassing. Vita and I had packed up our belongings from our previous posting in Warsaw, Poland, a few weeks earlier. The crate had to be trucked to Gdansk, wait for a ship, then be carried across the Baltic Sea down to Amsterdam, transferred to another cargo ship, then sailed down the coast of Europe, the entire West African coast, around the southern tip of Cape Town, and on to the South African port of Durban. Then it had to be transferred to a rail car and hauled to Zimbabwe.

The shipping clerk had said eight weeks at best; perhaps three or four months. My predecessor in Harare had assured me that the Zimbabwean government would issue my work permit as a foreign correspondent long before then.

The crate made it in three weeks.

Now I was in Harare, trying to explain to Tambadini why this unexpected delivery did not constitute an act of ugly American hubris.

"Mr. Tambadini," I said in an attempt to lighten the situation, "I'm five foot seven inches, and I don't think anybody has ever said I tried to act like a big—"

"We have just met, Mr. Tucker, and yet I know your kind very well," he cut me off, looking at his fingernails. "You come from America, a country that disparages black people. You are a rich man. You come here, you see poor little Zimbabwe, where even the people who administer the government are black, and you have assumed that we need you. You think we are so grateful to have you among us that you think we will exempt you from our laws. It is the way of the white man in Africa." His tone had changed to an icy disdain.

"So we have a system for people like you. We impound your goods in customs until you are approved, at the rate of a hundred U.S. dollars per day. If we decide to approve your application—and this could take months—then you will pay us and you may receive your goods. But you will pay us, Mr. Tucker, for your arrogance."

He was making a speech, and I got the idea it wasn't the first time, but I was still disconcerted. His insistence on characterizing a routine transit mix-up as a deliberate racial slight was unsettling, and the idea that I was a rich man might have been amusing in another context. But telling my editors they were about to be fined several thousand dollars was not a prospect I relished. So I took a deep breath and ate humble pie.

"Sir, if my company or I have made assumptions, I am terribly sorry, but they are not the assumptions you say. My paper, the *Detroit Free Press*, has been here seventeen years, the longest of any American media company. We have been in Zimbabwe since independence, since black Zimbabweans seized control of their own country. When every other American newspaper left to go to South Africa after apartheid, my newspaper stayed here, in a country that is ninety-nine percent black. The city I report for is the most predominantly black metropolis in America. It is seventy-five percent black. The managing editor of my newspaper, the man who sent me here, is a black American. The black lady waiting in the hallway, the one with the dreadlocks and the blue dress, is my wife. If my paper, my predecessor, or I thought it was necessary for me to come here to apply for a work permit months ago, I would have done so. It is unfortunate this shipment has arrived so quickly. But it is not for the reasons you suggest."

Tambadini looked out the window. "Perhaps," he said, and waved a hand, dismissing me. Two days later, the work permit was approved. But I would remember that little encounter in the years ahead, a warning light going off before I even knew to look for one.

THE RACIAL CONFRONTATION of that morning was more a tired refrain than a new angry incantation for me, for race had been the defining issue of my life. I did not grow up learning of Tambadini's home country, a small nation in southeastern Africa that was then known as Rhodesia, but my homeland in the Deep South was mired in an oddly parallel racial struggle. In the 1960s, when blacks in Zimbabwe were fighting for independence from a white colonial regime, black people in the American South were fighting for their rights. The reaction of white Rhodesians and white southerners, particularly in my home state of Mississippi, was just about the same. For a while, for the few who noticed, the two struggles seemed to play in syncopation.

A year or two before Rhodesian prime minister Ian Smith declared in 1965 that whites would rule Rhodesia for one thousand years, George Wallace in Alabama had bellowed: "I draw the line in the dust and I say . . . segregation now, segregation tomorrow, segregation forever!" in his gubernatorial inauguration speech. Martin Luther King Jr. published "Letter from Birmingham Jail" the same year an African nationalist and schoolteacher named Robert Mugabe was jailed in Zimbabwe. When Smith was using the Selous Scouts to terrorize blacks, the Ku Klux Klan was burning crosses across Mississippi. One night, they staged cross burnings in sixty-four of Mississippi's eighty-two counties, just to show they ran the place. A man named Byron De La Beckwith shot Medgar Evers in the back; mobs of young white men beat marchers, activists, and the Freedom Riders. In one of the most notorious incidents of the era, Klansmen killed three civil rights workers—"two Jews and a nigger," in local parlance—outside of Philadelphia, Mississippi.

While Rhodesia was hit with sanctions by the United Nations and became an international pariah, it was Mississippi that most horrified Americans. Nina Simone didn't sing "Georgia Goddam," Anne Moody didn't write *Coming of Age in Alabama*, and later the movie wasn't called *Louisiana Burning*. It was we, in rural white Mississippi, who seemed to insist on becoming the South's symbolic heart of darkness.

It was in this season of segregation and despair that I was born in Holmes County, the poorest, most predominantly black county in the poorest, most predominantly black state in America. The land straddled the low-slung hills of central Mississippi and the fertile edge of the Delta, a place where three of every four faces were black, a place so impoverished and forlorn that it sometimes seemed only the soil was rich. Stands of pine trees mixed among the muddy creeks and towering oaks and then the land sloped away, down a kudzu-covered place called Valley Hill, the last incline for more than a hundred miles. The Delta's flat fields stretched into the distance, a vast plain of black dirt and stagnant backwaters that ran all the way to the levee and the broad brown river, the ever-rolling Father of Waters, that gave the state its name. On a slate-gray afternoon in November—rain falling in a steady drizzle on the endless rows of picked-over cotton stalks and the trailers left by the side of the road and the sleepy wooden churches and the graveyards of the faithful and the tin-roofed barns and the shotgun shacks—it was a place that soaked into the marrow of the bones and pooled there, never to leave.

We lived in Lexington, a community of about two thousand, and later outside the larger town of Starkville, eighty miles east, where we raised sheep and cows. My father, Duane, was the local assistant county agent working his way up in the Cooperative Extension Service, a state and federal agency that helped farmers with crop and livestock problems. My mother, Elizabeth, whom everyone called Betty, played piano or organ in the Southern Baptist church. My older brother, Duane junior, whom everyone called Shane, and I would sometimes tag along with my father in his pickup truck as he went from farm to farm, turning from the narrow paved highways to gravel roads, the long trails of red and brown dust swirling out behind us.

Late at night on our small farm, I would curl beneath my sheets to listen to the train whistle blow for the clearing. I would sneak outside and watch it pass in front of our house in the moonlight. I stood in the yard, dew soaking my feet, and looked up past the oaks and pines to the stars above, feeling the earth rumble with the train's passing. I loved the place at such moments, I truly did. The sway of the trees and the whisper of the wind created a language all their own, and the night seemed warm and beautiful and secret.

On the long summer days and endless evenings, on rainy winter afternoons, with nowhere to go and not much to do, I began to lose myself in books and stories, imagining a world far from our sleepy pastures. I would start turning the pages and our house would fade away, replaced by another world that came from nowhere. Before I was thirteen, I read *Treasure Island* and *Huck Finn* and all of the Hardy Boys books and the Old Testament (when I was bored in church, which little boys often are) and *Lord of the Rings* and things that were way over my head, including Ernest Hemingway and *Papillon*, the memoirs of Henri Charrière, a French inmate who escaped from Devil's Island.

Those worlds seemed as real and important as anything going on in our little town—and a lot more exciting. I longed not just to watch the train go by our house, but to catch an armload of the next freight train running and ride it out of there, traveling to some of the places I read about. Then I would go sit on the railroad tracks and wonder what the real fairy tale was. For at least 150 years, with the exception of one or two great-aunts, everyone in my family had been a farmer in rural Mississippi.

But an era was coming to an end, and even the Magnolia State's "closed society," as one landmark book described it, was finally opening itself to the larger world. As the calendar pages fell and the years turned into the late 1970s, the Deep South's more vicious forms of racism began to ebb. The racial confrontations that roiled the country moved to the urban North. With the civil rights crusades fading into memory, with southern apartheid at least officially dismantled, small-town black and white teenagers in Mississippi began to try something none of our ancestors had—to grow up together. It was painful, it was odd, and sometimes it was surreal.

The most bizarre example of the latter could be found on the college football field, the Deep South's Saturday afternoon altar. In the 1970s, the University of Mississippi's football team was integrated, but the school still proudly went by the nickname of "Ole Miss" (the phrase slaves used for the plantation owner's wife in the antebellum days—as opposed to his daughter, who would be the "young miss"). The school's teams were called the Rebels, a reference to Confederate soldiers. That moniker, selected in the 1930s, came into play when the student body's other popular choice of the era, the Ole Massas (as in the slaves' name for the plantation owner), proved to be something of a tongue twister: the Ole Miss Ole Massas.

Nearly half a century later, a football game in Oxford looked like this: A black descendant of slaves with "Ole Miss" written on his helmet would score a touchdown for the Rebels.

The lily-white school band would burst into "Dixie," the battle song of the Confederacy. Thirty thousand white fans would start waving the red and blue Confederate banner, the battle flag beloved by the Ku Klux Klan. And nobody acted like we all needed to be committed.

It could be profoundly weird off the field too. My family and our kind didn't care for Ole Miss (we were Mississippi State fans, a far more blue-collar crowd that rang cowbells after touchdowns), but in elementary and high school my parents scraped together the dollars to send me to one of the "private" all-white academies set up after integration, the last-ditch creation of the White Citizens' Councils. The irony was in the music we played at our all-white homecoming dance: Earth, Wind and Fire; Kool and the Gang; Rick James; the Gap Band. The most popular comedian, with no one in second place, was Richard Pryor. When I took to the football field on Friday nights, I wore a bandana under my helmet, like J. C. Watts, the star Oklahoma quarterback, and a pair of wristbands emblazoned with number 22, which I had cadged from my hero, a Mississippi State wingback named Danny Knight. Watts and Knight were black, I idolized them both, and neither could have come to see me play because the only black person allowed on our school grounds was the janitor.

After school, I worked in a grocery store called Market Basket, stocking shelves and carting out groceries, and it was one such working afternoon that finally opened my eyes and ended my youthful career as someone who tossed off racial epithets. I was stocking shelves with a guy named Theron Lawrence, a student at the public high school. Theron was black, older, and infinitely cooler than I had any hope of being. We decided to get a Coke, punch out on the time clock, and take one of our allotted fifteen-minute breaks. It turned out we had both seen the horror movie *Alien* the previous weekend. We were doing what teenage guys do, talking it up, laughing, retelling the scary stuff, when I brought up the part in which actor Yaphet Kotto slugged the creature.

"Boy, did the nigger knock the shit outta 'im or *what*?" I chortled.

Theron's laughter stopped.

I was aghast. You were supposed to use the N word only among white people. Jesus, but I knew that. Theron looked down for a minute, then glanced up at the clock. "Looks like break time about through," he said, standing, and then he was gone.

Sitting in that chair, my blue store apron on and a stupid look on my face, I think I understood for the first time that the word I used had said nothing about Theron, about the actor, or even about black people in general. It said boatloads, however, about me. And I didn't like what that said at all, because I liked Theron. I thought of him as my friend. I liked bagging groceries for Mary Banks, the store's chief clerk. She was funny, warm, and personable in the way that southern women are. She called me "honey" or "sugar" (pronounced "shugah"). And yet she was black, and that meant a whole raft of things that existed in a universe parallel to my own, none of which I was supposed to consider good or admirable.

When I put down my adventure stories and started reading about my home state, books by William Faulkner and Richard Wright and Eudora Welty and Willie Morris, I began to get a sense of where I was. It would eventually form one of the central lessons of my personal and professional life: I had been raised in the heart of the most racist state in America, and as a child, I had accepted the perverse as normal. This is not a happy thing to learn about yourself or about the place where you grow up.

So while Mississippi was changing, I was too, and in ways I couldn't always name. The small-town lethargy, the religious hypocrisy, the racial chasms and complaints, the numbing poverty—all of this was home, and it came to weigh on me a great deal. I began to drive my beat-up car around late at night, down little country highways and dirt roads and back down shuttered Main Street, and nothing had changed except the night was an hour older, and I would wonder if I was ever going to go anywhere or do anything.

But fate is sometimes kind, and I had the good fortune to meet Willie Morris, the famous Mississippi author, at a college baseball game. He was the first person I ever met who wrote books for a living, and he had made a career for himself far outside the state's borders. I thought that was the summit of ambition. I told him I would like to write and travel as well. He and a professor named Tommy Miller steered me to a job at the *Oxford Eagle*, the smallest daily newspaper in Mississippi (circulation 2,500). I covered high school sports, murders, child abuse cases, city council meetings, factory layoffs, local elections, and a death penalty trial. I investigated a murder-suicide in a little town called Water Valley with such vigor that Yalobusha County sheriff Lloyd Defer tipped back his hat and interrupted me to ask, "Son, what kinda flesh-eating ghoul are ya tryin' to be?"

When I wasn't working, I was taking classes at Ole Miss on a scholarship. (They had the state's best English program, no matter what I thought about their symbolism, and out-of-state tuition was a number beyond my imagination.) At graduation, I was named the university's most outstanding journalism student. The stories I wrote for the *Eagle* had won all the regional awards for which they were eligible. I had job offers from something like a dozen newspapers.

It wasn't difficult to choose—I picked the one farthest from home. This turned out to be *Florida Today*, a little daily on Florida's east coast. I worked all the time at my new job, seven days a week, and moved from that paper to Gannett's national wire service to the *Miami Herald* to the *Detroit Free Press*, all in three years. When I wasn't interviewing people, I was on my motorcycle, or climbing mountains out West, or dancing at clubs until four in the morning. I let my hair grow out into a ponytail. I got an earring, a couple of tattoos, and a new set of clothes. My accent faded. I was out of Mississippi and had my foot flat on the gas pedal, heading anywhere at a hundred miles an hour.

2

LET'S STAY TOGETHER

ALL ESCAPE PLANS have a flaw, and mine was so to-
tally conventional, so boring, that I never saw it coming. I fell in love with the girl next door.

It happened when I was living in a loft in downtown Detroit. The six-story building was an old warehouse. It housed a
Greek pizzeria on the first floor, a small dance club on the second, and four more floors of unvarnished lofts. A noisy college
student lived in the loft next door to mine on the fifth floor for
a time; when he moved out, I posted a note on the employee
bulletin board at the *Free Press*, mentioning that an apartment
was available close to work.

No one responded for several days. Then a clerk in the paper's library whom I knew slightly asked if she could take a
look during lunch hour.

"I just want to see if it's someplace better than where I'm
staying now," Vita Gasaway explained.

She was a widow, outgoing and funny, a five-foot-two black
woman who exuded a certain Motown attitude just walking
down the street. She had long braids, pride in her dark complexion, and an easy, infectious laugh. She was eleven years
older than me and had come of age in Detroit in the 1960s,
when some of the city's musically inclined black teenagers
were revolutionizing popular music. Most any Saturday you
could go to the Motown Revue at the Fox Theater, right there

on Woodward, and see Stevie Wonder, the Supremes, Smokey Robinson, the Temps, the Four Tops, and, best of all, Marvin Gaye. These many years later, she was bemused by the fact that she lived next door to a white boy from Mississippi. We were friends for two years before we thought of dating. She worked almost more hours than I did—as a paralegal by day, and at the *Free Press* library in the evenings. One Saturday night in the summer, when it was too hot to sleep, I pulled an old chair out on my fire escape. I saw her sitting at her window, taking the breeze too. Her loft had no fire escape, and thus no way to sit outside.

I waved to get her attention.

"I'm not trying to be cute," I said, "but do you want a drink? It's cooler out here."

"Just what a girl needs," she said. "A fresh breeze and a glass of wine."

She came over, and I helped her step out of the huge, wide windows onto the steel fire escape. There were crowds of people in the parking lots and streets below, streaming out of the clubs and bars. The lights of the Renaissance Center spiraled up sixty or seventy floors a few blocks over. The Detroit River lay just beyond it. The lights of Windsor winked from across the water.

"This isn't bad at all," she said, and I relaxed, leaning against the rail.

It became a steady date. In the summers, we would pull a couple of old chairs out there, cook hamburgers on a diminutive grill, sip wine, and watch the people below. In Michigan's bitterly cold winters, we rented movies on Sunday afternoons and hooted at the screen, throwing popcorn at bad dialogue. In between, we took the motorcycle for afternoon rides to Ann Arbor. There was a jazz dive called Bo-Macs a few blocks from our lofts, a place where I ran a tab. Vita would come in there on a Friday evening, wearing a killer red dress, her braids falling down her back, and say, "Hey, baby love," in such a way that I would nearly forget my name.

I listened as she told me her family history, which also had its roots in the Deep South. Her father, Phil Griffin, grew up in south Alabama, a postage stamp of a place called Enterprise. There was not much of what you might call upward mobility for a black man in those days. So Phil, already in his twenties when the Depression hit, joined the Great Migration of rural blacks to the urban north. Married, with three children and more on the way, he moved to Cincinnati and then to River Rouge, a suburb of Detroit, before moving into the city proper. He was a painter of cars at a time when almost every other automobile manufactured anywhere in the world came out of Detroit, and he moved his family from house to house as his salary improved. His wife, Ida Helen, was a seamstress of leather covers for car seats and then of softer fabrics for sofa cushions. They had fish fries on Friday evenings, played cards with friends, and kept a small vegetable garden in the back-yard.

When Vita was a little girl, they would make the meander-ing trip down south each summer to visit relatives. Once across the Mason-Dixon, her father would sometimes stop the car when he saw black prisoners on a chain gang. He would of-fer cigarettes to the boss man, asking that they be distributed to the inmates. He would urge his children to smile and wave at the hammer swingers, offering them some small moment of kindness. He told his children of the injustice that led many of the men to be in stripes. These roadside courtesies ended abruptly at the Mississippi state line. In fact, Phil Griffin re-fused to stop his car in the Magnolia State at all.

"You had to pee in Memphis and hold it all the way through Mississippi," Vita remembered. "That place was so bad that, as a black person from Detroit, you were actually grateful to get to *Alabama*."

It would occur to me, sitting there beside her, that she had been scared of all the people I had grown up with and loved. It was an unpleasant sensation, but we came to share an unspo-ken understanding that the past did not have to dictate the future. We let our relationship develop—in fits and starts, with breakups and reunions—like most any other couple. Of course, some people gave me grief for dating a black woman— did I have some sort of Deep South fetish? Was I trying to prove something? This bothered me a great deal at first, but I learned to ignore it. Once people know you're from Mississippi, I discovered, they tend to place you in a box. (The number one thing people have said to me at dinner parties all over the world: "You don't look/act/sound like you're from Mississippi." It's as if, even in Beirut, people expect me to walk around barefoot in overalls, whistling "Dixie.") Such generalizations lead to misunderstandings, because most people not from the Deep South assume that white and black cultures there are polar opposites, which is inaccurate. Things were *perverse* for more than three centuries, they were violent and disturbed, but daily life among whites and blacks was and is not in diametrical opposition. In fact, it seemed to me there was a distinct cultural overlap between white and black rural southerners, from the foods they ate to what they did for a living (farm), the land they worked, and the ponds they fished— even to a type of personal warmth that other people in the nation simply didn't share. Exhibit A in this theory is Bill Clinton, a small-town Arkansas boy affectionately (or sardonically) referred to by black comedians, and even Toni Morrison, as the "first black president." He's even in the Arkansas Black Hall of Fame.

I had never really thought about this before I moved to Detroit. But the longer I dated Vita, the clearer it became that I often had more in common with her and many of Detroit's working-class black residents than I did with most of Michigan's white folks. What they called soul food in Detroit, for example, collard greens and black-eyed peas and corn bread and baby-back ribs and fried chicken, was the same fare I had grown up on. (The last meal my grandmother cooked for me was pork neck bones and collards; the first dinner I ate at Vita's mother's house was fried catfish and collards.) The sense of humor was similar, as was the pattern and pace of the spoken language, something more languid and indirect and expansive than the clipped English of many of my white *compadres*. Baptist was the most common religious affiliation, for better or worse. And I came to notice that black people (particularly those of a certain age) tended to nod or say hello or somehow acknowledge one another in passing, just the same as white rural southerners did. Northern urban whites most certainly did not. In high school, I had worked at our small-town radio station on Sunday mornings, running the control board for black gospel groups who would fill the studio with terrific live music. When I went to church with Vita at Third New Hope Baptist in Detroit, almost always the only white face in the crowd, I didn't feel as out of place as I might have looked. I already knew almost all of the songs, the arrangements, and the style of preaching.

On our first date, Vita was charmed when I opened the car door for her, pulled back her chair at the restaurant, and helped her with her coat. Nothing fancy; just the old-school southern courtesies, but a manner of respect that resonated with her.

This didn't mean I was entirely aware of what was happening between us. I had to move forty-five hundred miles away to discover that the girl next door was the one for me.

The *Free Press* named me as their European correspondent, and I moved to Warsaw. As I wandered Europe, Russia, and the Mideast, traveling alone from one city or conflict zone to another, the loneliness that accompanied me made it clear—I missed my best friend and next-door neighbor. She had become, in so many ways, the love of my life.

While I was stuck for several weeks in Sarajevo during the blistering summer of 1993, when the Bosnian war was at its height and the city was under a vicious siege, I ran over to the Associated Press office during a lull in the shelling and the shooting. I peeled off my flak jacket at the door and, sweating profusely, picked up the satellite phone. I caught Vita at her office.

"Name the most romantic place you can think of," I said.

"Right now? I'm in the middle of a meeting."

"The line is eighteen dollars a minute, baby. Now would be good."

"Well—wait—okay, the Greek islands."

"When can you meet me there?"

"Are you serious?"

"I suppose I could call somebody else if you're busy. What was that girl's name? You know, the one who lived down the hall—"

"September," she said, laughing now. "Just after Labor Day."

"Great. I'm a working man, you know. You'll have to fly coach."

"*Coach?* You mean as in economy? All my other international suitors send me first-class tickets. With champagne."

"What was that girl's name again? The one who stayed down—"

We met at the Athens airport in mid-September. We took a steamer out to Santorini, which was nearly empty in the off-season. The hotel we found was perched on one of the island's famous cliffs. We soaked up the sun each day, ate fresh fish each night, and forgot the rest of the world.

One night just before we were to leave, we took our rented motorcycle for a ride after dinner. Vita climbed on the seat behind me. It was late, and we swept up the empty roads alone, the moon breaking out of the clouds, the pale light floating across the cliffs. I pulled to a stop in the gravel on the side of the road, the ocean hundreds of feet below.

"I think," Vita said over my shoulder, into my ear, "that I could stay here for the rest of my life."

We were married at our house in Poland the following September.

My family boycotted the ceremony—they didn't approve of our marriage, to put it mildly. Vita's father had died, her mother was too old to travel, and her brothers and sisters sent their regards. It was her second marriage and seen as something of a lark.

"What does she want with that little white boy?" Vita's mother, Ida Helen, asked Kathie, Vita's youngest sister. "Is the girl just lonely?"

"Mama," Kathie sighed, "black people do not move to Poland because they're lonely."

We jumped the broom in a rollicking party in our backyard, on Warsaw's Pilicka Street, Al Green's chorus from "Let's Stay Together" on the invitations and twenty-eight guests from eight countries on four continents jamming to what sounded like a Belle Isle street party back in Detroit. The house came down when Patricia Wicks, Vita's best friend from childhood, showed the inebriated Polish wedding photographer how to bend over and dance to "Shoop."

I wasn't bothered by my family's snub of our wedding. In fact, very little bothered me anymore. I had developed a certain harshness after leaving Mississippi, a play-it-as-it-lays mind-set that was attuned to the bitterness in the world. I had the working idea that there was a higher form of truth to be found in the world's most impoverished and violent places, a rough-hewn honesty that could not be found elsewhere. Life had a tautness to it there, a sheen that seemed to say something about the way the world was, not how anyone wanted it to be. That was what seemed true and honest, and that was what I tried hardest to write about.

Given that, I found myself in the world of foreign correspondents and roving reporters. It was the first time in my adult life that I felt like I was where I belonged. I loved it—the travel and challenges, the friends flung out in a wide orbit of countries, getting on a plane time and again to write about the most compelling international events of the day—and at the end of each trip, there was Vita, my best friend, wife, and confidant. We went dancing till the clubs closed, had champagne brunches with friends that lasted all afternoon. So when Nancy Laughlin, the *Free Press* foreign editor, called our home in

Warsaw one snowy evening and asked if I'd like to take the paper's Africa posting, I said sure. It was the most wide-open job in journalism as far as I was concerned. To Vita, the chance to live on the mother continent was irresistible. We had all of our belongings in storage back in Detroit shipped to Zimbabwe.

We had no intention of returning to the United States.

3

THE GIRL-CHILD

AN OLD LAND ROVER came bumping down the red
dirt road and slowed to a stop. Two police officers got
out. It had taken several hours, but the young man
Herbert sent running for help had finally reached the nearest
police outpost. In rural Zimbabwe, where villages are scarce
and paved roads are few, that was more marathon than sprint.
He had hitched a ride on a bread truck for the first few miles,
got off when the truck turned at an intersection, then walked
and hitched again for several more miles until he came to a
dusty clutter of one-story concrete-block shops. He walked
past the butcher's and the beer hall, turned through an open
field, and came to a police barracks. He told an officer a newborn child had been found.

The officer sighed—this was not the first time this had
happened—and placed a call to a police station in the nearest
town for a truck to be dispatched. More than twenty miles
away, all on dirt roads, the truck took a while to appear.

The officers eventually made their way, the young boy as
their guide. Herbert was relieved. The child was in great dis-
tress. The women had rocked and comforted her, but she
needed a doctor, and soon. One of the officers took the child to
a clinic, perhaps five miles away, where she would spend the
night. The other officer stayed to ask questions. Abandoning
a child was a criminal charge. Attempted murder might be

24

added by a stern prosecutor. Had there been pregnancies in the village? Had any young girls suddenly gone to visit relatives? No, none, said the women. Herbert concurred.

The officer walked the paths, looking for something, anything—a note, a scrap of clothing—that might serve as a clue. There was nothing. Then he followed his partner to the clinic, where he questioned the staff. Had there been deliveries? Did they know of anyone who had come in for pregnancy or health counseling? None. He returned several weeks later, asking the same questions, trying to catch someone in a changed story, but got the same results. Three months later, he would close the case. More than two dozen infants had been mysteriously abandoned in his precinct alone in recent months.

"The children are not there in the evening, then they are in the morning," he said later. "Some are found close to roads. Others are dropped into sewers or ditches. We only find the corpses when people tell us about them. I think it is the mothers who leave them, because the fathers are gone, but it is only my theory. Who can say where they come from?"

The wave of abandoned children was unprecedented in the nine hundred years since the Shona-speaking people had built *dzimba dzimbabwe*, the magnificent stone fortress on the southern plains that formed the cornerstone of the national identity. There had always been isolated cases of abandonment, children set down in the forests for the animals to find—after colonialism, parliament adopted something called the Infanticide Act to provide for such cases—but only during the long war for independence had there been anything remotely similar.

In the mid-1970s, when the war was at its peak, Rhodesian troops would raid villages suspected of harboring rebel soldiers, guns blazing. Everyone would scatter. Parents would be killed or separated in the cross fire, losing children in the chaos. Most children had some form of extended family to care for them. For those who had no one, there was Chinyaradzo Children's Home in Harare. Stella Mesikano had been a worker at the orphanage during the war and she later became the matron, or director. In 1980, she began keeping a bar chart on graph paper showing the number of abandoned children brought to Chinyaradzo. Each year was carefully shaded with different colored pencils. In 1980, the year independence was declared, ending fourteen years of conflict, the bar was colored in black and showed that 40 children had been admitted. The next year was pink, and the number of children dropped to 23. It held at that level, or dropped to the low teens, for a decade. Then it shot to 35 in 1991. By 1994, it was up to 56. The orphanage was set up to handle a total of 58 children but had taken in 159 in four years. Other orphanages or children's homes began to take in the overflow. As Mesikano's chart began to move toward the edge of the page with each new year, she began to lose the enthusiasm for keeping detailed statistics for a government that had so little interest.

By the late 1990s, the administration of Robert Mugabe was skittish about acknowledging the depth of the AIDS disaster, and unable or unwilling to administer a program that might care for the nation's most vulnerable charges. The state was allocating only about five Zimbabwean dollars (then the equivalent of about thirty American cents, a rate that would drop by more than 60 percent in the coming months) per day to feed, clothe, educate, and care for each orphan. This was to provide about one-third of the total cost of administering the home. The government plan called for other agencies or donors to cover the other two-thirds. The agency that was to administer Chinyaradzo, and raise most of its funds, was the Child Protection Society (CPS). During what would come to be recognized as one of the largest wave of orphans in human history, the agency was almost completely moribund. "The organization currently does little research or advocacy on behalf of children," an internal study reported. "The CPS has become somewhat stagnant . . . there has been no director for a number of years."

As more orphans came in but more money did not, Mesikano became the de facto fund-raiser. She got help from a local Rotary club and a handful of Western aid agencies, most notably from the Canadian division of World Vision, the U.S.-based Christian charity, and the Qantas Cabin Crew Team, volunteers from the Australian airline.

The orphanage appeared modern and clean, for Mesikano and her staff worked hard. But there was only so much to be done with three dimes a day per child. Flies settled on the children, food, and dishes. The in-house clinic had shut down for lack of medicine. Diapers were old washcloths folded into triangles. Food was cornmeal mush and a lumpy porridge. Most of the fifteen to twenty infants in the ward at any one time had chronic diarrhea. Because many of the workers had little training in hygiene or lacked the proper sanitary materials, diapers were not properly disinfected before being put on another infant, allowing bacteria and disease to slink from child to child.

In January 1998, a newborn named Memory Chinyanga was sent from the orphanage to the hospital. She had not been well, though the workers at the orphanage could not list any specific illness. She died a few days later. The listed cause of death was dehydration. As was the standard procedure, no one at the orphanage saw her again. Her corpse would have been taken to the city's overburdened morgue, eventually wrapped in a white sheet, and put in a wooden coffin. A truck would have taken her to a potter's field on the outside of town. Her corpse would have been lowered into the red dirt soil. Prison inmates would shovel soil on top of her coffin until she lay under a rounded lump of earth.

A few days after Memory died, an infant a few cribs over was also sent to the hospital. Her name was Tatenda Jeselant (her first name means "we give thanks"). She had chronic diarrhea and was vomiting all day. She died two days later.

The next week, the workers called for a van to rush young Godfrey Muparutsa, not yet two years old, to the hospital. He never came back. The doctors said he died of pneumonia, a rather elastic term used to connote any inflammation of the lungs or to note they had become filled with fluid. Was its origin a virus? Bacterium? No one could say. There were no autopsies performed. There were no inquiries as to how three children in a state-run orphanage died in four weeks. There were no newspaper headlines, no staff shake-ups, and no change in procedure, for AIDS had rendered this scenario routine.

The calendar turned to February, and an infant named Shingirai Nyamayaro was brought in by social welfare officers. She had been abandoned, origins unknown. She developed diarrhea, which, because the orphanage could not afford rehydration packets or antidiarrhea medications, could not be stopped. She became dehydrated and died after a very short stay in the hospital. Then Munashe Tsekete fell ill. His breathing was raspy. He coughed a lot. They took him to the hospital, where he stopped breathing altogether. Five Chinyaradzo infants or toddlers were dead in eight weeks. Munashe's official cause of death was listed as "difficulties in breathing."

Joe Bhebbe, another infant, went a few weeks later too.

A month passed, and so did the short lives of Frasia Chateuka, who died of pneumonia, and Ashley Mhlanga, who "could not breathe."

Early one evening in the dry season of 1998, several weeks before we first encountered the orphanage, a van arrived. Darkness was falling as the social welfare officer walked in, calling for Mesikano. He was holding the infant Constance had found. The clinic in the rural area had no place to keep her, he explained, so the police officers had driven her into Harare. The girl-child was squalling to high heaven.

"She still had blood on her, they hadn't cleaned her up," Mesikano would later remember. "She had a clip on her umbilical cord, a stump. But she looked healthy. She had nice black hair, very full. She was actually sort of pink and plump."

She and a couple of the other women set to work cleaning the child. They soaked her in a small tub of soap and warm water, washing off the blood and dirt. They put antibiotic cream on the ear wounds. She had a small, fleshy stump on the outer edge of her left hand, a sixth finger. They looped a thread around it, pulled in opposite directions, and popped it off. They put cream over that, too. Then they looked over her body and facial features in an attempt to guess the new child's ethnic heritage, a popular orphanage pastime.

They could rule out that she was Shona, the nation's largest ethnic group. She lacked the deep black skin and broad facial structure for that. Nor was she a mixture of black and white; she was much too dark to be biracial. Someone looked at her burnt-tan complexion and her deep-set eyes and suggested she was from Mozambique, the country to the east. Then again, someone else said, she looked almost like the Ndebele, the nation's second largest ethnic group, cousins of the Zulu peoples of South Africa. But that downy hair on the back of her ears—didn't Indian babies have that? Perhaps, but then there was the puzzle of her small, rather flat nose.

Mesikano finally laughed and gave up the game.

"She is a child of Africa," she said. "That much we know."

It was up to her as matron to name the new children. This was a great power, of course, and she did not take it lightly. She wanted something pretty, for the little girl now sleeping peacefully in her arms was a thing of beauty. She finally settled on Chipo, a popular girl's name in the region. It translates from Shona as "gift."

"I wanted her to have a pretty African name, something she would be proud of all her life," Mesikano would later say, explaining her name selection process. "I wanted something to remind her of how special she is, and the circumstances of how she came to be. She seemed a gift of the land itself."

A worker opened the home's daily medical chart, where they kept a log of each child's health and condition. She wrote "Chipo" on a line of the ledger, putting a star next to her name. "New admission. 3.1 kilos (6.8 pounds). Brought in by social welfare officers. Wound on ear but the baby looks healthy."

The entries in the log read something like a status report of the ward. It showed that Chipo was one of fourteen infants, nine crawlers, and thirty-one toddlers in a three-room ward. Of the fourteen infants, six were in bad shape.

Caroline Razo was "coughing and crying in the night. She is severely wasted," the log read. Tinashe, whose last name was not recorded, had diarrhea and was vomiting. "Keep an eye on him," the nightly report noted. An infant named Gladys had some sort of unknown fluid oozing from her ears. Ester was on antibiotics and Tatenda needed amoxicillin, which, the log noted, they did not have.

The next day, three infants were rushed to Harare Hospital.

Caroline was gasping for breath by this point, desperately crying, waving her arms to and fro. Then she stopped gasping and died in the van while they were still in traffic. Tinashe was admitted minutes later, for similar difficulties in breathing. Yemurai had an ugly knot on her right arm.

For her part, the girl-child named Chipo was placed in the second crib to the right of the entrance. A bright yellow note card was put above her crib, noting her name, her date of birth, and the day she was brought in. Workers scarcely had time to pick her up, though, because the week after Caroline died, Collins Murehwa began vomiting, over and over again, until he was spitting blood and not much else. He was taken to the hospital, where they could do nothing for him. He vomited until he died. Clara Mlambo didn't last much longer; her tiny body withered and dehydrated until her lungs seemed to collapse and her heart stopped. Sandra Mahohoma didn't have a chance, coughing and gasping day by day until her strength left her.

Thirteen infants were dead in six months, the worst mortality rate in Chinyaradzo's history. There was little Mesikano could do but get used to it. There was no money to train her young staff. Many of them were teenagers or twenty-something girls who had been raised at the home and had nowhere else to go. They were officially known as trainees in a one-year course called "Elementary Hygiene and Child Care." In reality, they worked for room and board and the equivalent of five American dollars per month. There was no money for medicine, except what donors happened to provide. As the AIDS crisis wore on and the death toll of young parents mounted, the numbers of abandoned children soared. Chinyaradzo was becoming something it was never intended to be—a dumping ground for unwanted children.

"When I started in the nineteen-seventies, we just didn't have abandoned children," Mesikano said. "Now, ninety percent of the children we have are abandoned, no mother, no father. It seems impossible to me but it is true. Others have one relative, but who cannot care for them. We were set up to be a place for infants, a stopgap. Then the maximum age was raised to five. Then to twelve. Now, to be honest, we raise a lot of children. There's no place else for them to go."

Chinyaradzo's children were wards of the state, last in line for treatment, care, and medications in the nation's slowly deteriorating health care system. With no money for vitamins, tests for HIV were out of the question, and for more than financial reasons. There was no way to treat it. The fear attached to the disease was almost literally unspeakable. The scale of death was something lifted from the realm of Poe; the denial approached the world of Kafka, and still there were no guidelines for health professionals or caregivers to be tested for their own HIV status. Mesikano not only had no idea which of her infants was HIV-positive, she had no way of knowing if any of her young workers had the disease either, and thus was helpless to monitor the spread of the disease through the ward. The bitter truth came at the end of such calculations—even if Mesikano could have had every child tested for HIV, she knew in her heart that she would choose not to do so. The tests used in Zimbabwe, the ELISA and Western Blot, were outdated, and often gave false results, either positive or negative. Mesikano knew that for a child to test positive was to condemn the toddler to a quick death—the stigma was so deep, and the ignorance of how to handle AIDS patients so profound, that she was certain that any child who tested HIV-positive would be left to die.

The deadly cycle of ignorance, fear, and disease did not take long to run its course. Rejoice Neshuro, her name so pretty but her body so contorted, died in the hospital of dehydration. Then Nyasha Dziva died of pneumonia and dehydration. Workers were helpless to stop Abigail Mazviona's diarrhea. A few days later, she began vomiting. They didn't know how to stop that either. She spit up until she couldn't anymore, and then she died.

Sixteen children were dead in seven months.

The calendar turned to midwinter in Zimbabwe, when the temperatures drop into the low forties at night. In Harare, at more than four thousand feet above sea level, the chill can go to the bone. Chinyaradzo had no central heating, like most places in Harare. Its concrete-block walls and tiled floors held little warmth after sundown. The infants would be bundled into layers of heavy knit clothes and tucked under blankets, but the chill worked its way into their lungs.

In crib number two, lost in a green knit outfit and bonnet, the girl-child did not thrive. She began to turn away from her milk. One day, she threw up. Then again. Then over and over, crying and wailing as she spit up whatever was in her stomach. No remedy could stop it. Her bowels turned to diarrhea. The hospital van came for her, and she was rushed to the hospital's intensive care unit. She was badly dehydrated and had lost nearly a pound since being brought to the orphanage. She spent seven days in the ICU.

Then she was returned to Chinyaradzo.

She took a little milk. She did not cry so much. But neither did she smile or giggle. She scarcely responded when touched. Workers noticed this and tried to coax a grin from her, but they had little time for just one child, given the poor health of so many.

Then one morning the child stopped eating altogether. Her temperature soared to 104 degrees. She labored to breathe. She would open her mouth to cry out but no sound would emerge. She was rushed back to the hospital and again placed in the intensive care unit. Again she stayed for seven days.

The doctor wrote one line across the top of her dismissal papers: "Feed this child!" Her weight had dropped to four pounds, twelve ounces. Her growth chart, plotted on a grid, was supposed to gradually head up, like an incline. Instead, it plunged downward like a ski ramp.

Upon her return to Chinyaradzo, her lungs expanded and then expanded again, trying to draw in more oxygen. They became infected with a virus that would lay undetected until it developed into full-blown pneumonia. Her bronchial tubes became infected and inflamed. Her heart, weakened by severe malnutrition that was turning to marasmus, beat ever faster.

Marasmus describes a condition in which the body, starved of food, begins to take molecules of protein from muscle tissue and use it to fuel other bodily functions, burning a sort of emergency gas tank. The condition had stripped her emaciated frame to four pounds, three ounces.

In short, her body was now eating the only thing it could: itself.

4

FITTING IN

BEFORE I LEFT the United States in 1993, I had known a couple of friends of friends who had died of AIDS. In Zimbabwe, it seemed everybody I met had lost at least one, if not several, family members to the disease. By 1997, Timothy Stamps, the nation's health minister, said five hundred Zimbabweans were dying of AIDS each week in a nation of just eleven million. He likened it to "the crash of a jumbo jet each week, every week." There were more than sixty thousand children who had lost both parents, and more than half a million who had lost at least one.

Vita and I had heard these stories, initially thinking they were gross exaggerations. The country seemed too peaceful, too complacent for such waves of death. Zimbabwe was poor and had its problems, but on balance it was one of the most developed, least troubled nations in sub-Saharan Africa. This earned it the informal sobriquet "the Switzerland of Africa," which European diplomats counted as a compliment. Their counterparts from West Africa said it with a sigh; many of them privately considered Zimbabweans to be some of the most boring black people on earth.

But that was of little consequence. Zimbabweans had walked a hard road from oppression to independence, and in just two decades they had succeeded in carving out a solid future for themselves. Harare looked just like what it was—a small town built by Rhodesian colonialists, a kind of ersatz British transplant—but it had a sleepy charm. A few modern office buildings and hotels formed a modest skyline. Outside of that ten- or twelve-block area, few buildings were more than three stories. The light industries were all on the south end of town, along with the poorest townships, which were now politely referred to as "high-density suburbs," although they were all within the city limits. The "low-density suburbs" were to the east or north of the city center. Most of the houses were one-story, ranch-style places. They had been built in the 1940s to 1960s—the older ones tended to have tin roofs—and realtors cheerfully advertised they had been built with asbestos.

There was an enclosed mall downtown, next to the Meikles, Harare's best hotel. Across town, low-slung strip shopping malls featured ice cream shops, pizza delivery outlets, and chain grocery stores, including a French franchise called Bon Marché, where you could pay with a swipe of your credit card. There was the corner post office, a sprinkling of good restaurants, churches, hospitals, golf courses, tennis courts, and a health club or two. Two shopping centers featured terrific movie theaters, as nice as or nicer than most in the United States.

The most expensive neighborhoods, the ones with houses big enough to include personal living space for us as well as my office, unfurled in towering groves of eucalyptus and pine and jacarandas. The plots were half an acre or larger. And, we discovered, every single one had a set of small, concrete-block buildings at the back of the property where the domestic staff lived, usually set behind a boundary wall from the main house. Servants were paid a pittance, were expected to work long hours, and were not to come onto the main property after working hours. We toured twenty or twenty-five houses, looking for one that didn't have such an arrangement, for we neither needed nor wanted live-in help. We looked at smaller houses in different neighborhoods. They all had some sort of domestic arrangements too.

We finally gave up, since the only solution seemed to be taking a house and then firing the staff, which hardly seemed a blow for social progress. We settled into a house that was someone's idea of a Spanish-style hacienda. It had vaulted ceilings, arched doorways, stone floors, and big glass doors that swung open onto a patio. I set up my office in a large room off this end of the house, not thinking that the owners might be concealing a tin roof behind the red tile façade. They were. In a rainstorm, the din was so loud that I had to go to the back of the house, under more solid construction, to conduct interviews on the bedroom phone, balancing a laptop computer on my knees to take notes. There was also a small swimming pool, complete with a fountain and a palm tree by the side. It rented for the equivalent of $1,400 per month, which included the residence and salaries of the husband-and-wife team, Mavis and Judah Ganuka, who tended the place. We doubled their salaries, which delighted them, but it still only amounted to about $100 each per month. Judah celebrated each month by drinking up his extra pay as soon as he got it; Mavis saved hers to build a small house on her family's land in the rural areas.

We made a flurry of new friends; Charity, who worked in the local film industry; Angus and Chris, my colleagues at the Associated Press and Reuters, respectively; Bill, who was a senior officer at the U.S. Agency for International Development, and his wife, Dumisille; Patrick and Yvonne, an African American architect and his wife who had come to work for a while in Harare; Adam and Sekai, an Australian television journalist and his wife, a Zimbabwean writer; and Heather and Steve, another interracial couple. She was a Zambian clothes designer, he a Canadian airplane mechanic.

My work assignment also changed. My paper's parent company, Knight Ridder, took over several foreign bureaus from its member papers. The Africa bureau was one of them, leaving me with a new set of bosses in Washington, not Detroit.

Harried by these personal and professional changes, the usual travel (I averaged about two hundred nights a year on the road), and lulled by Harare's drowsy demeanor, it was nearly a year before it became apparent to us that the raw numbers of AIDS deaths were fact, not hyperbole. We thought we might volunteer to help out in one of the orphanages, maybe even take some children into our home on occasion. We had mulled over the idea of adopting in the past, and considered that possibility here. We thought such an overture would be welcomed, considering the vast numbers of orphans. We were quickly and politely put in our place by Tony Mtero, the director of the Harare office of the national Department of Social Welfare.

Tony was a slender, soft-spoken man who had spent a decade studying in the United States. He was also the fiancé of one of Vita's friends in town, Gloria, a fellow African American expatriate. We met them for dinner one night in one of Harare's nicer restaurants. When the drinks and appetizers came, and Vita said that we wanted to volunteer in an orphanage, perhaps even adopt, Tony nodded and stroked his mustache, as if considering a complex problem of algebra.

"Well, you can't adopt," he said, between nibbles on the food spread before us. "The law does not allow adoptions by foreign nationals."

"Oh," Vita said. Her voice fell half an octave as she said it, a change in timbre that I knew mirrored a drop in her hopes.

"Well," Tony said, "there's one way, but that requires the national minister of social welfare to personally approve an exemption, and let me tell you, that doesn't happen. Maybe once, twice a year."

"Oh," I said this time, looking at Vita across the table and raising my eyebrows half an inch, a gesture that said, *This isn't going the way we thought.*

"I don't mean to be rude," Tony said, putting a hand on Vita's arm. "People would be suspicious, though they will not tell you that. They will wonder why Americans would want a Zimbabwean child in their home." He turned to me, smiling to ease what he considered to be a blow. "And they're going to particularly wonder why you, Neely, would be interested in a black child. A boy or girl, it makes no difference. It's seen as something very odd here. I know that in the United States there is that controversy about whites raising blacks. But this is different. White men who want to be around black children . . . well, the perception is there is something unnatural there. Some sort of sexual abuse, likely. Perhaps more importantly, even before adoption by a white person would be considered, there is the matter of ancestral ties. There are totems, the symbols of something you might call family clans. A child without a totem—well, such a child would be considered to be lost. He or she would have no way of communicating with their ancestors. You are not African"—now he turned back to Vita—"nor are you, in this context, and therefore you cannot know how an African child should relate to these ancestral spirits. It is one of the most elemental staples of life."

He laughed, perhaps uncomfortable to be discussing such issues. Gloria said, "But there's fostering. There's volunteering."

"Oh, yes," Tony said, his tone lifting. "I do not mean to paint such a gloomy picture. I believe you might become foster parents to a child while you are here. In particular, we have a program for volunteers to take children out of the orphanage for the weekend to let them spend some time with a family. That would be a huge treat for them."

We ordered dinner then, laughing about Tony's time in the United States—he had been in Minnesota and had not known the world could be so cold—but came back to the topic at the end of the evening.

"We'll be delighted to foster, to bring some kids home for the weekend, at least for the weekends I'm in town," I said. "The house we're renting has a big yard and pool. The older kids will love it. But just out of curiosity, with the AIDS situation being what it is, why is the law on foreign adoptions so restrictive? I mean, from everything I read, there are more orphans than anybody knows what to do with."

Tony gave a gesture that was half nod and half shrug.

"It's a matter of debate within the field. But the general

policy is to actively discourage adoption by foreigners. The matrons at the orphanages will be delighted for you to take children home, because they have too many kids and too little money to care for them. Social workers, though, are the ones who make the decisions about a child's permanent status. They have caseloads in the hundreds. They don't even have cars to make their rounds. They have to be in court often. And there is what I told you before—it is against the social norm. Even among Zimbabweans, adopting a child not related to you is very uncommon. We see only a few such cases a year. The social workers know all this, and they know that, ultimately, their decision will have to go all the way to the national minister of social welfare." He rapped his knuckles on the table to emphasize the last few words. "That is the presidential cabinet. It is the same as if you had to get a piece of paper into Bill Clinton's White House. No social worker wants to approve a case only to have it rejected from higher. It will look like they made a mistake."

"You mean it will look like they took a bribe," Vita said.

Tony glanced at her, then Gloria, and smiled.

"Exactly so."

After dinner, we went into the restaurant parking lot, still chatting, and Tony shook my hand. "Don't be misled—we welcome your offer of help. I will call the matrons of the orphanages to let them know you will be coming, so they will not be startled."

We went the next morning.

The first stop was Harare Children's Home. Established by the Methodist Church in 1923 as the Rhodesian Children's Home, it catered to white children until independence. Now almost all black, the tidy campus was run on a series of bequests and trusts. The superintendent gave us a glossy brochure and a tour. We made a modest donation, and she walked us through the Gwen Ward Memorial Hall, the Underwood House, and so on. We entered one room where children were looking through glossy Western magazines, cutting out pictures, and pasting them onto brightly colored pieces of construction paper. One little girl with braids said I could help her. She was pleased to inform me that she was five years old. Her name was Elizabeth, but she said I could call her Beth if I wished. I started cutting out pictures and told her that my mother's name was Elizabeth too.

"Your mother has my name?" she asked with a smile. "So can I go home with you?"

"Well . . ." I was stuck. It suddenly dawned on me that I was not here as a reporter, dutifully taking notes and moving on. I was here as someone who might actually do just what she said.

"I just got here, Beth," I said, trying to get myself out of this. "We're visiting today. That lady over there, that's my wife, and we're just sort of looking around and cutting out pictures and things."

"So you're going to leave me here?" she said. I stammered out some sort of reply, tried to smile, and said I had to go look at some other parts of the home.

The older children showed Vita and me to their quarters, where they slept two or three to a room. After two hours, several children were asking us to take them to our house. Elizabeth stuck close to my right leg, smiling impishly, making sure I had not forgotten who was first in line. The superintendent called us into her office and closed the door.

"Did you see any children you liked?" she asked hopefully.

We got into the truck a few minutes later and shut the door. It was quiet.

"Jesus Christ," I said, finally cranking the engine. "I feel like I just kicked six kids off a lifeboat from the *Titanic*."

"And held them underwater for a while," Vita said.

We drove to Emerald Hills Children's Home. It was in Mount Pleasant, one of Harare's nicer neighborhoods on the north end of town. The facility had large dormitory wings, for it also was home to the city's deaf and hearing-impaired children. We went into the office of the matron, Ernestine Wasterfall. She was a serious, kindly woman, and I liked her immensely for her candor and warm demeanor.

"Most of our children are infected with HIV," she said. "Many already have AIDS. There are also many who are mentally or physically retarded. They need all the medical aid, not to mention love, that they can get." We toured a ward of terribly ill children who were so listless they could scarcely blink as we passed. The advanced stages of AIDS were apparent. They were severely wasted away, their heads seeming to loll on tiny bodies.

We went onto the grounds, where it appeared word had been passed along that a couple of Americans were coming. The children stood in clumps, giggling. They followed us from here to there as Wasterfall showed us around. I saw several young boys kicking a ball back and forth. I joined the game and was quickly surrounded by a cluster of three-foot-high children, all clamoring for me to pick them up or take them home. As Wasterfall said, many were sick, stunted, or suffering from scabies. Vita was talking with several little girls, many of whom were smiling but shy.

We stopped back in Wasterfall's office an hour or so later.

"Did you see any children you liked?" she asked, raising her eyebrows in almost exactly the same way as the previous matron.

"All of them," I replied, mustering a smile. I explained that this was our first day, and there were still other homes we had promised to visit. I made another donation, the cliché of throwing bricks into the Grand Canyon bouncing through my head, and we left. It was impossible not to be sobered by what we had seen. Dinner that night was subdued; we ate in silence, not speaking at all.

The next morning we drove to the south of town, to Chinyaradzo. The roads in the nearby industrial park were jammed with huge trucks belching out stacks of smoke and pollution, forming a brown haze. We honked at the gate, and a young girl came out of a one-story concrete-block building to unlatch the padlock. The interior of the compound was an open-air playground, with brightly painted yellow and red seesaws, a pair of slides, a swing set with chairs for small children. The backyard featured larger equipment for older kids. The classrooms had posters on the wall, cutouts of birds and bunny rabbits, even Winnie the Pooh and Santa Claus. It was well kept, with some rooms not appearing much different from something you might expect to find in small-town America.

In the infant ward, there were two narrow rectangular rooms of cribs. There was an erasable board that listed the feeding schedules for each child. At the back of the first room was a partition, and behind it were stacks of old furniture, rocking chairs missing an arm or curved leg, dismantled cribs, and baby toys. There was a small kitchen on one end and a changing room at the other, connecting to a room for toddlers.

In one crib was Christian, a chubby two-year-old in a pair of blue overalls. He was nicknamed the Old Man for the comically serious way he seemed to overlook the other children. There was a tiny infant named Robert, one of a pair of twins, who rarely awoke. Yemurai, who had recovered from her hospital trip, was a biracial baby with an endearing smile and a bad case of eczema. Tsongai was a chunky little girl who liked to bang her toys around.

I wandered back over toward the door and down by the windows. There were four cribs. The only one that held a child was the second one. I reached under the clothes and picked up the infant, looking at the card on the wall to get her name.

"Chipo," I said.

She was wrapped in a bundle of white cloths. She had dark brown eyes and delicately curled eyelashes that were so long she seemed to blink in slow motion. She kept three fingers of her right hand in her mouth. Her toes looked like little erasers on the end of miniature pencils. She seemed to weigh nothing at all. I tickled her chin. Nothing. "Hey, pretty girl," I whispered. She blinked. I playfully bumped the end of her nose with mine. She blinked again. Then she reached out with her left hand and, in a wobbling gesture, wrapped it around my little finger.

It is difficult to say what happened to me then. I had reported in a lot of places a lot worse than this one. I once spent the better part of a day in a slum hospital in Baghdad, a desperate place where the temperature soared above 120 degrees, the infants subsisted on less than fifty calories a day, there was no medicine, and a fifty-two-day-old infant named Maram Hassan lay on a feed sack that passed for a bed sheet. She was starving to death, even as her mother waved flies away from her mouth and eyes. I held the child and talked to her mother, and wrote a story about the child's doomed fate. I didn't lose sleep over it. Nor had I worried about Esmet, a six-day-old infant in northern Bosnia whom I held briefly in a refugee camp. Beset by the subzero temperatures, malnutrition, and the violence of the war, his mother had not bothered to remember his name.

"It doesn't matter," she said. "It's going to be dead in a few days."

I handed the dying child back to her and filed a story about them that night. It was eight hundred words and no big deal. Before dawn the next morning, heading out in a driving snowstorm, John Pomfret, my colleague from the *Washington Post*, and I were driving back to Sarajevo, munching chocolate bars and bellowing songs along with the tape deck to stay awake.

These were two among dozens, if not hundreds, of similar experiences in dozens of countries across the years. There was the man whom I watched executed on Florida's death row, back when they did it with the electric chair; there was Alija Hodzic, the wartime caretaker of the Sarajevo morgue, who came into work one morning to see that his dead son had been dumped on the floor. Developing a detachment from the suffering you witness and write about is a professional necessity, of course, but it can also become a job hazard of sorts. You can just keep going for so many years, not allowing yourself to feel anything, until you arrive at a place where your emotional connections have gone dark, lights out, all blown fuses that don't work anymore. It's not like you know when it happens. It's a steady erosion that diminishes your heart, drop by drop, bit by bit.

Keep moving, I had told myself time and again. *Don't think.* But when the child's fingers closed over mine, some long-forgotten part of me seemed to stir. I didn't know what it was. I just felt something. "Hey, baby, come here," I called to Vita. "Lookit this little punkin."

Vita took her in her arms, rocking her, as enchanted as I was. She asked the staff about this little newborn. "Oh, Chipo," they said. "She's not a newborn. She's more than three months old." They recounted the story of her discovery and subsequent hospitalizations. They said she had a cold and was not feeling well.

She seemed to doze after a time, and Vita lowered her back into her crib. We were so taken with the children that we wound up staying for the afternoon. We helped spoon-feed the other infants at noon and helped put them down for naps. With sixteen children in such a small area, it seemed at least one was always crying, thus waking the infant in the next crib, and so on, until it went around the room like a chain of dominoes. We also noticed, as the day wore on, that the veneer of the place was thinner than a bad coat of paint. Vita had gone to change one child with a young clinic worker, alarmed at the foul-smelling diarrhea. The child was not cleaned properly and another washcloth, what passed for a diaper, was pinned on. The windows had no screens or were filled with ragged holes. Flies settled onto children, the damp spots around their eyes and noses, the mush meal that was lunch. The adjacent kitchen was rusted. It had no hot water and no refrigerator. Uncovered baby formula sat on the counter, drawing more flies.

I spent most of the afternoon on the play mat with the infants, rattling toys, changing the occasional diaper—this astounded the all-female staff—but more and more often, I found myself drawn back to the little girl who had been abandoned the day she was born. "She's so *tiny*," Vita said, looking down into the crib.

I motioned to her to come outside. We stood in the empty

playground, leaning against the red and yellow swing set. The sun was out, and the day was breezy.

"I like that little bitty one, Chipo," I said, smiling.

Vita nodded. "Me too."

"You want to ask the matron if we can do like Tony said, that program where we take her home for the weekend, maybe be her foster parents?"

"Of course," Vita said. "I mean, she's so sick. She's not going to live without a lot of help."

"True," I said, taking a deep breath, "but she may not anyway. I was talking to Mrs. Mesikano, the director. You know how many infants they've lost this year? Sixteen."

Vita mouthed the number back at me. "*Sixteen?* She's going to die if we don't do something. She is, I know it." Her face had a narrow tic by the corner of her mouth and she had tears in the corners of her eyes, just that quick.

I found myself impatient, if not a trifle exasperated. Vita was a realist, but she had not been traipsing around refugee camps for the past several years. A lot of adorable little kids die, I was thinking, regardless of what we or anybody else does about it.

"And she may not make it anyway, sweetheart. Don't get me wrong—I think she's adorable. I think she's the most gorgeous child in the sub-Sahara. I'm all for taking her home for as long as we can. But look at where you're standing and let's do the math. We are in Zimbabwe, ground zero of the deadliest epidemic known to mankind. We are at an orphanage in a high-density township. If AIDS were a bomb dropped out of an airplane, it would hit us on the head. This child is grossly malnourished, she has respiratory problems, she has little or no responses. I've picked grapefruit that weigh more than she does. The odds of her being infected with HIV, I would guess, run about seventy to eighty percent. Vegas wouldn't put odds on her making it twelve months."

"There are times," Vita said coldly, "when you can be such a son of a bitch."

"I'm having this conversation now so we don't have it later on," I hissed, suddenly angry. "I am not going to take this child home for weekends and then stop it if she's got AIDS. I may be a son of a bitch, but I will not—under any goddamned circumstance—take this child home and then bring her back here because we don't have the guts to watch her die."

Vita turned away. She had had two miscarriages during her first marriage. The doctor had said the damage from those made it impossible for her to ever carry a child to term. That was why we couldn't have children. It was something I knew about when we got married. I didn't care then and I didn't care now. I had thought we might adopt. But then Tony's message at dinner shot down those hopes, the misery of the orphanages brought back unpleasant memories, the odds of the young girl were not making things better, and now the sunlight showed tears glistening on Vita's face. I softened my tone, trying to remember that I wasn't working in some refugee camp, where emotions were something that had to be curtailed.

"Listen, I just want you to think about what it would do to you, and to us, to get attached to a special-needs child," I said. "Yesterday we were thinking about bringing a few needy kids over for a few weekends. Maybe even fostering. Yeah, hey, fostering, why not? We can still do that with any child we've met. But this, with this little girl, is very serious. I meant what I said. I will not take her home and then let her be abandoned a second time."

"What makes you think," Vita said, brushing past me, "that you're the only one?"

MESIKANO—STELLA, as she insisted we call her—was delighted we had chosen to take home one of her most fragile children. A "trial weekend" was set up for the next day, Friday. We spent that day at the orphanage, helping out again. Late in the afternoon the workers bundled up Chipo into her green outfit—the knit cap nearly swallowed her head—and the women clapped and cheered. Few children left the orphanage, and even a weekend out was cause for celebration.

Once home, Vita began to get her undressed for a bath while I went to heat up some milk. The shortwave radio was beeping at the top of the hour. The BBC news came on, bringing news that jolted me back to work. Laurent Kabila, the self-declared president of the Democratic Republic of Congo, was facing an uprising in the eastern part of the country, the same place where the rebellion that brought him to power had begun two years earlier. Since the current unrest was centered in Goma, a city just across the border from Rwanda, it was reasonable to believe that the Tutsi-led Rwandan government was involved. It made sense.

In the Rwandan genocide of 1994, radical militias from the Hutu ethnic group, known as the Interahamwe, had unleashed one of the deadliest episodes of the twentieth century, leading a slaughter of more than half a million Tutsis and moderate Hutus. The instrument of choice was the machete, and they did their work in just one hundred days. The death toll may have been as high as eight hundred thousand; no one really knows.

The Interahamwe was shoved out of Rwanda by a Tutsi-led army. The killers fled over the heavily forested border into Congo, then known as Zaire, where they received shelter and support from Mobutu Sese Seko, the longtime dictator. From there, they continued to stage murderous raids back into tiny Rwanda. This set off the Tutsi-led rebellion to overthrow Mobutu, and the installation of Kabila as the new ruler.

But once in power, Kabila renamed the nation the Democratic Republic of Congo and turned on his Tutsi backers. He began giving shelter and support to the same Hutu militias that had terrorized Rwanda in the first place.

Another rebellion in the east, therefore, almost certainly involved a Rwandan attempt to neutralize Kabila. There was a message on the office answering machine from one of my editors, asking when I was planning to go in.

I started flipping through the pages of a thick catalogue called the *Overseas Airline Guide*, a monthly listing of international flights around the globe that is something of a Gideon Bible among correspondents. I was checking out how I could get into Kinshasa within the next forty-eight hours—Harare-Johannesburg-Kinshasa, or maybe Harare-Nairobi-Kinshasa—when I heard a shout from Vita. I went to the bedroom. "Look at this," she said, unwrapping the folds of cloth from Chipo's body.

"Jesus Christ," I said.

Undressed, her belly protruded as if she'd swallowed an inflated balloon. Her arms and legs looked like spider limbs. The skin over her stomach and hips had gone a pasty shade of brown. I recognized the onset of marasmus, the staple disease of desperate refugee camps. She would open her mouth, her face contorted with pain and rage—but no sound would come out. We would pat her on the back for fifteen seconds and then a fierce wail would emerge. She would stop a few minutes later, exhausted, chest heaving, and stick three fingers of her right hand into her mouth, her comfort gesture. A few minutes later, she would start screaming again.

We had bought a small infant tub to bathe her in, but she was lost in it. Vita ran a sinkful of water and cleaned her there, soothing her swollen belly with a warm cloth, running it over her arms and hands and fingers and feet. Chipo just looked at her. She had almost no responses. She did not smile and had never laughed. We had bought the smallest infant's shirt we could find; it fell to her ankles. I finished warming up the infant formula and put it in a bottle. She could scarcely suck the milk from the nipple. So I went to the store and bought several syringes. I sterilized them, poured in some warm formula, and squirted a few cc's into her mouth. She looked up in surprise when the spray of milk hit her tongue, then let it dribble off her chin. Then a few drops went down. She swallowed, looked confused for a minute, and then held her mouth open. I laughed and gave her another splash, and then another.

I was rocking her to sleep when she began coughing. I patted her back, as if burping her. It didn't help. She seemed to be gasping for breath. She opened her mouth, tears rolling down her cheeks, but no sound came out for so long that her face turned red. I patted her back, harder now, calling her name, and finally she burst out in a howl. Thick mucus was coming from her nose. I wiped it away, but her nasal passages seemed clogged. Her chest began heaving.

I felt a trickle of fear slide down my neck. "Vita!" I shouted, nearly running now. "She can't breathe! She can't breathe!"

Vita had been taking a shower. She wrapped a towel around her chest and took Chipo, looking at her nose. Without hesitating, she laid her down on the bathroom counter. She bent and placed her mouth crossways over Chipo's, as if giving mouth-to-mouth resuscitation. Then she blew. The blast of air went into Chipo's mouth, through her sinuses and down her nasal passages, expelling clogged mucus onto Vita's cheek. She took a breath and did it again. Chipo was screaming then, loud enough to hurt the ears, but vocal evidence she could breathe again.

I returned her to my shoulder, rocking her back and forth, wrapped in warm, soft clothes and blankets. She finally drifted into sleep, only to awaken thirty minutes later gasping for breath, as if she had been underwater. I would give her some more warm milk and she would doze. Then the whole process would start over. That night, we placed her in an infant-carrying basket and put it between us in the bed so that we could more closely monitor her breathing.

At some point in the night, she had another coughing fit. I took her in the bathroom and repeated the procedure Vita had used earlier. I felt the wet slap of mucus on my beard. She cried in outrage. "It's not such a hoot on this end either, little girl," I said, washing phlegm out of my ear.

The next day passed in this manner, too. In between feeding and naps and rocking Chipo, I began to pack my bags and monitor reports out of Congo, trying to get my attention focused on a daunting assignment. The rebellion was advancing across the country with lightning speed. Foreign nationals were fleeing Kinshasa. The American embassy, aware of the CIA's long and sorry history in the country during the Cold War, told its five hundred nationals to flee the country or "face attack or detention."

Journalists, meanwhile, were trying to get in as fast as everyone else was trying to get out. Since there was no direct flight from Harare to Kinshasa, I booked a flight to Nairobi on Monday, and then on to Kinshasa the next day.

We slept with Chipo between us again on Saturday night. We didn't leave the house all day Sunday, keeping to the steady, unnerving routine of helping her to breathe, to get some sort of nourishment, to ease her screams. It was long after nightfall when we reluctantly took her back to the orphanage, as required. Helen Tanyayiwa was heading the night shift. We helped her tuck in one infant, then another, under their sheets. The night was chilly, and we bundled up Chipo in a forest of blankets. She was dozing again.

"I'll see you tomorrow, little baby," Vita whispered, giving her a light kiss on the cheek, so as to not wake her. I added my own, and then we slipped outside. We started the truck and drove home in the darkness. The roads were deserted.

"I wish I weren't leaving just now," I said.

"She'll be fine," Vita said. "I'll go see her every day. We girls will manage."

I smiled. "I know. I'll check in on the satellite phone."

The next morning, Vita rode with me in a taxi to the airport. I slung my computer bag across one shoulder and gripped a small carry-on in the other hand. "I'll be back when this thing blows over," I said. "Three weeks, six on the outside."

"Don't get dead," she said, giving me a kiss at our standard parting line. Then she told the taxi driver to stop by Chinyaradzo before heading home.

5

"BREATHE, BABY, BREATHE"

THE INFANT WARD was in high clamor when Vita walked in, with children crawling on playmates or eating or being changed or crying in their cribs. The second crib on the right was still. Vita looked down to see Chipo wriggling silently. She was struggling to breathe. Vita pulled open the child's clothes and was stunned to see Chipo's heart ricocheting off her chest, each beat etching a sharp tattoo against her rib cage. She could scarcely open her eyes, the lids puffy and discolored. Her diaper was filled with diarrhea. It appeared no one had touched her since the previous evening.

Vita didn't hesitate. She picked up the soiled infant, rushed out of the ward, turned into another short hallway, and barged into Stella's office. "I'm taking her to the hospital," she said. Stella looked up, startled. She stood up, looked Chipo over, and quickly agreed with Vita's decision. Protocol was for a worker to take the sick child to the hospital in the orphanage's van or to have the hospital send an ambulance. Vita had no legal authority to admit the child to a hospital. But the situation was critical, and Stella gave Vita directions to the public ward of Harare Hospital.

Vita got back in the waiting cab and ignored that. She told the driver to rush to the Trauma Center, a privately run, cash-only clinic that offered the country's best medical care. They pulled up to the emergency entrance in a screech. The gatekeeper peered inside, saw a black woman with a child, and refused to open the gate.

Vita responded with a Motown flair for the direct. "My baby is sick!" she shouted, coming halfway out of the car. "Now open this gate before I beat your behind into the asphalt!"

Startled, the man did.

Inside, the doctor on call took Chipo from Vita and placed her on an examining table. Chipo was in a frenzy by now, screaming and shaking her arms and legs. The doctor looked at Vita, slowly shaking his head.

"It's her heart," he said.

He gave her an injection to calm her, then transferred her to the Avenues Clinic, the town's premier hospital. He scribbled a note that she was to be taken to one of the only pediatric cardiologists in the country, Isidore Pazvakavambwa.

When Dr. Pazvakavambwa touched Chipo, she screamed as if her skin were on fire. Vita was so upset that nurses had to lead her from the room. She sat in the gloomy hallway until Dr. Paz, as Vita began calling him, appeared. He was an albino, his pale face almost hidden beneath a large safari hat and thick glasses. When he learned Vita was not the child's birth mother, he was touched by her devotion, for his own youth as a social oddity had taught him something about the fate of left-behind or ostracized children.

He asked for Chipo's history. Vita relayed the tale of her birth and hospitalizations. He said the child had been born prematurely, perhaps by as much as a month. Her vital organs were very weak, especially her heart. She also had pneumonia and bronchitis. "If she makes it through tonight, the immediate danger will be past," he said. "But that is only a chance. She is a very sick child."

Vita rushed to buy diapers, bottles, clothes, and formula—the hospital did not provide any—and settled in for the vigil.

Chipo had been placed in an outdated oxygen tent, actually a clear plastic shell that fit over her head. She was so small that it could have covered her entire body. There were two other children in the four-bed ward, with equally concerned mothers. They regarded Vita with glares. Her clothes, the goods she had bought Chipo, and her direct manner in talking with the doctors and nurses were conspicuously Western and upscale. She didn't need to be told she was resented. It was the first time in her life that she didn't feel like an African American. The looks she got made it clear: She was an American, period.

The women turned inward then, and each settled in for the long hours ahead. There was little Vita could do but tap on the plastic shell when Chipo was awake and make eye contact. "Breathe, baby, breathe," she coaxed. Time dragged by into the small hours. It was 2 and then 3 A.M. The hallways were dark and deserted. It was quiet. In spite of herself, Vita gradually nodded off. She came to, sitting bolt upright in a chair, just after daylight. Chipo was asleep, her chest moving slightly up and down with each breath. Vita closed her eyes and said a prayer of thanks. Dr. Paz was delighted when he came by on his morning rounds. By that afternoon, he even allowed Chipo out of the oxygen tent for a few minutes so that Vita could walk her back and forth in the hall. Her body was warm, a sensation that delighted Vita, but her breathing was shallow and fast. Her eyes seemed a listless shade of brown. Her head lolled back on her shoulders. She went back under the shell, into the hiss of the oxygen.

The next day, the shell stayed on for twenty-two hours. The day after, twelve hours. By this point, Vita had all but moved into the ward, returning home only to shower and sleep for a couple of hours.

"I have a question for you," Dr. Paz said to her late one afternoon. "Chipo is well enough to go home. But she is so small, her lungs and heart so weak. If I sign the papers for her to return to Chinyaradzo, I am signing her death warrant. She will not live if she is returned there. I want to know if you and your husband would take this child in. I do not mean for a while. I mean to stay for always. If you say yes, I will inform the home and the Department of Social Welfare that this will be my recommendation."

"You mean she would be ours?"

"If you wish."

Vita, who had given up on ever having children, felt a swoop of hope pass through her, a sensation like the flapping of the wings of a small and unseen bird.

"Of course we will," she said.

The next morning, Vita found herself taking Chipo home in a taxi. She had tried to call my hotel in Kinshasa but could not get through. This was particularly unnerving, because Chipo would never have been released at that stage in a Western country, and now Vita had the child alone—in better conditions than the orphanage, and perhaps even better than the hospital, but still alone. She nervously eyed the combinations of liquid medicines Chipo needed to combat the pneumonia and break up the fluid in her lungs. It was difficult. Like most every infant, Chipo would take a teaspoon of medicine and spray it back out, but her life depended on that medicine getting into her bloodstream. Vita would let one blast of medicine splatter onto her shirt, then get another and coax it down, time after time. She tapped her on the back four or five sessions a day to try to dislodge the phlegm. She grew unnerved and exhausted, for Chipo rarely slept more than an hour at a time.

After several days, the disorientation of sleep deprivation became apparent. There didn't seem to be a way out. The intensive-care session had no doubt saved Chipo's life, but there was no hospital in Zimbabwe Vita trusted enough to call for help in an emergency. She had learned that distrust firsthand.

The previous year, a minibus had plowed the wrong way down a one-way street, smashing into her car head-on. It cracked her collarbone, which the paramedics snapped in two when they lifted her out of the car by picking her up under the shoulders. A crowd gathered as she lay on the grass next to the wreckage. She felt a tugging on her boots, at first thinking it was the paramedics. But it persisted, and she opened her eyes to see that a bystander had knelt down and was stealing the boots off her feet, tugging hard to get them off. Once he got them, he stood up and walked away. No one stopped him. Then the paramedic stuck an ungloved finger into the open gash on her leg. "Uuhh, that's deep," he said. Later, after doctors set the fracture, they allowed an artery to fuse onto the snapped collarbone. It wound up requiring a trip to Johannesburg and a four-hour operation, all to set a broken bone.

She was grateful to Dr. Paz, but in fact she was dependent on him now. Chipo had little documentation that she even existed, much less a birth certificate or traveling papers. The first-rate hospitals of Johannesburg were just a ninety-minute flight away, but there was no way Vita could get Chipo there. Fortunately, Mavis Ganuka, the housekeeper who lived on the grounds, was enchanted with Chipo. She had raised five children of her own. She didn't hesitate to tie Chipo onto her back, in the traditional mode of child transport, and go about her chores. Chipo, soothed by the intimate body contact, would drift to sleep. In a gradual rotation, the two women made it through one day, and then one more.

HALF A CONTINENT AWAY, I was not calling home every day. I had fallen into a different world. Kinshasa was filled with the pandemonium of a city expecting a military invasion. Congo was a sprawling country, but to effectively seize control of what little government apparatus there was required only that Kinshasa be taken. The rebels knew this and, rather than fight their way through each section of the country, were making for the capital.

I flew into Kinshasa with my buddy and frequent travel partner, Ann Simmons, the Nairobi bureau chief for the *Los Angeles Times*. Since our papers did not compete for readers, we often watched each other's back on difficult assignments. We landed in Kinshasa's tumultuous airport, where men shoved and fought to grab luggage to take to a friend's aging car, euphemistically called a taxi. Then you paid a hefty tip so that you might leave with your luggage. It only took a day or two in the city before we discovered we were an almost comically unpopular pair. My passport was American, which was bad enough, but the only thing people noticed about me on the street was my close-cropped beard and long ponytail. *"Frenchman,"* they spat. Since France had been one of the colonial exploiters of Congo, the French were perhaps more despised than the Americans at this emotional juncture. Ann was a British national but had an equally problematic appearance: She was six feet two inches tall, slim, and had the dark skin of the West Indies, thanks to Caribbean parents. She was also graced with a long, slender neck. The combination made Ann a striking woman anywhere she went—and in Kinshasa, it made her appear strikingly Tutsi, the hated Nilotic "invaders."

The rebel army, whatever its soldiers' ethnic composition, was closing in. They took the hydroelectric dam that gave power to the city. They would cut the power off, then turn it on and shut it off again to proclaim their approach.

In return, Kabila announced he wanted to arm the general population to defend themselves. The streets went electric. Shops belonging to Tutsis, or people thought to be Tutsis, were torched. Large bands of young men roamed the avenues, pointing sticks at passing cars as if they were holding rifles. Businesses were shutting down, except for travel agents' offices, which were drawing steady lines of expatriates.

There was a rally scheduled for 10 A.M. the next day at the city stadium. We went to the stadium half an hour early, when people would be streaming in but not yet stirred by speeches. We agreed to stay less than fifteen minutes. It's a rule of thumb of sorts among correspondents that if your car is not attacked upon arrival in a hostile neighborhood, you've probably got a few minutes before a crowd forms and emotions soar. In most places, the idea is to get off the street, into a shop or even a market stall, where you are not immediately visible.

As we pulled into the dirt-and-gravel parking lot of the stadium, set in a poor section of a very poor city, there were no such stalls or closed spaces. There were only streams of thousands of young men, apparently none over thirty and most in their teens. Some were squaring off into military squads. They tried to march, with exaggerated goose steps and set faces, while a man in front screamed directions.

We told the driver to stay in the car, roll up the windows, and not open the door for anyone but us. "If you see us come running," I said, "be ready to go." We stepped out with our interpreter, who went by the name of Jean-Peter. I clicked my watch over to its stopwatch mode so that we would stay no longer than the fifteen minutes we'd decided on. We headed for a group of men who were flying banners and chanting "*Vive* Kabila!" then, in Lingala, "Death to the Tutsis!" We stepped over a large pipe, the crowd around us growing thicker as we approached the chanting men. The noise was deafening. A tall man was walking alongside me, shouting in French. I shouted back, tapping on my chest, that I was American. He stood between Ann and me and shouted, "The Banyamulenge [the word for Tutsis born in Congo] are animals! They are savages who must be exterminated! They want to come in, stay forever, and colonize us! They must go home to Rwanda!" He gave his name as Steve Mukena, an electrician, and as I wrote I glanced at my watch. Seven minutes. Someone yanked on my hair. Jean-Peter was trying to hold several men back, leaning up against them with his shoulder. An alarmed look came over his face in response to what he was hearing. He looked at Ann, then me, and shouted, "Leave this place!" He then turned and yelled back at the men who were shouting at him. It was impossible to hear anything. I grabbed his arm, Ann locked her arm in his other one, and we began to try to move backward through the crowd. The men saw this for what it was, an awkward retreat, and responded with jeers and whistles. Someone shoved me in the back. Someone kicked at my leg. We moved faster, Ann letting go of my arm to step over the pipe, and I felt a sharp whack across my shoulders. It felt like a stiff rubber hose or a slender stick, but I didn't turn to look. A man spat in my face. Rocks began flying. A hand was in my back, steadily shoving. *Jean-Peter*, I thought, *give me a break. I'm going.* The man with the hose or stick skittered alongside of me, lashing my back, then the back of my knee, causing it to swing out in front of me. From the other side, a man began kicking me in the ass with his foot. I acknowledged none of this, just concentrated on moving forward and not falling down. I turned to tell Ann something, and Ann was not there.

My stomach fell into a pit. I turned to yell at Jean-Peter that we had to find her, but the man shoving me in the back wasn't Jean-Peter. It was a young man, his mouth turned into a snarl, his shirt ripped, his eyes glazed. I turned to look for the car and it wasn't there. I was, in fact, standing amid rows and rows of cars that I didn't remember from when we had parked. I turned, looking for our car, but my nerves were rattled and the shouting was intense and I suddenly couldn't remember what color or make it was. I had just seen the thing for a second when we got in that morning. I cursed myself now for not having paid closer attention. Dust was kicking up from all the feet. Sweat was pouring down my back. The man who had been kicking me reached out and kicked me again, aiming at the side of my knee. I blocked him with my arm, still scanning the crowd, starting to move again, and then I saw the top of Ann's head, moving above the others, perhaps fifty yards away. I loved her just then for being so tall. I made my way as quickly as I could, ignoring the lashings, and caught up with her and Jean-Peter as we reached the car. We got in. "Get moving!" Ann snapped at the driver, but he pointed over the hood of the car. I turned, and there was a soldier at the front bumper, an AK-47 pointed at us. He glared, swung it to the left, and stepped aside. The driver edged forward, then hit the gas.

> >

AT TEN IN the morning the following day in Nairobi, U.S. ambassador Prudence Bushnell was conducting a polite meeting with several Kenyan trade officials on the eighteenth floor of the Cooperative Bank building, a high-rise with long rows of windows on each floor, affording views of the entire city. She had a brief news conference for local reporters, then they served tea. Two doors down at the embassy, State Department employee Frank Pressley was talking to his colleague Michelle O'Connor about a broken fax machine in the General Services office. He noticed a commotion outside. They were at the back of the building, with a view of the parking lot, and he could see men running. A tremor ran along the walls and windows, as if there had been a small explosion. People joined him at the window.

Then there was a tremendous blast that seemed white at its core, and the shock waves roared through ten blocks of downtown Nairobi. Vans were blown off the street, cars flipped into the air. Eighteen stories up, the windows shattered, the furniture flew across the room, and Ambassador Bushnell was thrown to the floor. Ufundi House, a five-story office building between the embassy and the bank, collapsed like a stack of pancakes. In the embassy, Michelle O'Connor was decapitated. A passing school bus was lashed with flame, killing several children on board. The twenty-two floors of glass in the Cooperative Bank building blew out, the shattered panes spinning two hundred feet above the street, and then they tumbled down, down, falling sheets of glass that cut pedestrians in half and gouged out their eyes and sliced off their arms and fingers. Pressley, knocked unconscious, came to on the floor of the embassy, looking at blood on the walls and O'Connor's remains. He looked down. "I saw my body sticking out of my shirt," he later told a Manhattan jury. His jaw and part of one shoulder had been torn away from his body.

There was a vast silence, and then the air seemed to

condense and everything rushed together, the screams of the dying and a dense plume of dust and smoke rising into the air. Desks and chairs dangled out of the windows of the Cooperative Bank, then plummeted to the parking lot below. The deadliest attack on a U.S. embassy since the Beirut bombing in 1983 was over, but the death toll was just beginning.

In Kinshasa, almost halfway across the continent, Ann and I were still scrambling around town, preparing for the invasion. The rebels were now moving hard for the city's airport. The word was that the airfield would shut down the next day, if not that afternoon. At a sullen little outdoor cafe, I used a cell phone to call my desk back in the States.

"Thank God," said editor Joyce Davis when she heard my voice. "The bombing is all over everything. I've been trying to reach you for two hours." I stood up and scanned the horizon, hating to be scooped on a bombing in Kinshasa by an editor in Washington, but saw no plume of smoke. I sat down, wrote "bomb" on my notepad, and turned it around so Ann could see it. "We were just getting our cell phone so I could call in," I said, stalling for time.

"They're saying at least one hundred dead, likely more. That building behind the embassy just collapsed."

I stood up again, by now alarmed that Ann and I were twiddling our thumbs while our colleagues were across town, covering the story of the year. "Right, right. Which embassy was that again?"

"Nairobi, of course, the U.S. embassy," she said. "And at Dar es Salaam too. A smaller one there. Ah—wait. It's on CNN again. My God, that building is just flattened. People are screaming. It looks terrible. How quick can you get there?"

"Real quick," I lied, furiously scribbling notes for Ann: "U.S. embassy bomb—Nairobi—100+ dead." She took one look and started for the taxi. "There's just one small bit of bad news, Joyce, which is that they're closing the airport here."

"*Closing* it?" Joyce shouted. "How can they close the

airport? You mean you can't get out? You mean you're going to be stuck in Congo?"

"There is the small matter of an armed invasion," I reminded her. "And I didn't say we couldn't get out. I said we're going to have to run. I'll be on a plane in three hours or know the reason why. I'll call you back."

Ann and I split up, trying to double our chances of finding a flight leaving the city, bound for anywhere. There was no small jet to charter—Nairobi was more than fifteen hundred miles away, which would require a refueling stop in rebel-held territory, which would likely get us shot down. While I went nowhere checking that out, Ann found two of the last seats on the only flight leaving Kinshasa that evening—an overnight Sabena Airlines flight to Brussels, Belgium. Then there was a connection back down to Nairobi, another eight hours. We would arrive at 9 P.M. Saturday. That was just enough time for me to rush into town, talk to three people at the bomb site, and file a story in sixty minutes or less. Ann, with a West Coast deadline, had an extra three hours. It wasn't pretty, but it would mean we would file in time for Sunday's paper, the week's most important edition. The only seats left were first-class, and they cost $3,900 each. That was if we could get to the airport in time. The flight left in two hours.

We threw clothes in bags and money at the checkout desk, then ducked into the car. The roads were jammed in a turbulent, horn-honking melee. Evening cooking fires arose from roadside stands where vendors were selling fabrics, fruit, or raw meat. The stalls spilled into the roadway at narrow junctures. Buses belched exhaust. At two traffic lights, young men pounded on the windows or yelled from across the street, screaming at us to go home, for Ann to go back to Kigali, the Rwandan capital.

"I'm going to miss this place so much," I said.

The airport was a mess. Cars pulled up to the dilapidated terminal, where crowds of young men clamored to carry your luggage, whether you wanted them to or not. We got out, shoved people away from the trunk, popped open the lid and grabbed our bags, and pushed our way through a loud foul-smelling crowd to the Sabena ticket counter. We stood at the back of a crazy-quilt mélange of a line that was peopled by men and well-dressed businesswomen. There were Nigerians, Guyanese, Brits, Americans, South Africans, French, Belgians, Ethiopians, Lebanese—a multicolored potpourri of foreign nationals who wanted to be on the other side of the border. In the crush, people tried to edge their way in front of one another, or slip under a rope and leap to the front. For any foreign correspondent, the prospect of calling back to the desk and explaining that yes, a plane with 250 people just took off and no, I wasn't on it, is not a happy one. So we shoved and jostled and threw elbows with the best of them, sweating in the heat, until we made it to the counter and got our boarding cards in hand.

As darkness fell, the plane and baggage were checked for bombs. We sat on the steaming tarmac, under guard from U.S. Marines, while all carry-on bags were opened and searched. We lumbered down the runway two hours late. The pilot then announced, in English and French, that we would be making an unscheduled short stop in Luanda, the Angolan capital. Fighting in that nation's long civil war had started up again, and there were a couple of evacuees who had to be picked up as well.

I thought about that for a minute. Then I turned to Ann and said, "Isn't Luanda south of Kinshasa?"

"Of course."

"Isn't Brussels north?"

Ann got it. "We're going to miss our connection to Nairobi."

Ten hours later, we were running down the corridors of the Brussels airport, just in time to see the flight attendants seal the doors on our plane. I shouted. I railed. I slapped my $3,900 ticket on the counter and demanded they open the door and let us on. The clerk behind the counter said they couldn't do that; besides, the flight was fully booked. "Then tell someone who didn't pay $4,000 to scoot over," I shouted.

The bluster went nowhere. We watched as the plane backed away from the terminal and rolled down the tarmac. "We get through Kinshasa and get stiffed in Brussels," Ann said. "Go figure."

We were rerouted on a flight to London, where we cooled our heels, watched the Sunday paper go to press without us, and waited for another overnight flight. I called Vita but got the answering machine. I wasn't concerned. We had often been longer than this without talking. I was sure she and Chipo were fine.

6

AWAY FROM HOME

NN AND I split up once we got to the Nairobi airport. I tumbled into a taxi, groggy from the second
overnight flight in as many days. A few minutes later,
when we were still at the edges of the savanna on the outskirts
of town, the driver pointed out the pall of dust and smoke that
still hung over the horizon, a haze that gave a funereal air to an
overcast winter morning. We made our way through the oddly
quiet streets, and I got out. The ruined hump of Ufundi House
was a twisted hunk of steel, collapsed concrete, and mounds of
dirt that was two stories high. Israeli and Kenyan rescue workers stood on top of the debris, working with a 150-ton crane to
lift huge chunks of concrete. The steel rods that had been set
inside them reared into the sky, exposed, like angry tentacles.
Rescue teams lowered tiny microphones into crevasses, listening for tapping on walls or muffled whimpers from people
trapped alive. Others worked with shovels and picks. Many of
the victims were secretaries who had been sitting at their
desks when the roof caved in, mashing their bodies into the tables in front of them and then burying them beneath tons of
rubble.

"I lifted a slab of concrete and there was a head beneath it,"
said Jackson Muthomi, an engineer who was walking off the
pile of rubble, nauseous. "I kept pulling the stuff, the bricks,
the concrete, away from the body, and then the middle section

turned into this bloody mush, all the intestines and entrails or whatever is the proper name were spilled out, the liver or something, and there was shit coming out of the intestines and there wasn't any more body below it."

The adjacent embassy was sealed off. Rescue workers from Fairfax County, Virginia, detailed to the State Department, searched the floors while Marines stood guard behind hastily erected cordons. Across Haile Selassie Avenue, police and FBI investigators were hauling chunks of automobiles and battered bits of steel and concrete to a parking lot that had been converted into an open-air investigation center. Thousands of people stood around the perimeter of the scene, dumbstruck.

Red Cross officials said there was still hope of finding someone alive in the rubble. There was a woman trapped far below the surface, Rose Wanjiku, who could be heard by rescuers. They began digging for her. At the hospital, thousands of the wounded, and thousands more of their relatives, filled the corridors and sprawled out onto the grass of the courtyard. The waiting rooms were filled and the rooms were jammed.

The morgue was awash in bodies and blood. More than forty unidentified and badly mutilated corpses were splayed out, two to a table, uncovered. The stench of decaying flesh and formaldehyde washed over me like a bad memory from Sarajevo. Families trickled in, stepping around pools of dried blood, looking to identify missing relatives. They covered their noses with kerchiefs. There was a sudden movement near one of the bodies, and an elderly woman plopped down next to the corpse of a mutilated young woman. Almost all her clothes had been blown off. Her body was pierced and burned by dozens of gashes that sliced through her arms, legs, face, neck, and torso. One breast had been severed. Her hair was set in delicate braids, still pulled back into a ponytail. Her toenails were painted a light purple. The older woman swooned with grief, her high-pitched trill bouncing off the walls.

Two bodies over lay a man's corpse, similarly pierced, but with his head split open between the eyes, as if the top half had been cleaved in two with an ax. The brain was gone. One of his eyes had popped out and lay against his cheek.

Over the course of several days, the scenario of what had happened that day would slowly emerge. Shortly before 10 A.M., a small truck carrying several men pulled to the front of the embassy, where three-foot-high barriers prevented them from pulling onto the sidewalk. The guards waved them to the back entrance. Once there, they were refused access to a drive that led to the embassy's underground garage. The driver sped over a small curb but was blocked from going farther by a drop-down gate. Several men emerged from the truck. A couple of U.S. Marines came over. Guns were drawn, the men firing several rounds before throwing a concussion grenade—the first, small blast Pressley heard inside the embassy. Then some of them ran. Others detonated a huge bomb set on the back of the truck, some five hundred pounds of explosives.

The blast killed more than 240 people, 12 of them Americans. The bomb in Dar es Salaam, which went off five minutes after the Nairobi bomb, killed 10 Tanzanians. More than 4,800 people were injured in both blasts, the deadliest attack against an American institution abroad since a suicide bomber killed 241 soldiers at the U.S. Marine base in Beirut in 1983. The first arrest was of Mohammed Sadiq Odeh, a Palestinian national who was detained in Pakistan while trying to cross into Afghanistan on a forged Yemeni passport. He admitted to taking part in the bombing, but that was about all anyone knew at the time. It would be two years later, after the World Trade Center had been leveled, before the connection to Afghanistan would fully resonate.

That first day, very little was clear. I made it back to the hotel with seventy-five minutes to file a fifteen-hundred-word story, munching chocolate and drinking Cokes to stay awake. Then I used the satellite telephone to call Vita before editors started calling me back with queries and clarifications.

"Where have you *been*?" she shouted.

"Half of Africa and a quarter of Europe," I mumbled. "The Nairobi embassy blew up. Didn't you hear?"

"Sort of," she snapped. "I'm a little preoccupied. Chipo nearly died." I sat up. Vita sounded as tired as I felt.

"What?"

She gave a quick synopsis of the past week, the emergency room and the hospital and the marathon of caring for her at home. She ended with Dr. Paz's recommendation that Chipo live with us.

"What? You mean to stay?"

"To stay."

"Jesus, baby. I had no idea. Why didn't you call me?"

"Where? How? Who can ever find you? It took two days and three operators to get the hotel in Kinshasa, and you had gone. You're always in some remote spot or another, or in transit, and no one can ever track you down until you call in. I finally got your message and figured you'd show up in Nairobi sooner or later."

That stung. Sitting in my hotel room, I had the sensation of how the child had felt in my arms, how weightless she had seemed, how hard she had struggled just to breathe. That feeling when she took my finger in her hand returned, and I looked out the window. How could I have left? What had I been thinking? Chipo would have died had it not been for Vita, I realized, which was another way of saying she would not have lived had it been left to me. It was difficult to speak.

"Is she stable?"

"Well, yes, I think so. But she doesn't sleep more than an hour at a time. Mavis is helping. The social workers are coming tomorrow to do a home study. But Dr. Paz said no more Chinyaradzo for Chipo."

The speed of it all was overwhelming—I had left home seven days earlier, when we were committed to doing what we could on weekends for a child we scarcely knew. Now we were set to become caretakers of a terribly ill infant, as Dr. Paz had left no room for doubt about the magnitude of the responsibility he had asked of us. I found myself trying to say, again and again, that I would not have traveled if I had known she had been so desperately ill, but it seemed flat and defensive, if not just a lie; who was I kidding? Vita knew better than anyone that my job defined my life. It wasn't a paycheck. It was all of me, a careening mixture of energy, creativity, and curiosity. It was my drug.

Meanwhile, social workers had told Vita that, with Dr. Paz's letter, traditional restrictions on adoptions would be greatly eased. Fostering and adoption would be mere formalities for a child in Chipo's condition. The fostering process, Vita was told, would be concluded in a few short weeks. The adoption would be a matter of paperwork.

There was no time to take stock of all we had just taken on, and little inclination to do so. We hung up a few minutes later, when Vita had assured me that everything was all right. I worked the words *parents* and *father* around in my mouth, trying to get used to them. I ordered champagne from room service, trying to summon the energy for a small celebration. But I fell asleep in my chair, fully dressed with all the lights on, waiting for my desk to call back, too exhausted to drink the stuff.

I awoke three hours later with violent stomach cramps. I made for the bathroom, and my left knee, the one that had been whacked in Kinshasa, collapsed under me, sending me to the floor with an awkward thump. I crawled to the bathroom and was indecently ill. I peeled off my shirt, drenched with sweat, and looked in the mirror. I had nasty bruises across my back from the lashing I had taken in the parking lot. My head spun; my joints ached so badly I couldn't stand up. After half an hour, I gave up trying to make it back to the bed. I curled onto the bathroom floor, using a towel for a pillow. In this fevered state, nightmares of startling clarity came sliding by. In the dream, I was walking through the morgue again, but it was not the mutilated young woman with the purple nail polish whom I saw on the table. It was a young girl I had once seen in the morgue in Sarajevo. She had been wounded in a shelling. She could not have been more than five. The hole in her chest could not have been more than an inch wide. She was not the first person I watched die, but her face was the one that hung in my memory, her black hair falling from her forehead, her mouth open and soundless, her head bouncing as a man swept her into his arms and ran screaming into Kosovo Hospital. It was the one image of war that my mind ran in a loop at times of great stress or depression. Now it played it back to me but transposed her corpse to the Nairobi morgue. A tiny body lay on the adjacent steel table. As I moved closer in the watery movement of dreams, I could see that it was Chipo. Her body was badly mutilated. She lay in her own dried blood.

I awoke with a violent start. Sweat was pooling in the small of my back, my navel; I ran a hand across my neck and it came away soaked. Then I was ill again. I staggered around the hotel room, shaking my head to clear the mental fog, opening the balcony window for fresh air. I soon lapsed back into sleep, only to see the same images. I snapped back awake and, this time, stayed that way. I called the hotel's concierge at 4 A.M., asking for a doctor. I got a return call from an Italian voice thirty minutes later. He said to meet him in his office at 7:30 and gave me directions. I watched the hands on the clock inch forward for three hours and then heaved myself down downstairs into a taxi.

"Food poisoning," he said, after prodding about for a few minutes. "Your heart is very slow. I have counted it at thirty-eight beats per minute. Your pulse is weak and your blood pressure is very low. Have you been sick like this before?"

"I had something like typhus once, in Iraq. They never figured out exactly what it was."

"Well. You are dehydrated, I think, and what I would call clinically exhausted. You look terrible, you know." He scratched out a prescription for antibiotics, for things to calm my stomach. "Stay in your room for a couple of days, lie still, fly home. You will feel very bad. But don't worry, I do not think you are going to die."

I mumbled that this was good news, but added I was there to cover the bombing, not to go on safari. I couldn't sit in my hotel. He shrugged. "Carry a plastic bag," he said. "Because you're going to be one very sick man."

In the days ahead, as the fever worsened, I reported the major events of the story like everyone else. Rose, the woman trapped in the wreckage, died just hours before she could be rescued, while her husband stood by the mound of rubble, praying in vain for a miracle. FBI agents swarmed into the Hilltop Hotel, an $8-per-night, all-male residency hotel in a hardscrabble district of Nairobi, where the bomb was apparently put together. Six or seven men had stayed in rooms A-107 and B-102, assembling part of the bomb, then hauled it downstairs and onto the back of a flatbed truck. They had finished the bomb there, then drove to the embassy. Three of them apparently died in the explosion. (Four men were later arrested and convicted in a Manhattan trial.) Osama bin Laden's World Islamic Front Against Jews and Crusaders issued a warning through an Arab newspaper: "The coming days will guarantee, God willing, that America will suffer a black fate."

Meanwhile, I lost eleven pounds in four days. I was so dizzy I took to writing stories with one eye closed and the other squinted nearly shut to keep my equilibrium. And more and more often, I found my mind going back to an incident that had occurred the second day I was in Nairobi.

I had stopped back by the morgue. There were families lingering about, those who had hope and those who had resigned themselves. At the entrance to the unit where they were bringing the mangled remains from the bomb site, there was a man I recognized from the day before. He was wearing a black suit, white shirt, tie, and vest, with a carnation in the lapel. Amid the stench and the flies, curious, I introduced myself. He said he was John Mungai, pastor of Nairobi's Apostolic Faith Church. I had no need to interview a man of the cloth at that point, and as I prepared to take my leave, he said quietly, "I am not here as a pastor. I am here only for Margaret," he said.

I told him I did not understand.

"My daughter." He paused, fumbling with his wallet. He produced a picture. It showed a young woman with a radiant smile. She was wearing a white blouse with a lace collar. She had her hair neatly pulled back in braids, a good complexion, and cheerful brown eyes.

"She's very pretty," I said.

"She is, yes," he said. He began talking in the present tense. "She is our daughter. She is twenty years old. She is studying at the secretarial college there at Ufundi House. I believe it is on the third floor. She takes the bus each day, and then she takes the bus home each night. She lives with her mother and me.

"She took the bus last Friday, and there was the bomb. We waited at home. We were sure she would come, but she did not. We went to the hospital, then the clinics. Then we came here."

He inspected each load of carnage for something that might have once been his daughter, even detached limbs. He toured the room of corpses each day to make sure he had not missed her.

"We pray and have hope for her, of course," he said. "But I only wish that she will be found now, so we can give her our final love and goodbyes." He grasped my hand to shake it, and then he leaned closer and whispered, "She comes to me every night in my dreams, my brother, and she is crying for help. I see her trapped under the rubble. She is crying for help, but no one can assist her. I can hear her but not find her, cannot get to her." He stared, not more than a few inches from my face. I didn't know what to do. We were in a crowd of neatly dressed men and women, whom I assumed were members of his extended family, as well as a few reporters and photographers. It was an oddly personal moment in a public setting, and Mungai seemed to be suddenly aware of this. He let go of my hand.

"Do you have children, Mr. Tucker?"

The question caught me by surprise. It was the day after Vita had called with the news about Chipo.

"Yes," I said, at last. "Well . . . yes. I do. A daughter."

"How old is she, may I ask?"

"She's not even one."

"She is well?"

"She is beautiful."

"You should love her, every day," he said softly.

7

VITAL SIGNS

I HAD BEEN gone nearly a month by the time I staggered home to Harare. What I found was alarming. Vita had not slept much more than an hour at a stretch for weeks and had a thousand-yard stare worthy of any combat-weary Marine. Chipo would seem fine for a few hours, then her breathing would turn ragged and desperate. Her breathing was so uneven, and her crying and thrashing so fierce, that during the nights Vita put her in that infant-carrying basket and then placed it on the bed beside her. The basket prevented Vita from rolling onto her during the night, but it also kept Chipo close enough so that she would know, even by smell, that someone was with her. When I returned, we slept with Chipo between us in the basket. The crib we had bought went unused.

Her breath was faint as mist and almost as hard to hear. I would move her about the house with me through the day, carrying her around in an infant's car seat, setting her by my desk while I put together my expenses from Kinshasa and the bombing. Vita had been trying to get Chipo to eat as much as possible, and showed me how to warm up the formula, hold it for Chipo, and try to coax down every last drop. I took over the night shift, while Vita tried to get some much-needed sleep. In the small hours, when Chipo struggled to draw breath, I held her against my chest and lay back in a reclining chair, pulling a blanket over both of us. I would begin to doze, lulled by watching her chest rise and fall, rise and fall, tiny waves in the ocean of sleep. I was somehow convinced I would be jolted awake if the rhythm stopped. I kept a log of her sleep patterns, in case a physician should need them. A sample entry: In bed at 9 P.M. Awake at 10:45 P.M., 12:10 A.M., 1:20, 1:50, 2:55, 4:20, 5:40, and finally 6:20. At each of these, I would scoop her up, pat her back to clear her congestion, and walk around the house, rocking her back to sleep. I took to going outside and talking to the night guard, Tofa Kachidza. He had two children of his own. He would sometimes carry Chipo for a walk around the grounds, singing softly to her in Shona, while I splashed water from the swimming pool onto my face to stay awake. Just after daybreak, I would be heating water in the kitchen to make her formula and a nutrient-rich infant cereal, called Cerelac, that was her breakfast. I sat her on the kitchen counter in her carrying basket and she would watch me bump around the kitchen, three fingers in her mouth, her other hand curled around a milk bottle that she was still too weak to hold. Sometimes she would try to fit both her fingers and the bottle into her mouth at the same time, a gesture that seemed to combine her need for comfort and her hunger. I would sing whatever came to mind at that groggy hour—vaguely remembered nursery rhymes, jazz standards, even Johnny Cash ballads that popped into my head from my own childhood.

"I keep a close watch on this heart of mine," I sang to her one morning while the coffee was brewing, thumping my leg with a hand for the song's *chugga-chugga* train sound, my face six inches from hers. "I keep my eyes wide open all the time."

She stared back, transfixed.

Vita came into the kitchen.

"*What* are you doing?" she asked.

"Trying to get some response out of her."

"Well, try not to make her scream. Jesus, you're gonna scare her doing that."

"I sing that bad?"

"The dogs howl when you sing, honey."

I was at a loss, as neither Vita nor I had any real experience with children, to say nothing of special-needs infants. Vita had been the good auntie in Detroit, hosting her young nieces for sleepovers. I had changed the occasional diaper for a single-mom friend in a pinch, but that was about it. We didn't even have a decent baby book. Vita had already bought the only child-care editions in local bookstores, but they were badly outdated. Some friends sent theirs, via express mail, that detailed problems with sleep and malnutrition, and we studied those.

Given Chipo's persistent breathing problems, I stopped in town to buy a book on infant CPR. I went to three stores. There wasn't one. Vita finally got one from Dr. Paz's office, a 1996 pamphlet produced by the National Sudden Infant Death Syndrome Council of Australia that had been shipped to Zimbabwe. The emergency number to call was 000, which I took to be the Aussie equivalent of 911. I had no idea what it was in Zimbabwe, and Vita's experience with the paramedics in her car accident rendered it moot anyway—calling that ambulance crew would have been somewhere between useless and frightening. So I turned my attention to the booklet. There were diagrams of how to give your infant heart compressions (you use just two fingers), how to turn the child on her side and clear an airway, how to clear a throat with a finger. You were then to place the infant on her back, support the jaw, give five quick breaths over the mouth and nose, then fifteen compressions (about 2 centimeters, ¾ inch, in depth, the book said). Then you gave two more breaths and repeated the process.

That Chipo's life might depend on how well we performed such a task gave me pause. I logged onto the county's agonizingly slow Internet connection and went to the *Journal of the American Medical Association* Web site. I typed in a search for *pneumonia* and *infants* and got dozens of hits—almost all relating to HIV treatment. It turned out pneumonia in newborns and infants was something of the bellwether of warning systems about HIV infection.

I found it disturbing. No one knew anything of Chipo's biological mother, or father for that matter. But some basic mathematics came into play on her odds of having the virus. One in four pregnant women in Zimbabwe who went to clinics for prenatal exams tested positive for HIV—that was, in fact, the medical test that formed the basis for the country's estimated HIV infection rate. So Chipo, like any child born in Zimbabwe at that time, had a one in four chance of being born to an infected mother. The nature of her discovery, however, suggested that her mother had been in difficult circumstances, therefore making the odds higher.

There weren't many definitive studies out there on mother-to-child HIV transmission in sub-Saharan Africa, so it was difficult to tell what Chipo's chances were if her mother had been infected. The studies available seemed to show that about 39 percent of infected women passed the virus to their children. There were three ways this happened.

The first was when infants were still in the womb. The virus could breach the placenta under certain conditions, particularly if the mother had vaginal or cervical infections. Such infections were rare in Western countries but far more common in the Third World, where women's health issues do not receive the same priority. In Zimbabwe, the preference for "dry sex" further increased the odds for inflammations and infections in the vaginal wall. (Dry sex is a manner of intercourse in which the vagina is kept as dry as possible, mostly with the insertion of various sachets or douches just prior to intercourse.)

The second and much more common method of transmission was during the trauma of delivery. The amniotic sac ruptures, labor starts, the child begins to move through the birth canal, perhaps aspirating blood and other fluids. The longer the exposure to the mother's blood, the greater the chance for infection. Chipo was delivered to Chinyaradzo with her mother's blood and parts of her umbilical cord and placenta still present two days later, a period of time that I was sure the medical journal's editors did not even contemplate.

The third manner of infection was through breastfeeding, which accounted for about one-third of all mother-to-child transmissions. Such as it was, this was Chipo's one break—by abandoning her immediately, her birth mother had eliminated that possibility.

The most troubling indicator by far was her medical chart since birth. It read like a textbook study of the most virulent form of the disease.

Her weight had plummeted by more than 33 percent in her first few weeks. Her breathing was irregular and weak. She was racked with diarrhea. She had had pneumonia at least once; perhaps it was what had sent her to the hospital before. I read the report "Identifying Infants at Risk for HIV Infection" with a growing sense of dread. "Infants born to HIV-infected women should be identified promptly so that prophylaxis can be initiated before these infants are at risk for PCP (pneumocystis carinii pneumonia for children)." Well, she already had pneumonia—but did that mean she was HIV-positive?

It got worse the longer I read, until a paragraph at the end of a list of bulleted items seemed to leap off the page: "Growth failure and neuro-developmental deterioration may be specific manifestations of HIV infection in children." Chipo's weight chart, headed steadily downward, was only too fresh in my mind—as was her nonresponsiveness.

In infants, HIV progresses in two distinct forms. The first and most common, at least in Western countries, is that it behaves much like it does in adults; after infection, the virus can wait for several years before it causes full-blown AIDS. Children so infected would not be particularly ill when young and would likely survive until their teenage years.

The second type, comprising about 20 percent of pediatric AIDS cases studied in the West, is severe and quickly lethal: "Severe immunodeficiency develops quickly within the first year or two, manifested by multiple opportunistic infections and frequently major cognitive dysfunctions as the virus invades the brain. These infants never thrive, and their prognosis is grim. Nearly all die in early childhood."

I sat in my office in silence. Chipo was asleep in her infant's seat next to me. I watched her for several moments and felt far more helpless and scared to the marrow of my bones than I ever had been before. The odds she had so far survived and was now facing sank in on me then, far more clearly than they had that day in the orphanage. I made a three-line grid across a yellow legal pad. Above the top of grid on the left-hand side, I wrote "Just a little sick." Above the middle column, I wrote "HIV+ (slow)." In the third, I wrote "HIV+ (severe)."

I tapped the paper with my pen. In which grid would a reasonable analysis of the information at hand lead one to place a check mark? I considered that for a moment. I didn't like the answer. So I closed the door to the office, picked up the phone, and called an old friend in Detroit.

Kathryn Moseley is a pediatrician and board-certified neonatologist, a doctor who specializes in the care of critically ill infants, and her practice focused on black children. She was educated at Harvard and the University of Michigan. Her car's vanity license plate once read TWO-KGS, the weight at which infants could be discharged from intensive care. She was also a good friend. She picked up on the third ring at her office at Henry Ford Hospital in Detroit.

She burst out in a cheer when I told her Vita and I had a baby girl at home, but grew serious when I told her that she was a special-needs child. Chipo now weighed a little more than four and a half pounds—

"A newborn!" Kathy interrupted.

"She's closer to four months," I said.

"Oh," she said. "That's not good."

"No. And she's got pneumonia."

"Oh."

"And she's been hospitalized twice—well, three times now,

for the pneumonia, for vomiting uncontrollably, for dehydration and diarrhea. She started out weighing six pounds and eight or nine ounces. She was at four pounds and three ounces when we took her to the hospital."

"She *lost* two and a half pounds in less than ten weeks?"

"Um, yes. Correct. Her stomach was bloated. It looked like marasmus to me, but I'm not a doctor, and it wasn't necessarily diagnosed that way. Also, she can't sleep more than an hour at a time."

"What does your doctor there tell you?"

"That she's really pretty sick."

"Can you bring her to see me? Or somebody in London, something like that?"

"Not a chance. She doesn't have any paperwork."

There was a pause.

"I don't think I have to tell you that this is not very good," she said. "How is her color? Her responsiveness?"

"Her color has improved since we brought her home. She doesn't look anemic, if that's what you mean. But she doesn't smile or giggle. She'll follow you around the room with her eyes. She'll hold your finger. She cries every fifteen minutes."

"Good," Kathy said. "She's telling you she doesn't feel well, which sounds like just the reaction she should have. Bad is when they get too weak to cry."

I asked her about HIV tests and the implications for treatment.

"Well, if you were in the United States or Europe, of course I'd say yes, get one immediately," she said. "But you're not, so there's no sense talking about it. Get one when you can, but there's no need to rush down there today. The tests for infants are relatively new, and the older types of tests, which is what I bet they have over there, test false, either positive or negative, a fair amount of the time. But at a basic level, she is or she isn't infected. Neither one affects what you should be doing for her on a day-to-day basis at this point."

"Which is?"

"Feeding that baby!" she nearly shouted. I had to laugh in spite of myself. It was almost verbatim the mandate that a doctor had written on her medical chart two months ago, what Dr. Paz had ordered, and what Vita had been doing religiously. "The better nourished she is, the faster her immune system will develop. That doesn't change her HIV status; it helps protect her against it. She'll sleep more. She's waking up every hour or so, I would imagine, because she's so hungry. Every time she opens her mouth, put something in it."

I was at the store an hour later, raiding the shelves of almost every little glass bottle of Gerber they had. I bought three canisters of Nan, the infant formula, and boxes of infant cereal. We had been feeding Chipo at a heady clip and giving her formula constantly. But now the great feeding campaign began. I was up with her at six, mixing the cereal with hot water, a teaspoon of peanut butter stirred into it for the extra protein, and off we went. Patricia Wicks, Vita's best friend since childhood, flew in from Dallas with a suitcase of the latest American baby food and vitamins. Chipo would sit in her high chair and eat and chew and chew and eat until she passed out on a cereal high, slumped over her bowl.

One week passed in this manner, then two, then three. Chipo would seem to improve for an afternoon or rally for an entire day, looking more alert and crying less often. Then she would lapse into coughing spells and withdrawal, either sleeping or taking little interest in her surroundings. Our attempts to coax her into smiles and giggles continued to play like bad vaudeville to a tough crowd. She looked at us without expression, as if two slightly deranged adults had taken leave of their senses.

HAD THE ADMINISTRATION of Robert Mugabe dealt seriously with the AIDS or orphans problem, the country would not have deteriorated to the point it had. But the government had been ignoring warning signals for more than a decade. AIDS was rarely discussed by high government officials; when it was, it was listed as a disease "created by whites to harvest blacks," in the words of vice president Joshua Nkomo at his adult son's graveside service. Those bitter 1997 remarks were one of the first times a high-ranking government official acknowledged the disease was killing members of his family.

Orphans, meanwhile, were almost completely ignored. In 1995, already several years into the epidemic, government officials developed the National Policy on the Care and Protection of Orphans. It set out comprehensive guidelines for how social workers and rural communities should handle the influx of children. For the next four years, while the country skyrocketed to the top of the world's list of worst-hit AIDS countries and the number of orphans doubled, Mugabe's de facto one-party state (the Zimbabwe African National Union–Patriotic Front [ZANU-PF] controlled all of the executive branch and 147 out of the 150 seats in parliament) could not bring itself to pass the measure, much less implement it. For its part, the Ministry on Education stuck to its policy of barring children without birth certificates from attending school, according to aid organizations. That kept almost all orphans and abandoned children from receiving any education, thus ensuring that a large part of the population would grow up with almost no training or viable job skills.

Instead of boosting medical care as the AIDS scythe began to swing across the country in the 1990s, the government allowed its state-sponsored system, once the envy of the continent, to fall into shambles. More than 450 doctors left the country between 1990 and 1998—our landlord was one of them. Between January 1996 and June 1997, some 890 nurses resigned, one report found, complaining of government salaries that scarcely covered their rent. At the time, ZANU-PF allocated less than 2 percent of the national budget to health care, about half of what they spent on defense.

But if the government was apathetic, the efforts made by extended families and individuals to care for orphaned children was nothing short of astounding. A 1999 UNICEF survey in the Masvingo and Mwenezi provinces of southern Zimbabwe found that there were 11,514 orphans or other children in need of protection in those areas. More than 11,000 had been taken in by relatives—over 95 percent. The Chief Charumbira Community–based Orphan Care Programme in Masvingo, making do with very little government help, was one of many programs undertaken by very poor people to try to care for the rest.

To understand how severely taxed the country was to handle the crisis, consider one small comparison. Rwanda and Zimbabwe began the last decade of the century with almost the same percentage of orphans. During the next ten years, Rwanda suffered one of the most murderous episodes of the century. Zimbabwe was completely at peace. At decade's end, according to the U.S. Agency for International Development, the percentage of orphans was higher in Zimbabwe than in Rwanda. The percentage of children who had lost at least one parent was more than 25 percent in both countries. In Zambia, also devastated by the AIDS epidemic, the percentage of children under the age of fourteen who had lost at least one parent stood at 34.3 percent.

UNICEF and other international agencies painted a numbing picture of what was happening across the southern swath of the continent. "The most striking situation of the HIV problem is of unusual family structures, a grandparent surrounded by grandchildren, adolescent-headed families, often siblings and cousins bonded together, dying adults being cared for by their children. . . . Orphans run greater risks of being malnourished and stunted. . . . Often emotionally vulnerable and financially desperate, orphaned children are more likely to be sexually abused and forced into exploitative situations, such as prostitution, as a means of survival."

The year after Chipo was born, a major international development agency called PACT organized a conference in Zimbabwe to look at the orphan crisis. The agency pulled together seventy-eight public and private groups, local and international nongovernmental organizations and charities, to figure out how things had gone so terribly wrong. The final, official report of the conference stated: "Regardless of the seriousness of the orphan problem, the government continues to ignore the orphan crisis." There were actually three government policies in existence, none of them implemented: an Orphan Care Policy, the Child Protection Adoption Act, and the Social Workers' Act. "Government departments dealing with orphans cannot cope. The National AIDS Coordination Programme is focusing on AIDS awareness and does little for orphans. . . . The Department of Social Welfare can only assist about 3,000 children per year. . . . To make matters worse, Social Welfare lacks resources (it is owed about US $545,000 by government) and therefore whatever help it gives is far below what is needed."

The Zimbabwean zeitgeist was summed up in "Mabasa," a mournful tune written by Oliver Mtukudzi, one of the nation's most prominent musicians, that the radio stations played over and over. Translated, the main lyrics are a lament of the crisis:

> *Tears run dry*
> *We mourn quietly*
> *Death has now lost its meaning*
> *Funerals no longer have the necessary dignity*
> *Everyone around us is dying*
> *Who will sympathize with whom*
> *Since each of us has death in our homesteads daily?*
> *Who will mourn whom?*
> *Who will bury whom?*

In these early days with Chipo, despite the recommendation of Dr. Paz, our legal custody of her was as thin as the paper on which it was printed. Three days after Vita brought Chipo home, while I was still covering the Nairobi bombing, a social worker named Douglas Chapara had come to do a home study. Since the department had no automobiles, and since Vita couldn't drive to go get him, he was driven to the house by department director Tony Mtero, the man whom we had had dinner with. He wanted to make sure things were done properly in this unusual circumstance.

Chapara asked Vita the standard litany of questions— background, reason for wanting to take care of a child on an emergency basis, income, education, marital status, and so on. He inspected the house and Chipo's living conditions. He took notes for two hours. Then he filled out a yellowish slip of paper that had three printed lines. It was titled "The Children's Protection and Adoption Act (Chapter 33). PLACE OF SAFETY: PLACEMENT UNDER SECTION 15 OF THE ACT. (Section 8 of the Children's Protection and Adoption Regulations, 1972)." It was made out to: "Mr and Mrs. N & V Tucker— You are authorized to receive and retain BABY CHIPO a child/young person alleged to be in need of care, in accordance with the provisions of section 17 of the Act. The said child may be detained during the validity of this authority and until he may be brought before a juvenile court in terms of section 18 of the Act."

It was a standard form—only the names had been filled in—and Mtero signed it. It was, by statute, valid for no more than two weeks.

His final question to Vita, as he stood up to go: "The father, is he an absentee one?"

Vita called me in Nairobi five minutes later. While my colleagues kept reporting the story—the United States fired missiles into Sudan, an alleged terrorism sponsor—or went back to the Congolese crisis, I flew home. I was in Chapara's office before closing, making a friendly introduction that I hoped showed I was no absentee.

TWO WEEKS LATER, on the morning of the fourteenth and last day of the commitment order, a Friday, I drove to a complex of tin-roofed, one-story buildings set in a dusty courtyard in downtown Harare. The halls were gloomy corridors of blank walls and chipped paint. The offices were tattered rectangles with simple desks and overflowing file cabinets. This was the Department of Social Welfare.

I went inside to find Chapara. I had tried calling for two days and had not been able to get through. His office had been moved, it turned out, and I had no idea where it was now located. There was no one at the front desk, so I knocked on doors and asked for directions. It took fifteen minutes, but I found it. No one answered a rap on the door. It was locked. I waited ten minutes. Then I went down the hall, knocking on doors until I found the deputy director, Florence Kaseke. I introduced myself and asked if she knew when Chapara might return. She did not. I asked her who might, and she said she did not know that either. I waited another fifteen minutes, then wrote a note with my number, tucked it into his door, and left. I called two hours later and got no answer from the switchboard. I returned just before noon, but no luck. The same at two. And at three.

I finally caught him at twenty minutes to five, walking out of the building. I asked if he would sign another custody order, and he explained that it wasn't his case any longer. Surprised, I asked for the name of the new caseworker. He said he did not know. It was closing in on the end of the business day, and I was nervous about letting our custody order expire, even for a weekend. Kaseke, the deputy director, had smiled when I introduced myself, but it had been one of those transparently false barings of the teeth that bureaucrats the world over seem to keep in their left-hand pocket. Wondering what to do, I saw Mtero crossing a corridor and dashed after him. He signed a new order and promised to look into who had the case now.

August turned into September, and we took Chipo into Dr. Paz's office for her twice-weekly checkup. Vita plunked her down on the stainless-steel scale, and the balance teetered at nine pounds, one ounce. She had more than doubled her weight in four weeks. She looked like a bowling ball that had sprouted arms and legs. At nights, her lungs no longer seemed to have that same ominous rattle. I bothered the Department of Social Welfare two weeks later, and they gave us another emergency placement order. Her weight moved up another half pound. She began to sleep two hours at a stretch.

Days later, I was back at work, this time traveling to Uganda. I sat next to Johnnie Carson, the former U.S. ambassador to Zimbabwe, on the flight from Harare to Kampala. I tried to get my mind back on Africa's political and social situation. Carson was going to Kampala, I suspected, to monitor national elections. I was going on the hotfoot because FBI agents had raided a local Islamic charity on the suspicion that it was a front for a group of suspects in the embassy bombings. I checked into the Grand Imperial Hotel as an impromptu victory party for a candidate was sweeping through the streets. Adonia Ayebare, my trusted colleague and interpreter in the region, and I rushed around the town's Muslim neighborhoods for three days, trying to sort out what the FBI did, and did not, have as evidence. I was in my room one evening, writing on deadline, when the phone rang. I said hello, still tapping the keyboard.

"CHIPO IS SMILING!" Vita shouted down the phone line.

She had been changing Chipo's diaper when she leaned down and tickled Chipo's stomach with her nose. Chipo's eyes sparkled and she turned up the corners of her mouth.

She had dimples. Who knew? She was nearly six months old.

8

MISSISSIPPI REDUX

I WAS PUSHING Chipo in a stroller around our Harare neighborhood one Sunday morning, taking in a little fresh air and sunshine, when we approached a lady who stopped dead still. "What are you doing?" she said, dispensing with "hi" and "hello."

"Walking," I said.

"I mean with that baby," she said, her face trying to crinkle into a smile.

"Still walking, ma'am."

"She's your baby?"

"Every day," I said, and kept moving.

I knew what she meant, even though I didn't acknowledge it, because it was already a question I was getting from Zimbabweans from time to time. Lingering glances, stolen looks, the occasional stare. I knew perfectly well what it all meant: *What's that white man doing with that little black baby? Did he just call himself her daddy? Who does he think he is?* Vita never got this, of course; she and Chipo had almost exactly the same complexion. And when people in Harare would find out that she was adopting Chipo, it scarcely raised an eyebrow. People seem to understand maternal instincts much more easily than they do paternal ones, especially when those fall across the color line. I got it all the time in all sorts of ways, primarily from black people, although I suspect this is true because curious white people were probably leery of their questions being construed as racist. It wasn't always a hassle—most of the time the questions were good-natured—but there were many times when complete strangers did not hesitate to question me in public about the child in my arms.

Like the time I took Chipo along to buy a carry-out pizza one Tuesday evening, as friends were coming to watch Monday Night Football. It came on cable live at 3 A.M. Tuesday in Harare. I would tape it when I was in town and a small group of friends would come over that night for pizza and beer. I set Chipo on the counter while waiting on our order. I was the only customer around, and the young female cashier reached out to touch Chipo's hand, smiling, and said, "Whose little baby did you bring with you?"

"Mine," I said.

Her eyebrows arched. "That's your baby?"

"Yep."

Her smile frozen in place, eyes darting, she considered the texture of Chipo's hair, her complexion, the width of her nose, then looked up at me with a shy glance. "Is her mother *really* black?" she finally whispered.

"Very," I said, leaning over the counter with a conspiratorial tone. "She's from *Detroit.*"

"Ooohhh," she said.

I didn't mind letting people hang themselves in these situations, but it had nothing to do with why I immediately considered Chipo to be my daughter. The talisman to this small secret is buried in my family history; its only remaining symbol is the last name that I somehow carry.

When my father was only a few days old, as it happens, he was abandoned by his father, a man named Clayton Tucker. Clayton and my grandmother, Gladys, lived in the red clay hills of north central Mississippi, at a tiny intersection of dirt roads called Gum Branch. It was on the edge of the Tombigbee National Forest and was not and is not on any map, but it exists nonetheless, and this was where she moved back onto the small family homestead.

The prospects for a deserted teenage mother and infant child in rural Mississippi during the Depression were not good to say the least. So it was a great relief when Gladys married a thin, wiry man named Pete Gazaway. Gladys and Pete migrated across north Mississippi in search of jobs, my father in tow, for more than a decade. They moved from logging camp to share-cropping stead to working on Parchman Prison's farm before finding some stability running a small country grocery store in the Delta. Pete was a small but ferocious man. He once got in a fight with a much larger man (what they called a "whoppin' big sum'bitch" in those parts) outside a livestock sale barn near the town of Louisville. It was going bad for Pete until he grabbed the man's head and bit off a chunk of his ear. A doctor tried to intervene, but Gladys knocked him flat. She and Pete later divorced and she moved out to Texas, estranged from us. She existed to me as a voice on the phone every so often, as she would call and berate my father whenever she got both mean and drunk, which was not an infrequent occurrence. She called one afternoon and blurted that she was getting married again that night, this time to a German immigrant. She called back at midnight, pickled, and said, "Well, I just shot the son of a bitch." That marriage didn't last either; gunfire so soon after the nuptials is always a bad sign, even this far down south.

My mother was from faded southern gentry, I suppose. Her great-great-grandfather had owned a Civil War–era plantation called Rest Easy. His name was Charles Brown, and family lore has it that somewhere around 1890 he ran off with a freed slave, a woman whose name was never recorded. The wife and children he left behind lost the plantation and the family money. My grandmother, Catherine, died when I was three years old. My grandfather, Augustus, worked most of his life on another man's cotton farm.

It's a fairly ordinary family history for a region so mired in poverty for so long, and the only thing remarkable about it is that I didn't know any of it until I was thirteen or fourteen years old. My parents were very conservative, and the airing of the family's dirty laundry, especially in front of the children, just wasn't done. I think I was in college before I actually heard the name Clayton Tucker. As a child, it never occurred to me that the man whom my father called "Daddy," Pete Gazaway, was anything but that. There was my parents' wedding picture in a faded family album, with Pete helping my father fix his collar before the ceremony, then another of him standing beside my father as best man. We spent every Thanksgiving with Pete and his second wife, Bonnie; they came to our house each Christmas Day. Bonnie was a short, slightly plump figure in a simple housedress, her black hair showing a little more gray each year. Her face was crisscrossed with lines from years working in the sun, but her eyes were always bright. She was one of seventeen children, never learned to drive, and could catch a chicken in the backyard and snap its head off before you could blink. It would be frying on the skillet within the hour. She didn't say much, but she slipped a quarter in my palm for candy at the country store every time we came to visit, giving me a conspiratorial wink. She was warm when you hugged her, and she hugged you right back.

She and Pete lived on a hardscrabble farm a dozen miles from our house, on a dirt road that I suppose you could say was near the community of Bradley, but it's probably more accurate to say it was way out in the sticks. In the summers, Shane and I would load up plastic buckets and burlap sacks into the back of our rattling old station wagon just after dawn. It was cool in the shadow of the trees at that time of day, the overnight dew soaking the grass and settling the dust on the back roads. The radio played country music, buzzing with static, as my mother turned off the paved highway and onto one gravel road and then another until we got to their place. We came upon the little wood-frame house with a chicken coop in the back and a box fan with streamers, blue and red and green and yellow, propped in the open kitchen window. We referred to the place as if it were one word, GrandaddyPeten-Bonnies. Bonnie would come out, wondering why we were so late. "It's already seven o'clock," she'd call out, frowning, "the day's half gone." She would put on a broad sun hat and we would walk down to a garden that covered three acres. The morning would unfold, the sun rising into a blast of heat, the humidity a living thing that would run a wet hand down your pants and under your shirt and clamp a sweaty hand over your mouth. The butter beans would go by, your back hunched over and aching, then the bright yellow squash, which we could sell in town for what Bonnie called "cash money." Then there were the long rows of black-eyed peas and string beans and corn and okra and greens and the watermelons. We spent the afternoon in the cool of Bonnie's house, shelling what we had picked. There was no air conditioner for many years, nor was there indoor plumbing until the mid 1970s. You went to the outhouse in the backyard next to the chicken coop. For showers, we went down the road about three hundred yards to the "old house," a shack that had a water pipe hooked up to the back wall. You stripped down and stayed close to the house, under the water, so that no one driving by could see you.

In the fall, we cut trees into firewood. Pete worked with us, a leathery man in overalls or work trousers and an old shirt, a Winston dangling from his lips and a pack in his shirt pocket. I loved him, of course, as he taught me about snakes and fishing holes and deer hunting. I would sit next to him in the woods late on chilly autumn afternoons, taking a break from chopping wood and soaking up the smell of his sweat and cigarettes and old clothes as he talked.

Years later, during a rare visit home, I drove out to their house one morning to help Bonnie make a set of fried apple pies for my parents. Pete had died several years earlier, and she lived alone in the house now. She still awoke before daylight and was waiting for me when I pulled up, a cloud of red dust from the road settling over the car. The chickens in the backyard were gone, as were the cows in the pasture. She was alone most of the time with her daytime game shows and "stories" (soap operas). We cut up the apples while sitting at the dining table, set two steps away from the kitchen, in the room where I had spent so much of my youth. She did not turn on the lights, content to let shafts of morning light stream in through the windows, dust motes dancing in the air. The screen doors let in a soft whisper of a breeze, carrying the first touch of fall. We talked a while, a conversation punctuated by her observations that I was a pretty lousy apple slicer, and I finally got the nerve to tell her something I had never told anyone: She had always been my favorite relative, I said, and I loved her as much as I did anyone I knew. She worked to keep the corners of her mouth from turning up into a smile, which was only partly successful, and told me I should watch out or I would slice my thumb off.

On the way home, I opened the tin box she'd put the turnovers in, removed the wax paper covering, and pulled out two for myself. They were the last Bonnie ever made for me.

Even though I know the full family history now, even though I realize that Pete and Bonnie were actually my former stepgrandfather and his second wife, I have never considered them as such. They were my grandparents, and I knew that because my heart told me so.

This sense of family, something that goes beyond bloodlines and shared last names, was strengthened in my generation. When I was five years old, my first cousin, Cathy Brown, came to live with us. Her parents were parting in an ugly divorce. On the day she came to our front door, my parents did not say, "Your cousin is coming for a visit." They said, "Your sister will stay in this room." She has never been referred to or regarded as anything else, in more than three decades. I stayed the baby of the family for years, until my parents met a young Indian immigrant named Vanishree Rudraswamy, who was trying to make it alone in this country. Vani now calls my parents Mom and Dad, comes home to the farm for holidays, and, when I introduce her to my friends I just keep it simple: "This is my little sis."

> >

FOR HIS PART, the two-bit bastard who gave us his name, Clayton Tucker, lived his entire life within ninety miles of us, my father found out years later. Clayton's children by other marriages discovered my father's existence only after Clayton died, his cast-aside son mentioned in some obscure papers buried in the bottom of a trunk. Clayton had never called my father, made contact, or showed any interest in us at all, though he could have driven to our front door within an hour or two.

My father was always happy to return the favor.

Other than mentioning his family details to my mother once—and only once—when they were dating, he never again mentioned his father. Not to his wife, to his friends, and never, not once, to his children.

The power of such a stance, held over decades of time, honed and refined to a sheer state of nothingness, impresses me still. It was the inverse corollary that verified Pete's role as father and grandfather. Taken together, it defined what family was and was not, what love was and was not.

I inherited that way of looking at the world. Though I spend large parts of my life tracking down obscure details for eight-hundred-word newspaper stories, though my files for this book fill two filing cabinets, I have never so much as lifted a finger to find out anything about my "real" grandfather. I have never even seen his picture. I have no curiosity to do so. In my family, Clayton Tucker, patriarch of us all, adds up to a little less than zero.

WHEN VITA AND I were married, I thought that was pretty much it for my family ties, whatever they might once have been. My parents and I had been estranged for several years preceding the wedding anyway, split by issues about race, long hair, earrings, and tattoos. It was obvious that they were not about to warm up to the idea of a black daughter-in-law. Interracial marriages had been illegal in Mississippi until 1969, and my parents' generation saw miscegenation landing somewhere between the unnatural and the downright sinful. But time has its way of working away at things. The year after we were married, Shane and my mother flew to Poland to visit us. While Shane and I went for a jog one afternoon, my mother pulled Vita aside on the couch.

"I just want you to know that I have prayed about this, Vita, and I was wrong about this race thing," she said. "I was just plain wrong. I don't know how else to say it. I was raised a different way, I guess. But I want you to know how very sorry I am about it. I apologize and hope you can accept it. I didn't intend to hurt your feelings."

"I didn't take it as something to do with me," Vita said carefully. "We had never met, so it couldn't have been something about me. If you had problems with black people in general, that sounds more like your issue."

"It was," my mother said. "But it isn't anymore."

The rest of the visit went well. They flew back home, and my family mostly just got on with things—although at a cautious, transatlantic distance.

But when Chipo came home with us, it initiated a remarkable family rapprochement. My father, who had grown up with the sting of being abandoned, took to her immediately. He applied for an expedited passport and bought a plane ticket to Harare. He seemed to forget that he hates to go north of Memphis or east of Tuscaloosa. He and my mother traveled for thirty-eight consecutive hours—Mississippi to Atlanta to London to Johannesburg to Harare—so that they could see their only grandchild. Race, the defining issue of life in Mississippi, suddenly became a minor thing. The differences we'd had seemed to be a memory of the distant past. During that visit, my mother related the story of Charles Brown, my great-something-or-other grandfather, the one who was said to have run away to be with a freed slave—the first time I heard that little family secret. Charles and his lover disappeared from family and Mississippi history, it appears, leaving a question mark that has lingered for more than a century. No one knew what became of them, my mother told us after dinner, while I listened in stunned silence.

Vita was very amused.

"Once a century, somebody in the family just *has* to run off and marry a black girl," she giggled at the table. "And here you were, thinking you were blazing a trail. You're just a family retread, sweetheart."

She kissed me on the nose.

Later, after my parents returned to Mississippi, my father went to his fiftieth high-school reunion. It was in Clarksdale, a drowsy little town lost in the heart of the Delta, mostly renowned for the extraordinary number of blues musicians who once resided there.

In the small banquet hall, those in the all-white crowd were in their late sixties, the generation of Mississippians who once had battled so fiercely against integration and the civil rights movement. After dinner, they were each given the chance to stand up and tell their former classmates the one thing—the most important and meaningful thing—that had happened to them in the half century since they were all classmates and teenagers.

My mother, sitting beside my father, silently wondered what he would say. He had been the first person in her family or his to go to college. He had also gone on to get a doctorate (in animal husbandry), and now everyone called him Dr. Tucker. He had risen in his chosen profession, the Cooperative Extension Service, to being the state's number two official, a position of some clout in an agricultural region.

When his turn came, my father stood up. He didn't mention any of that.

"I am most proud to tell you that I have a granddaughter, her name is Chipo, and she is from Zimbabwe," he said.

And then he sat down.

My mother was speechless. And then she could have kissed him.

9

CHILDREN OF THE DRY SEASON

JUST BECAUSE we considered Chipo to be part of the Tucker clan didn't mean anyone else did, however. The question before us was how to get approval from everyone in the Department of Social Welfare, all the way up to the presidential cabinet, for an adoption that would make her legally ours. The early assurances Vita had been given that all of this would go smoothly had quickly proven to be nonsense. I remembered Tony Mtero's words of warning about the process, and it stopped us from immediately filing an application to adopt. We knew that would be rejected outright. After debating on a course of action for a couple of weeks, and doing a little legal research, we decided to begin with a flanking operation. We submitted paperwork to become foster parents, the step Tony had mentioned that night at dinner. There was no law excluding foreign nationals from this, and while fostering still had to be approved by the department and legalized by the courts, it was not subject to the same rigors as adoption.

A new social worker, Florence Sibanda, did another home study, and we answered all the questions and filled out all the forms a second time. She was very nice but almost never in her office. She once showed me her case files—the thin folders were stacked more than a foot high—and said, "Mr. Tucker, your file is one of these. All of these people want to see me. If you need me to do something on your file, you must find me."

She wasn't kidding, and I wasn't shy. I probably spent more time following Florence Sibanda around than I have any public official in my professional life. All I needed her to do was sign and date the emergency placement order, an act that was becoming a thirty-second formality, every two weeks. The problem was that her signature was harder to get than that of a Mafia don. She would not make appointments, never answered the phone, never returned the dozens of messages we left for her, and didn't keep regular office hours. I tried to track her down at her office, at court, on her lunch hour, when she came to the building in the morning, and when she left at night. I would start stalking her every other Wednesday to make sure I found her by the Friday deadline—or, if I was out of town, Vita would. When it was my turn, if I had not found her by midday Thursday, I would take my cell phone, a notebook, and a couple of files to the department. I would sit cross-legged in the gloomy hallway and conduct interviews from there, sliding my feet to the side when people passed.

Neither would she provide a checklist of required paperwork for foster custody—things such as our marriage license, birth certificates, pay stubs, police clearance, personal references, and so on. Instead, she would mention two or three items she needed from time to time. We would go away, get those things, and come back with them, and then she would ask for two or three more.

For the police clearance, you had to buy your own fingerprint form at Kingston's, the state-owned bookstore, then drive out to your local precinct and be fingerprinted. Then you had to take it back to the Department of Social Welfare to be vetted. We went to the Borrowdale police station to be printed late one afternoon. An officer waved us into the back of the compound. A young woman was with him. She wore blue jeans and a disheveled look. He printed her, standing outside next to a water hose, rolling her fingers across the ink pad, then carefully across the white paper. He walked away for a moment. She looked at us, rubbing her hands beneath the water to get the ink off, sizing up what a pony-tailed white man and a dreadlocked black woman might have been doing to get arrested.

"What are you here for?" she finally asked.

"Fostering," Vita said. "You?"

"Sex."

"Don't tell me they outlawed it."

"Only if you sell it."

She walked off, and Vita nudged me, whispering, "Go on, baby, make her an offer. See if you can get some play." I tried to stifle a laugh, nudging her back, and then we were giggling— the first laugh we'd had in a month.

It was difficult to relax, even though Chipo's health seemed to be stabilizing. The situation at Chinyaradzo was as grim as ever. Tadiwanashe Mtero, an infant who had slept across the room from Chipo, died in the hospital due to diarrhea and vomiting. He was the fourteenth infant to die that year.

Not only was there still no inquiry, it had come to the point where the government almost seemed to resent the wave of abandoned children. Articles would pop up in the government-run newspaper from time to time, lecturing the overwhelmed public that they should somehow take up more of the responsibility themselves. "Communities Must Assist Disadvantaged Children," read the headline of one article in the state-owned *Sunday Mail*. It was buried deep inside the paper despite some astonishing information. "About 10,500 orphans went through the Department of Social Welfare in the last seven months. One of the children's homes in Harare reportedly admits not less than four abandoned children every week. These children are found by the police or members of the public. Since March this year, Harare Central District dealt with 91 cases of abandoned children." The numbers were extraordinary by any measure, and almost beyond belief in a nation of eleven million. But the statistics were at the bottom of the story. The lead, in the state-sponsored style of journalism, read as a government scolding to the proletariat. "Although Government has, through the Department of Social Welfare, tried to accommodate disadvantaged children in institutions, it has now run out of resources and most of the available homes are reportedly over-enrolled. It is now up to the communities to take the burden off Government and bring an end to the anguish of these children," the article began. Florence Kaseke, the same deputy director of social welfare in the Harare office whom I had met, was quoted as saying: "Our traditional system of caring for children in need of State care and protection is rapidly becoming inadequate, ineffective and unsuitable."

The article was striking for several reasons. The news judgment to bury it deep inside a paper that would sometimes strip a story about a decent rainfall across the top of page one was beyond me. Ninety-one children abandoned in six months in one province! It read like a typographical error. Further, the willingness to turn truth on its head was jarring—people were turning to state-run orphanages to help with abandoned children *because* their extended family networks were already overrun, as the UNICEF study had shown, not because they didn't want to be inconvenienced. And while the government was indeed facing high inflation and some very real financial pressures, none of it was because they were spending too much on orphans. It either did not matter or did not occur to President Mugabe that by dispatching more than eight thousand Zimbabwean troops to protect "the precious lives of the people of Congo" in that nation's ongoing civil war, he was sealing the fate of his own nation's most vulnerable children.

We had no illusions about making changes in this vast system. But, struck by the rapid-fire deaths at the orphanage, we did think that by focusing on the medical care of ailing infants in one ward, we might be able to at least slow the mortality rate there. Getting the infants to three years old seemed to be the trick; the death rate dropped off dramatically after that. So we made dozens of trips to Makro Cash and Carry, the city's warehouse grocery, buying more than three hundred large cans of powdered formula, dozens of bottles of vitamins, more than one thousand diapers, cases of baby powder and skin cream, garbage cans, laundry baskets, and an electric kettle for the kitchen.

One afternoon when I was delivering some of these supplies, not long after we had brought Chipo home, Stella mentioned that there was another case like Chipo's. A newborn had been thrown in a roadside trash bin in Norton, a farming village about thirty minutes outside of town. Vita and I were absurdly optimistic about our fostering/adoption chances at this stage, given how quickly Chipo had been placed in our home, and I was moved by the child's circumstances. Stella made a call to the local social worker, and I drove out there to see him.

Downtown Norton was a dusty street with a few scattered concrete-block shops and a farm supply outlet, with trucks parked out front and men lounging in the shade. It might have been a small Delta town from my Mississippi past. Then the road turned to gravel and twisted along past a row of small houses. There was a turn to the left, another to the right, and then I rolled through a row of shade trees and parked in front of a small rectangular building. Several dogs rousted themselves from the dust and sniffed my feet, tails swishing cautiously. This was the Ngomi Community Hall, with bench seats and a small stage at the front. Behind it was a tin-roofed addition, a single room with a concrete floor that served as the local branch of the social welfare office. There were five chairs, two desks, four filing cabinets, one typewriter, one telephone, and one employee. E. W. Matinyadze rose and shook my hand with a smile. He was a serious man, and he quickly told me what had happened.

Norton had several large trash bins set on the edge of town. Three days earlier, someone tossed in their garbage and heard crying. They peered over the edge of the bin and there, halfway buried in the trash, was a squirming newborn child. His umbilical cord was still attached and he was crying at the top of his lungs.

"The doctor said he'd been there five to seven hours, judging by the exposure problems he had, the big number of ant bites," said Matinyadze. "But good for him to be wriggling around! To be making that noise at that time! What a lucky chap. If he'd been sleeping and someone had tossed a bag on top of him, I doubt we'd have heard from him."

They had taken the boy to a hospital. Social workers had named him Ferai, a popular name that translates as "happiness." I stopped by the hospital to see him, explaining to the curious nurse that Matinyadze had said it was okay. She brought a white bundle of cloth, and deep inside was a sleeping little boy, his fingers as tiny as anything I'd ever seen, his eyelids so thin you could see the veins in them. I held him for a few minutes, thanked the nurse, and drove home.

"What do you think about a little boy?" I said to Vita, telling her about Ferai. We were exhausted with Chipo, but his circumstances were so jarring that it seemed cruel to say no. Vita took a deep breath, and then she laughed. "You know I would love to have a little boy," she said.

We waited for Ferai to be transferred to Chinyaradzo. We would do his paperwork by the book, we resolved, instead of Chipo's dramatic circumstances, so that no one could later accuse us of Western arrogance. When he didn't appear after a couple of days, I drove to the orphanage and asked Stella when he was coming. She made a couple of phone calls.

"Oh," she said. "Ferai, he died."

I looked at her.

"Yes, in the hospital there. It is very sad."

I did not know what to say. I left her office and got in the truck. I felt nauseous, fingers tapping on the steering wheel. He had been in my hands. Should I have taken him to the Trauma Center, as Vita had done with Chipo? Should I have gone back to see him each day? Well, of course, I could see that now. But they hadn't said he was sick. Just a bit of exposure, they said, and now he was gone, dead and buried.

"But I *had* him," I kept saying out loud.

I scarcely knew how to tell Vita. I pulled into the driveway and switched off the ignition. I sat in the quiet for several minutes.

I finally went inside. Vita was cooking dinner.

"Hey," she called out, with a half look over her shoulder.

I leaned against the refrigerator. "Ferai didn't make it," I said. "He died at the hospital. Never got to Chinyaradzo. Stella told me just now."

Vita stopped, perfectly still. She was looking straight ahead. Sliced onions popped and hissed in the skillet. The clock on the wall ticked a long time. Then she looked back at the stove and stirred the onions. Her jaw was set into a grimace. I left.

We never talked about it again. It was too depressing, too much of a reminder of Chipo's delicate hold on life.

But over the next several days, my sense of sadness and guilt intensified. If I had acted promptly, the boy would have lived. There was no getting around it, and the thought came to me unbidden, in the shower or in the middle of an interview or the first thing when I woke up in the morning. I could shake neither the sense of failure nor the sorrow that fluttered along behind it, like a whisper in the breeze.

We kept working at the orphanage, though, and soon we were drawn to a bright, happy little girl named Erica. She was nine months old. Her head was shaved so close she was almost bald. She had a lopsided grin, which she flashed all the time. She was light-skinned, likely biracial, and she too was completely abandoned. We applied for permission to bring her home. Stella looked up her paperwork, and weekend visits were approved.

Erica came home on a pleasant weekend in late September. Vita took her to the bathroom, undressing her as she had Chipo that first day. Erica was much healthier, but still underweight.

Vita wrapped her in some new clothes and took her into the kitchen, warming up some formula. Her health problems were quickly apparent. She was wracked with some sort of intestinal disorder that turned her waste into foul-smelling diarrhea. We treated this and tried to fatten her up with steady meals and bottle after bottle of formula, something she couldn't get at the orphanage. Vita rocked her back and forth on the couch, Erica tucking her head against Vita's neck, and they would both drift into a nap. In the afternoons, we put the two girls on a play mat together. They were small enough to sleep in the same crib. There wasn't much rest on those nights, as one of them was awake, or the other, or both, or all of us, but Erica came home with us for another weekend, and then another, and then they started fussing over the same bottle.

"They're already acting like sisters," Vita laughed.

Then the orphanage took Erica back.

There was a German couple that was adopting Erica, Stella explained over the phone, and they would be coming into Harare from the provinces the next day. We needed to bring her back right away. We were speechless. No one had ever mentioned this couple—and they were adopting her after we were told that was virtually impossible? All this talk about cultural ties and taboos, yet this couple we'd never seen at the orphanage was blowing through to pick up their child.

We let the girls sleep through their nap. When they awoke, we numbly dressed Erica and took her back to Chinyaradzo. We were glad for her to have a home, but we had thought she might have found one with us. Somewhere between sad and furious, both Vita and I smelled a rat.

I called the man when he came to town, and asked how he had done it. He said it was all pretty simple. He was working for a German nongovernmental organization in a province outside Harare. He said they went into the local Social Welfare office, filled out the adoption forms, were directed to Chinyaradzo, and picked out Erica. Then they returned to the province and completed the paperwork. It took about seven months, maybe eight, he said. He was very nice, he was entirely sincere, and said he would love to meet us but they were leaving the country the very next day.

I hung up, flabbergasted. We had been told time and again about the depth of bonding that was needed before adoption, that you had to foster first—probably for at least two years, a social worker had recently informed us—before you could dream of adoption. Chipo had been with us four months now, and the only custody we had was a series of those two-week emergency placement orders. Foster custody? Months away, if we were even approved. Adoption? Beyond the horizon. Yet this couple had wrapped up the process and would be out of the country before Monday. Worse, it appeared Stella had known this but concealed it. She watched us take Erica home time after time and develop a bond with her, and she didn't say a word.

"What happens if there's something like that about Chipo?" Vita said.

It was a problem that we could not solve and a fear that we could not fight. The people who would help us couldn't; the people who could help us would not return our phone calls. The only thing to do was sit tight, make no mistakes, and push forward, ever so slowly, on the fostering paperwork.

THE EXHAUSTION AND depression I had felt coming on during the Kinshasa rebellion and the Nairobi embassy bombings were deepening now into something I could not articulate. Chipo was sleeping better. Her weight had tripled. Vita was buoyed by her turnaround, by being with her all day, every day. But I was traveling constantly, and my worries for Chipo began to eat at me. I woke up in hotel room after hotel room in the middle of the night, automatically looking to see if Chipo was all right, but there was no one there but me. When sleep would finally come, nightmares wrecked it. I'd dream that Chipo had stopped breathing while I slept. I would wake up and she would be dead—just as Ferai had died while I tooled around town. Vita could endure these trips, relying on Mavis for help during the day, but they were wearing at her on the home front too.

When I was in Harare, Vita slept deeply, catching up on the time she missed while she had been handling everything. I woke up three or four times a night, drenched in sweat, no more at ease now that I was at home than when I had been on the road. Chipo now slept in a crib set next to our bed. Every time I woke up, I went to the crib, leaned over, and touched her cheek, her neck, her wrist, checking her pulse, her breathing. Then I would lie back down, telling myself to get a grip—and wake up again, ninety minutes later, in the same sweat. Nothing seemed very certain anymore. I began to feel so disoriented that writing a simple story became a migraine-inducing marathon. I had a brace on my knee from the thrashing I'd taken in Kinshasa, my weight dropped, and I was still bouncing around the continent, knocking out one story after another. I soon found myself in southwestern Nigeria, stepping onto a small boat with a group of violently discontent young men who were kidnapping Western oil company workers and seizing oil platforms belonging to Chevron and Texaco.

There were two groups fighting in and around Warri, a grimy but important riverside town in the Niger Delta. Young men from the Ijaw ethnic group, probably a majority in the area, pointed out that their bayou homelands were terribly polluted while the government and the oil companies took the riches for themselves. They began seizing oil platforms. I called home from Lagos, the Nigerian financial capital, the night before I headed down to Warri, finding Vita in an exuberant mood. She had seen the most beautiful little boy, just brought into Chinyaradzo.

"His name is Robert," she said down the phone line. "He is so beautiful, baby. His little feet and hands—and you should see his eyes!" She busted into a laugh. "Big brown things!" She was smitten, and it was infectious even on the other side of the continent. He was, like Erica, Ferai, and Chipo, completely abandoned, Vita was saying. "We waited too long to tell them we were interested in Ferai and Erica. I've already told Stella we want to bring him home as soon as you get here. I can't handle Chipo and him by myself. But this is the one, baby. This is going to be our little boy." She pronounced the last three words slowly, like water dripping on a rock.

"Okay, okay." I laughed. I couldn't imagine taking care of two infants at this stage of exhaustion. But we wanted another child, and it wasn't as though Robert could wait. The memory of Ferai still gnawed at me. "I've got this one story already lined up. Let me knock it out and I'll scratch the rest of the trip."

"Just get here, baby," she said, "as soon as you can."

TWO DAYS LATER, my colleague Peter Cunliffe-Jones, from Agence France-Presse, and I stepped onto a small boat with five young men, compatriots of the hostage-taking activists. A man sat down behind us and pull-cranked the Yahama outboard engine. He had a pump-action shotgun across his lap. The four other men carried three machine guns and a hunting rifle.

We moved out into the narrow bay, passing long rows of rusted-out oil tankers, and then the river widened into a broad channel, the landfall all undergrowth and bayous. The Atlantic Ocean was only a few miles ahead when the boat turned into a tributary that was maybe fifty yards wide. A dugout canoe was in a narrow turnout among the tangled mangrove roots, two young girls looking at us without smiling. Then, fast, we turned into another of the serpentine creeks, swinging out wide, the men alert at the bow, a muddy roll of water washing out behind us. I leaned over and shouted over the wind into Peter's ear, "Remind me why they're not going to take us hostage, too."

"Because they know our bosses wouldn't pay to get us back," he yelled.

We pulled into the Batan Flow Station, a small steel platform at the edge of a wooden jetty. Run by Shell on a lease from the government for more than thirty years, it was very clean and very modern. It was next to a village of wood-and-thatch huts called Diebiri, which was not. The people there had no electricity, no lights, no school, no clinic, and no running water. The tour continued through the bayous and backwaters, heavily armed teenagers meeting us on each jetty, the hostages never in sight. It was late in the afternoon when we docked back in our little bay. Before we could step out, the drivers were at the waterline, shouting and waving their hands. "There's been a terrible oil fire in Jesse," they said. "Hundreds are dead."

We ran to the car then, without pausing, speeding through Warri's jumbled traffic and onto a narrow highway. A towering column of oily black smoke loomed in the distance. Miles later, at the side of a road that ran along a heavily forested section of undergrowth, there was a path going back into the woods. We learned the details from local residents as we walked to a small clearing, approaching a thick column of flame that roared thirty feet into the air.

Two nights earlier, thieves had come to the clearing to tap into a fuel manhole station that serviced the nation's largest gas pipeline. They siphoned off a tankerful to sell on the black market. They left without closing the valve. Hundreds of thousands of gallons of gasoline gushed into the underground chamber, overflowed, and spilled outside, forming a shallow lake of high-octane gasoline. Since this was a rare and expensive commodity in Nigeria, hundreds of people from nearby villages along the Ethiope River rushed to scoop it up with cans, buckets, even pots and pans.

Then there was a spark.

No one still living knew where it came from. There was speculation it was a cigarette, a backfire from a cranked motorcycle. Whatever its origin, the spark turned the lake of gas into a river of fire. More than twenty-four hours later, flames from the ruptured pipeline station billowed in the twilight, illuminating dozens of corpses that were too close to the fire to be hauled away. One woman's body still had her baby on her back.

By the time we arrived, a bulldozer was digging a pit a few hundred yards away. There was a huge mound of charred bodies already in it. Bare-chested workers, sweat pouring from the heat of fire and the Nigerian afternoon, covered their faces with surgical masks and their hands with red rubber gloves. They loaded each corpse into a wheelbarrow, rolled it to the edge of the pit, then thrust the handles up. The body spilled out, rolling to the bottom.

Toward the river, less than a hundred yards away through the underbrush, low branches held the occasional scrap of cloth. There would be another scrap a few yards beyond, then another, and then a burned body lying in the weeds, fallen after stripping the burning clothes away. People had run for the river, thinking in their desperation that water would extinguish a gas fire. Some made it. They plunged in the water, but gas had seeped into that too. They flared out like matches. Their disfigured bodies lay in the tangled weeds and vines at the water's edge. Some had been split open by the heat.

I had to stop taking notes in pen. Rivers of sweat were running down my hands and onto the page, smearing the ink as soon as I wrote. I pulled out a pencil, scribbling down notes from a doctor at the scene. At least eight hundred people, perhaps more than a thousand, had been burned alive. It was the worst oil-related accident in Nigerian history.

Just after nightfall, a fierce thunderstorm descended, lashing roads with sheets of rain. There were maybe ninety minutes before deadline. I set my portable computer on my lap in the backseat and wrote as the car swayed back and forth, tapping keys by the light of the computer screen. By the time we reached the hotel, the rain had stopped. I pulled a chair and the satellite telephone into the hotel's courtyard. I aimed the flat satellite dish toward a satellite hovering over the Atlantic and hit the command keys to send the story to a computer line in Washington, where it would be relayed to my editor's desk.

The connection wouldn't go through. Not on the first try, not on the fourth. I tried a different connection in the States, a line that was based in Mississippi. In my travels, I had used it as a last resort and a good-luck charm. That failed too. Cursing, I moved into a clearing of palm trees and turned the dish in the other direction. This time, I was aiming it in search of a sister satellite to the east, all the way across the continent and hovering somewhere over the Indian Ocean. I hit the series of keys again. Nothing. Second try. Nothing. Third try—this time the little circular lights in the upper left of my computer screen happily blipped back and forth, the sign of a solid connection. I sat back, dizzy. I watched the story go through, then turned the computer off and leaned back in my plastic chair. I had not eaten in twenty-eight hours. My shirt, pants, socks—everything was soaked through and stinking with sweat. By now, the restaurant of our grimy little hotel had long since shut down and the driver was gone. It wasn't as though there were restaurants open in Warri at that hour, anyway. I locked the computer and satellite phone in my room and walked through the moonlight to the hotel bar. I ordered two cold Star beers, the Nigerian brand that came in big green bottles, and some peanuts. A heavyset prostitute, displaying a frightening amount of cleavage and a gap-toothed smile, sidled up next to me while I was waiting on the change.

"Let's do it for free the first time," she said.

"Let's not," I said, collecting my beers and limping out the door. I went back to the room, lugged out the satellite phone, set it up in the courtyard, and called home to check on Vita and Chipo and Robert. I was thick-tongued and exhausted and could not really think. I wanted to talk to somebody so that I could block out the heat and the smell and the scenes from the fire. The images played back to me now that I had a moment to rest. The corpses in the light of the flames, the bodies burned down to the tissue, the sound they made when dumped out of the wheelbarrows. The phone rang until the answering machine picked up. I started to leave a message, and then Vita came on. Her voice was more than sleepy. Something was wrong.

"It's Robert," she said.

"What's wrong with him?"

"He's dead."

It seemed to me then that I was in something like a car crash, dazed by the impact and unable to speak. I could neither formulate nor produce speech. He had not been that sick, Vita was saying. She had seen him two days ago, had stayed late. The next morning, he had not been well. He was gasping and coughing and crying. A young worker was assigned to take him to the hospital. She strapped him to her back, got a ride to the emergency room, and sat down to wait. When they finally called her name, he wasn't breathing at all. She had sat in the waiting room as he was dying, unaware of his condition and too timid to call for help. She gave the hospital the corpse and returned to the orphanage.

He was buried before Vita knew he was dead.

She was crying now, inconsolable. Never had I heard the hollowness in my wife's voice that I could hear now, even through the static. I could not think of a single thing to say.

As I listened to the sounds coming down the phone line and looked up at the moonlight through the palms, my mind seemed to go into free fall. I found myself remembering the corpses I had seen in various states of decay in the past six months—I stopped counting at twelve hundred—and then the past six years, the number of people I had watched killed or dying, the number of brutally raped women I had interviewed in how many different languages, the face of a condemned man strapped into the electric chair in Florida just before the hood was dropped over his head. I remembered the thought from long ago that had led me to this courtyard in southwestern Nigeria: the idea that there was some sort of truth to be found in the world's most sorrowful places. It was something I had viewed as critical to my understanding of the world, and I had pursued it since the day I had come of age in Mississippi and began to see things as they really were. And here I sat, many years and many places later. Surely I knew something by now. Surely I had learned some great lesson. I listened to the crackle of the phone. The only thing it said to me was that I had been gone. Not there. Ferai was dead because I had not been there. Robert was dead because I had not been there. Had it been left to me, Chipo, my very own daughter, would be dead because I had not been there. There are defining moments in your life, in which your measure is taken for good and you remember it always. So it was for me then. There was no court of appeal, and I had the rest of my life to think about it.

I hung up the phone. I leaned over in the courtyard and threw up.

10

"RESECTED"

THE FOLLOWING DAYS were as dark and deadening as any I had ever known. I kept moving, kept traveling, for reasons I was no longer sure of or could no longer recall. On the four- and five-hour plane flights across the continent, I no longer read the thick background files on an upcoming assignment. Instead, I found myself looking out the window at the storm clouds or the nightfall, nursing a glass of bourbon, and somehow two or three hours would pass, the files unopened on the seat beside me. After Robert's death, something ticked over in me, in Vita, and in our relationship. We never spoke his name, and yet his death seemed to hang over us, an unseen and unmentioned influence that seeped into our lives like the shade of late afternoon. We knew, in the unspoken way that couples communicate, that we would no longer try to bring another child home. That was all over, and the shaky breathing that kept Chipo alive came to seem a visible thing, a cobweb of existence that could float away in a passing breeze.

I found myself thinking, again and again, of John Mungai and his dead daughter at the Nairobi morgue. The image of the dead girl in Sarajevo floated in and out of my dreams. There seemed to be no way I could articulate such things even to Vita, my closest friend for nearly a decade. She withdrew into her own hurts and memories. Day by day, we found our worries for Chipo's health and for our custody of her slipping into near paranoia. The mortality rate of Chinyaradzo's infants continued to roll forward unchecked. Beauty Chiwasa, whom everybody called Sarah, and Mable Kachembere both died in the hospital of "coughing and diarrhea." They were the seventeenth and eighteenth fatalities of children under two in eleven months.

It was about this time, when riots rocked downtown Harare and police moved in with billy clubs and tear gas, that we began to realize how deep the rabbit hole we had fallen into actually went. This was just a few weeks before the Department of Social Welfare tried to take Chipo away from us, when we first began to realize that Zimbabwe's deteriorating political and social situation was not only a national tragedy, but a series of seemingly disconnected events that was going to, among a million other things, turn our attempt to adopt Chipo into a bizarre race against the clock. A crackdown on journalists was coming that would soon make international headlines, and I began to look for ways to get Chipo out of the country safely. This was me thinking as a father first, journalist second, which was natural enough—except for the fact there was still not a piece of paper anywhere that suggested Chipo was legally our child. At the time, I considered this to be more of an irritation than a matter of substance. But it was only a matter of weeks before I would encounter an irony worthy of Greek theater—my job, the thing that I loved so much, that had taken me wherever I wanted to go, would now become the thing that threatened to have Chipo taken away from us.

In the early days of January 1998, Mugabe's administration had raised the state-controlled price of cornmeal by 21 percent overnight. It set off riots that left six people dead. Now, in late October, the administration again raised the price of bread and meat by 30 percent. As with the previous price hike, it was done by fiat. A week later, it put into play a 67 percent jump in the state-controlled price of gasoline, effective immediately.

Riots ensued.

Taxi and minivan operators nearly doubled their prices for a one-way trip into the city center to about ten Zimbabwe dollars (then about twenty-seven cents). Commuters retaliated by heaving rocks and stones at taxis and buses rather than paying the higher fares. The owners of those vehicles responded by turning their automobiles sideways across the main thoroughfares, blocking routes into the city center. No one could get to work. Cars passing the barricades were stoned. Other cars were torched. Smoke began to rise. In Chitungwiza, Harare's most impoverished suburb, soldiers, not the police, were dispatched to handle mobs of young men who were attacking cars and taxi vans. The protesters responded by torching an army truck. Riot squads and heavily armed troops struck back in force.

It was the second riot to rip through the capital in eleven months, but urban ghettos were not the locus of the nation's discontent. More than 61 percent of the population lived below the poverty line, as per-capita income had fallen below what it had been a generation earlier. Most people, who still lived in the rural areas, were caught in a grinding poverty that led to malnutrition, increased infant mortality, and a withering life expectancy that was growing worse by the year. Zimbabwe had begun the decade ranked 111th in the United Nations Development Programme index. Eight years later, it had fallen to 130th.

It was in the midst of this crisis, one morning in late November, that Stella Mesikano called our house. She was upset. She talked to Vita for quite a while. I could hear Vita shouting all the way down the hallway and across the living room.

She finally hung up and stomped her way across the floor. "You know Kaseke, the deputy director down at Social Welfare?"

"Yeah?"

"Stella says she just rejected our foster application. She wants Chipo returned to the orphanage immediately."

"She does *what*?"

"Wants to send Chipo back!" Vita was leaning forward, yelling. "Thinks we bribed somebody. Told Stella our file was a 'nonstarter.' No way. No how."

"*Bribed* somebody?" I shouted back. "To do what, take home the sickest kid in the orphanage? So that we could go, what is it, four months, without our file going anywhere? This is bribery?"

Vita was blinking back tears, which was only partially successful, because they were leaking out of the side of her eyes and down her face, hard, shiny things born of equal parts fury and desperation. She stalked back to the bedroom, slamming doors as she went. Chipo was back there, I knew, and Vita was closing every door between them and whoever might come.

Shaking, I picked up the phone and made a call of my own. I had developed a friendly source in the department who would pass along what was really happening, instead of just what we were told. This source verified what Stella had said. Kaseke, it seemed, was developing a willful sort of amnesia. Now that Chipo was doing better, she seemed to forget that the child had been critically ill. She forgot that Dr. Paz had asked us to take her in. She told Stella that it was very curious that we had yet to be approved as foster parents, yet we had a child at our home. She began to suspect—yes, yes, it had to be true—that someone had *sold* Chipo to us.

She stamped our file "rejected." Refused to process paperwork. Called Stella and told her to have us return Chipo. Stella, looking at more kids than she could handle, told her that didn't make sense. She was, in fact, bringing Kaseke to our house in two days for a meeting. That didn't guarantee anything, she warned Vita; it just meant that we had another couple of days and a chance to argue our case.

I couldn't help but marvel at the way Kaseke had chosen to do this. It spoke volumes about how the department worked and how we were regarded. No one had said a word to us about alleged improprieties. No one had hinted there was something amiss. Kaseke, a short, heavyset woman, had smiled and been pleasant, at least to our faces, when we were in her office. Then one day she called Stella, who didn't even work for the department, and told her to go get Chipo. Given her legal status as a court officer mandated to look out for abandoned children's best interests, her position was all the more remarkable. While in the orphanage, Chipo had lost more than one-third of her body weight, been hospitalized three times, and nearly died. Since she had come home with us, her weight had nearly quadrupled and she had learned to smile and giggle, to touch and respond. That the court officer in charge of her welfare thought it was in her best interest to go *back* to the orphanage didn't make any sense.

But given my experience with the government's information minister, with her, and with the sullen anti-Western editorials beginning to appear in the state-run media, it was becoming clear that Mugabe's administration wanted very little to do with Americans, a position that would soon would be staked out in neon. There was no reason to doubt that she meant what she told Stella.

Still, there was no way Chipo was going back to that orphanage, whatever Florence Kaseke thought. There is the way the world is supposed to work, and the way it often does. I'd seen enough countries falling into anarchy to know that sometimes people are forced into desperate circumstances when the law becomes elastic. But this was something I reported about, not something that I knew firsthand. I found myself amazed at the difference between the two now that I was on the other side. Either we would have to somehow persuade Kaseke to change her mind, or we would have to run with Chipo, an act that some people might refer to as kidnapping.

In this light, we put together an emergency plan. It was very simple. I called a friend who lived across town. She was a single mom with young girls of her own and a flurry of nieces and nephews. I told her the situation. I asked if, in the event of a full-blown crisis, we could leave Chipo at her house for a short time. Hers would be a safe house of sorts, I explained.

"Of course," she said. "I've got so many little girls around here, nobody will notice one more, anyway," she said.

I thanked her, hung up, and called a different friend. He went to the rural areas every weekend to visit his family. I repeated my explanation and request, this time asking if he might take Chipo home with him, a remote safe house and emergency option number two.

"Not a problem," he said.

The next day, with the meeting with Kaseke less than twenty-four hours away, I talked to a third Zimbabwean friend about the next step of the plan. If things got nasty, she, Vita, and Chipo would go by bus to Beitbridge, the border crossing into South Africa. A number of market women crossed there every morning, buying trinkets and tourist goods, then bringing them back to sell in Harare the same day. Our friend would don the typical market-woman attire—wrapped skirt, long shirt, head wrap—and tie Chipo to her back, as if she were her sleeping child. Passports were seldom examined for the traders, and even if they were, the guard would not expect a child Chipo's age to have documentation. In theory, they would cross the border first. Vita would make sure they were across safely, then do so herself. Our friend would walk into a bathroom stall and hand Chipo to Vita. Meanwhile, I would keep my pale face out of the mix, fly to Johannesburg, rent a car, and drive to pick up Vita and Chipo. Our friend would buy a few trinkets, walk back across the border, and take the bus home.

"Nice plan," she said, and then her lips pursed into a crease. "But what do you do then?"

"Nice question," I said. "I have no clue."

But to tell the truth, I didn't think it would ever get to that. I was pretty sure that if Florence Kaseke tried to take Chipo at the end of our meeting, Vita would knock her flat with a haymaker to the chin, then stand over her like Muhammad Ali over Sonny Liston, daring her to get up and try it again.

> >

THE GATE BUZZER sounded a little after nine.

Mavis had cleaned the house till it shone. Judah had the lawn trimmed and manicured. Vita had scrubbed Chipo so clean, she was nearly pink. I had set out the medical records, emergency placement documents, and other Social Welfare paperwork on the coffee table in chronological order.

With the stage set, Vita asked Mavis to prepare tea—a required bit of social etiquette—and I buzzed open the gate. I stepped into the drive to welcome Stella and Kaseke as they pulled up in the orphanage van. I opened the doors for them, helping them step down to the pavement, my best southern manners at full throttle.

A few moments later, we were all sitting in the living room around the circular coffee table. Mavis poured tea, and everyone tried to act as though they weren't nervous, that this was something we did every morning. Chipo sat on Vita's lap and pulled at her dreadlocks, giggling. Stella made small talk, admiring the palm trees outside the open glass doorway with a flutter of her hands. And then she said, "I was just telling Mrs. Kaseke how fat Chipo is now! Look at her little cheeks! When she left the orphanage, she was so tiny!"

Vita seized on this opening with a recitation of Chipo's dietary habits. I held up her growth chart, as if we were hosting an infomercial. I handed Kaseke the records from the Avenues Clinic, from the Trauma Center, bills that totaled more than the government spent on the entire orphanage for a month. I handed her the section 15's, each signed and stamped fourteen days apart. I noted that they had been signed by two different social workers, Chapara and Sibanda, as well as her boss, Tony Mtero.

Kaseke, smiling, distant, crossing and uncrossing her legs at the ankles, was polite but hardly swayed. It was clear in an instant that she was the person who administered the department on a daily basis, regardless of Mtero's higher job title, and thus she was the person who carried the most weight. That wasn't good, because she dismissed our little demonstration of Chipo's recovery.

"But there are many children in need of care," she was saying, sounding tired already. "Chipo is not the only one."

There was a pause. I could feel a web of heat spreading along my back to the base of my skull. There was a thin bead of sweat on the back of my neck.

"And that's why we work at Chinyaradzo," I mumbled. Vita, as if on cue, reached onto the table, picked up copies of papers showing our donations of food and of medical and sanitary supplies, and handed them to Kaseke. I could see her face was beginning to have a glassy sheen of sweat as well, even through her makeup. "I'm very well aware of the level of needy children, Mrs. Kaseke," I went on, gaining speed and confidence. "In fact, we'll be happy to bring another child home. Two, if you like, since the need is so great. Tell you what. Why don't you select the child, Mrs. Kaseke? You pick a child and we'll foster it. The child can be in our house by nightfall."

Vita, leaning forward, arched her eyebrows at me but said nothing.

I was sincere in this off-the-cuff offer, but it was also a not very subtle trap. If Kaseke sent a child home with us, then she would be vulnerable to bribery charges herself. Therefore she would have to defend us against such allegations in the future. It sounded good, but I didn't hold out much hope, which was good, because it fell flat before the tea could cool off.

"Ah, but that's the thing, Mr. Tucker. You haven't been approved as foster parents. The law is quite clear. No child in state custody can go to a home that is not approved in advance. You have not been approved, and yet you have a child. Many parents would like to have a child but do not. This looks very improper, for wealthy Americans to just have a child."

"And where are these parents, Mrs. Kaseke, who are lining up to adopt children?" Vita said, with some heat now. "From what I read of your remarks in the *Sunday Mail*, the government is out of money to care for children, and you admonish parents to come forward. We did so. Now here you are this morning, trying to take a child *back* into an orphanage that you acknowledge has too many children."

"But you are not Zimbabweans. The adoption law for foreigners—"

"Mrs. Kaseke, we have never applied to adopt Chipo, so let's not talk about our passports," I said. "Let's stick to the historical record that is laid out in the documents in front of you. What those Zimbabwean government documents show," I said, pronouncing each word slowly for emphasis, "is that we didn't ask to bring Chipo home. Vita rushed her to the hospital, not to our house. The doctor at that institution asked us to take her in, and your office approved it. Then we had one home study. Then we had another. There *is* a legal mechanism to keep children in emergency placement shelters, as it turns out, but we didn't know that until your department told us about it. Those orders are valid for fourteen days, and three different officers in your department have signed them. There is no limit on the number that can be granted and there is no statutory provision that the shelter must be the home of an approved foster parent. Meanwhile, we have applied to foster and have provided every bit of documentation Mrs. Sibanda has requested. The only medical opinion in the record is from Dr. Paz, whose letter says Chipo should be here—and specifically not at Chinyaradzo."

As the conversation went on, and on some more, Chipo wriggled from lap to lap. She bounced on Vita's lap, mine, then Stella's, and then Stella handed her to Kaseke. Chipo then did a very odd thing, which sounds invented but is not. When she sat on Kaseke's lap, she stopped giggling and smiling. It was a shift in mood as sudden as a door slamming. She just stared up at her, almost without blinking. Vita noticed it, then Stella, and then me.

"Hey, Chip, how about a smile over there?" Vita called, trying to lighten a very sharply worded discussion.

Kaseke tried to laugh. Then she tried to ignore it. Then she handed the little girl back to Stella, unnerved, and Chipo went right back to her happy-girl status. It was uncanny, and Vita and I exchanged looks. Kaseke didn't stay another five minutes. It was as if she thought Chipo had put a hex on her. She got up so abruptly that she left without any word on Chipo's status, leaving the situation almost as ambiguous as it was at the beginning of the meeting. She had never asked us about the bribery charges.

I followed them back to the van in the driveway, opened the door for Kaseke, and closed it behind her, smiling pleasantly, waving goodbye as they backed out of the gate. I walked over to Herbert, the guard during the day. I asked him to get a good look at the van and the people inside, particularly the woman in the passenger seat. He said he did.

"Good," I said. "Because I want you never to let that truck or that woman in this place again."

Things were about to get unpleasant.

11

Rain

THE RAINS descended on Harare then, washing out power
lines, phone connections, and television reception. Ditches
were turned into midafternoon streams, and water dripped
from trees and arose in a spray from passing cars. Thunder
would boom seemingly at the treetops, a *whoomp* that would
make you duck and would leave teacups rattling in their saucers.
Dogs scampered for cover. Then a crack of lightning hit with
the force of a detonation, and the windows vibrated and the
lights flickered and died, leaving only the sound of rain drumming on the tin roof.

In these desultory afternoons, we threw open our curtains
and watched the rain roll across the yard in sheets, bringing a
malaise of depression and uncertainty and poverty and the
sense of being a thousand miles away from the rest of the
world. In Rome or Manhattan people were going to work in offices and chatting on the Internet and having cappuccino. Here
the phones were down, the country was collapsing, and diver-
sions were scarce. Bookstore shelves were lined with cheap pa-
perbacks, celebrity memoirs, and last year's novels that had
been popular with distant, richer people. Hollywood movies of
the previous season played in strip-mall theaters, the last stop
on the international circuit of cinematic backwaters and after-
thoughts. Cafes near them would be jammed late on weekend
nights, echoing with the sound of bright chatter and clinking

glasses. A friend in Egypt bound up a package to send to me, but Cairo post office clerks refused to accept it. They looked at the labeled destination and said, "There is no such place as Zimbabwe." A supervisor ordered it opened and inspected for contraband.

Our rooms were filled with slender candles and fat candles and tall candles and short candles; their yellow light flickered in the evening gloom. Chipo would watch them, mesmerized.

And still the rains fell.

The swimming pool looked as if it were being sprayed by machine-gun bursts of raindrops. Palm trees twisted sideways in the gusts. The driving rain turned into ropes so thick I could scarcely see beyond our jacarandas. On the hillside above us, the rains built into a lake behind our boundary wall. The water was one foot high and then two, three, and then four, and then the wall toppled into our driveway in a cascade of rushing water and shattering brick.

In early December, I sent my editors this e-mail: "The local papers say Harare has been hit with the worst electrical storms in memory. Some sections of town, on priority circuits, are fine. But our phone lines are out or garbled beyond comprehension. E-mail, faxes, and phone calls have been impossible. Today our electricity has been out for fourteen hours. I am writing this on my last few minutes of computer battery power and sending via satellite phone, in which the batteries are also fading."

We ate in restaurants and took Chipo to the town's only bowling alley—the rattle and noise brought out round after round of giggles. Vita was the lead organizer of a fund-raiser to pay school fees for impoverished girls; it was an auction of decorated Christmas trees. We bought one for Chinyaradzo. Along with a television my visiting parents gave the older children, this qualified us as the season's largest patron of the nation's main orphanage.

"Children's home hard hit by serious financial problems," read a story on page four of the *Herald*. "Economic hardships and the AIDS scourge had seen the number of children seeking assistance shooting to unprecedented levels," the paper reported in its trademark style of fractured tenses. "The home relies on the generosity of the public and companies especially at Christmas. However, this year the home did not receive a lot of support."

Stella was quoted as saying they were now diverting children to other orphanages. Florence Chitauro, the minister of public service, labor, and social welfare, said the federal monthly allocation per child, then the equivalent of about $3.90, was all the government could afford.

Mugabe made his annual state-of-the-nation address. He said the country's problems were due to El Niño effects on the weather, thus affecting the tobacco harvest, and also due to a conspiracy of financial speculators that was driving the nation's currency down.

He didn't mention the bodies stacked up like firewood at the morgue.

There were times, in fact, when AIDS activists said it was still difficult to get most people in the country to adapt their habits to the new reality. Western companies filled warehouses with condoms that could be bought for the equivalent of two pennies apiece. In Harare, activists and AIDS workers said it was almost impossible to get men to use them consistently. "Most everybody in Zimbabwe knows what AIDS is and how you get it," said Andrew Mutandwa, a prominent health-care journalist. "The problem is, so few people act on it."

Irene Ncube, a tall, thin, pretty Ndebele woman, cut my hair every few weeks when I stopped in the salon where she worked. She would ask me where I had been traveling, or relate hilarious stories about her teenage daughter, and our conversations often made my appointments take much longer than a simple trim required. She was single and routinely castigated men for their carelessness when she talked about the dating scene. As she cut the back of my hair one day, I asked if she was being "careful" and if she'd had an HIV test. Her expression in the mirror looked as if I'd made a vulgar proposition.

"Neel! Condoms? An HIV test? Do you think I am a prostitute?" she whispered, shocked, in my ear. "What if it came back positive? I couldn't work anymore. I'd give up and die in two days. I'd be disgraced and then I'd be dead."

A few weeks later, I traveled to Rwanda. In the northwestern province of Ruhengeri, near the heavily forested border with Congo, more than ten thousand people had been killed in the past two years. Across the border, the rebellion raged on. Hrvoje Hranski, an Associated Press reporter whom I'd known since Bosnia, was shot through the chest while reporting in Kisangani. He was airlifted out and survived. He was the fourth Western journalist to be shot in Africa in recent months. One, Myles Tierney, had been killed in Sierra Leone.

In Ruhengeri, the Tutsi-dominated army swept everyone out of the hills, some 450,000 people, into "resettlement villages" in the valleys. The people could return to work their hillside fields in the day. After dark, the hills were a free-fire zone.

At dusk, the roadways were filled with a hushed procession of hundreds of thousands of men, women, and children, farm tools on their heads. Soldiers eyed them closely; few people spoke. Interviews seemed to be out of the question, although we had been given written permission by the local prefect to conduct them.

As we drove slowly through the crowd, one young woman in a simple green dress agreed to hop into our car. She lay down on the floor of the backseat so that she could not be seen. She talked as the driver moved the car forward slowly, one eye on the rearview mirror. I looked straight ahead and took notes. Her name was Anonsiata Mufankusi, I scribbled, she was Hutu, she was twenty-four. She had been run out of her mountain home a month ago. Her father and three brothers had been killed, she didn't know by whom—it was dark and the men were not in uniform. "They were killing everyone in the area and burning the houses. I ran. I can't say who the killers were." We came to a crowded section of people on the road, and I leaned over and opened the back door. She slipped out quickly into the throng, the car never stopping.

Four miles later, the guard at the camp gate stopped our car. He demanded we produce the woman. We had seen no soldiers, there were no telephones, and no car had passed. I cursed to myself, keeping my eyes locked on the soldier's, and wondered how he could have known. I gave him a slightly puzzled smile and lied, saying I didn't know whom he was talking about. The driver and interpreter, a Kigali man who used the name of Charles Africa, was sweating as the soldier barked commands back at me. He turned the car around and started to go back. I spoke sharply. I was furious that he had done the soldier's bidding. I said we would drive around for twenty minutes and come back, shaking our heads, saying that we couldn't find her. Charles didn't reply. "There she is," he said, finally spotting her green dress along the roadside. She got in the car. She smiled and said it was nothing. She waved as she went in the guard shack. The guard told us to leave. I said I had given the lady a ride there, I would give her a ride back. He ignored me. I pulled out the piece of paper from the prefect. The soldier turned and spoke sharply to Charles in Kinyarwanda, the principal language of Rwanda, then unslung his rifle and pulled it into the crook of his arm. Charles put the car in drive.

We left. There was nothing else to do.

We went south to Nyamata. More than 1,100 people had flocked into the village's Catholic church for sanctuary during the genocide four years earlier. The Interahamwe slaughtered them with machetes and machine guns.

Now their skulls were lined up, shelf after shelf, in an underground vault behind the church. In a side room, there was a charred husk of a woman. There appeared to be the remains of some broad object that had been forced into her vagina. She appeared to be clutching the remains of an infant. They had been burned alive.

There was a boy walking around the grounds. His name was Casius Niyonsaba. He was ten years old, Tutsi, and had a six-inch scar across the back of his head. His mother, father, and three sisters had been hacked to death in the church, just behind the altar. He took my hand and showed me where. He lived because his mother had fallen on top of him, he said. The machete blow that ended her life went through her body and sliced through the back of his head, leaving an indentation across his skull.

We drove a few miles to another church that had been similarly attacked. The skulls were in rows—51 rows, 11 deep—in a covered shed. The church's interior had been left untouched as a type of grisly memorial. The floors were filled with rotted sacks of grain, decaying sacks of clothes. There were broken bricks and bones and the fetid compost of dozens of bodies.

The caretaker, a slender, serious man in a ripped pair of trousers and an old shirt, led us inside. We stepped on bare spots of the floor that were not strewn with debris. The pews had been ripped out, but the slats that had supported them were still there. That was the way to walk above the remains on the floor.

We stood on the slats and the caretaker, who had survived the attack, told me the tale. I shifted my weight and a foot slipped off one plank, but I continued to write notes, racing to keep up with his account. I rocked my foot back and forth. It began bumping against something.

At first, I thought it was a chicken's rotted bones that had somehow not yet collapsed. Then I leaned down and peered closer. I blinked. It was the splintered remains of what appeared to be an infant's rib cage. My toe was resting just inside, and I had been twitching my foot against the bowed ribs.

I went outside then, and sat on the hood of the car until the photographer finished his work. Then we drove back through the dusty roads to Kigali. There wasn't a lot to say.

IT WAS IN this season of unending rain and melancholy that a brown envelope was delivered to our house early one afternoon. It was from Dr. Paz's office, and inside were the results of Chipo's HIV test.

Vita and I looked at the envelope as if it were a snake that had slithered onto the kitchen table. The enthusiasm we had felt in the previous weeks, when Chipo ate and ate and began to breathe more rhythmically, deflated like a balloon that someone had let the air out of. We knew the odds. Now we had to face them. There was no sound in the room, and the clock on the wall seemed to stop. I saw my hand reach across the table and pick up the envelope. I turned it over once, twice. My head throbbed. Then I ripped it open in a rush and tore out the piece of paper inside. I scanned the series of lines and forms and confusing medical language until my eyes came to rest on one word. It seemed to be iridescent.

Negative.

I threw the paper in the air with a shout. Vita doubled over, her face in her hands, and then she burst out laughing. In the celebration that followed—we ran around the house holding Chipo aloft, as if she'd just homered to win the World Series— I wondered if the woman who had given birth to her was still alive. Perhaps she had AIDS and knew it. Perhaps she had abandoned her for some other reason. The question lingered, then faded away, lost in the giggles and shouting and the burst of joy that seemed, for the afternoon, to shower over us like yellow rose petals falling from the sky.

12

PERSONA NON GRATA

OR SEVERAL DAYS afterward, a sense of relief washed
over me in what almost felt like muscle spasms. I would
stand at the Dutch door of the kitchen, the top half
swung open, watching the rain pelt down onto the brick courtyard, and my right shoulder would start twitching. Then it
would shift over to my back. It wasn't painful. It was like un-
winding the tuning knob on a guitar and watching the strings
uncoil. It was the end of the year, it was Christmas, and I just
couldn't find it in me to care about the job that had taken me
all over the world, the work that had turned my naive childhood dreams into an adult reality. I walked around the house,
holding Chipo high above my head as though she were a
diminutive superhero, swooping down over the couch and behind the plants, and she would laugh and laugh. We bought a
Christmas tree. We shipped presents. We met friends for dinner, for nights out dancing. I could sleep for three or four hours
without waking.

In the office, I kept staring at the test result as if it were a
winning lottery ticket. All of the problems she had had, the
pneumonia and the weight loss and so on, were also symptoms
of AIDS, and it just seemed such a long shot that they added
up to negative. We had her tested again and again, went for
checkup after checkup, and she was just fine. It made us wonder about the high mortality rate at the orphanage, and how

often something other than AIDS, something preventable, was actually the cause of death.

I happily did a story on Zimbabwe's renowned sculptors, whose works in soapstone and granite were fetching world-class prices in Europe and North America, then headed back to Rwanda for a reporting trip after the New Year. And therefore I missed the story in a small weekly tabloid in Harare, initially of dubious veracity, that would mark Zimbabwe's descent into political, economic, and legal chaos. Or, more properly, it was the government reaction to that story that would have so many implications for the country, and for our chances of adopting Chipo.

On January 10, 1999, an article appeared in the *Standard* reporting that twenty-three officers of Zimbabwe's army had been arrested for plotting a coup attempt against President Mugabe. The story was written by Ray Choto, who had once applied to work as my assistant and whom I knew both socially and professionally.

Ray's story said that the cadre of officers had been planning to oust Mugabe because of his one-man decision to throw the army into the Congolese civil war in August. Mugabe's decision had been timely. The rebels had been marching on the Kinshasa airport the day Ann and I were there, but Zimbabwean troops and aircraft rushed in and turned back the advance. The triumph of that moment had faded, however, and now the army appeared to be stuck in a drawn-out battle over the vast reaches of eastern Congo.

Domestically, this was terrible news. Mugabe had not consulted parliament, never mind the public, before dispatching the troops. The war was now extremely unpopular among family members of soldiers who were suddenly incommunicado a thousand miles from home.

Ray's story was important because it alleged that discontent about the conflict was far more widespread than just among family members of fighting men—it charged that the questioning had spread to army officers themselves. The highest-ranking

officer supposed to be involved was a colonel. There were also alleged links to a cabinet minister and a parliamentarian. Ray reported that the government had learned of the plot the night of
December 16, nearly a month earlier, when more than twenty
thousand "loyal" troops had been put on alert. It wasn't clear
whether the plot merely had been discovered that day or if
someone had made an attempt on the president's life. The accused plotters had been arrested and were now facing military
trial, the story said.

The *Standard* stripped it across the top of its front page. It
was the talk of the town, as you might expect, but it scarcely
attracted attention outside the country. Newspapers in South
Africa dutifully reported it on the inside pages, and wire services put it on the record, but that was about all there was to
it. This lack of response was largely because the alleged incident had transpired nearly a month earlier and had no obvious
impact on the country. And one had to keep in mind that Zimbabwe's independent papers trumpeted claims of government
failures in each edition, and sometimes these claims were over-
stated or poorly sourced.

I often talked with Iden Wetherell, the editor (and later recognized as International Editor of the Year by the World Press
Review) of the *Zimbabwe Independent*, one of the best papers in
town, and once asked him if he worried about government response to his paper's caustic articles.

"Oh, no," he had said at the time. "They dine out on what
we say about them. They consider it amusing, such as, 'Did
you hear what the *Independent* said about me this week?' "

All that ended on January 10. Ray's story hit like an A-bomb.

Army soldiers stormed into the *Standard*'s office and hauled
out Mark Chavunduka, Ray's editor. They went hunting for
Ray. Defense Minister Moven Mahachi could barely contain
himself in an interview with the BBC. "These are lies! *All lies!*"
He was screaming into the microphone. He shouted that journalists were "enemies of the state," the moral equivalent of
the Congolese rebels.

Mark was still missing two days later, and his newspaper was frantic. The paper's attorney pushed a legal writ into the nation's high court, demanding that he be released immediately, on the grounds that his detention was illegal—police are the agency that deals with civilians, after all, not army squadrons. The judge agreed and ordered the army to release Mark within thirty minutes.

They refused.

A few days later, Ray was arrested. Another judge, now thoroughly incensed, ordered both men released. That was ignored, too. After some more legal tussling, Mark and Ray were finally brought into court, where they were charged with contravening something called the Law and Order Maintenance Act. The irony was too rich to ignore—this was a draconian law introduced by the white-supremacist government in the 1960s to suppress African nationalists led by . . . Robert Mugabe. The journalists were charged with "spreading alarm and despondency" and released on bail to await trial. If convicted, they faced up to seven years in prison.

At a press conference, they told of their ordeal. They had been handcuffed, blindfolded, and driven around town. When their blindfolds were stripped off, they appeared to be in a basement cold-storage room. The officer in charge asked Mark what he saw.

"I said, 'Blood on the walls,'" Mark recounted.

They said their interrogators attached electrodes to their bodies, including their genitalia. Then an officer would flip a switch, delivering a sharp jolt of electricity. They said they were handcuffed, with burlap bags pulled over their heads, and then the upper half of their bodies was dunked in a barrel of water. In between these near drownings, the officers demanded to know their sources. Mark wrote out more than one hundred pages of statements.

Their faces were bruised and puffy. They had cigarette burns. Ray's feet were so swollen—he had been beaten on the soles of his feet with wooden rods—that he could barely walk. His right ear was leaking a clear fluid.

Mahachi, the defense minister, dismissed the idea they had been tortured. "It looks like they probably scratched themselves," he said.

By now, the government's response had elevated one newspaper story into a constitutional crisis at home and an ugly incident abroad. The incident was reported across Africa, Europe, and the United States. British Foreign Office minister Tony Lloyd summoned Zimbabwe's acting high commissioner in London, Pavelyn Musaka, to explain the affair. In Washington, State Department spokesman James Rubin denounced the torture.

I flew back to Harare the day Mark and Ray appeared in court. The place was in an uproar. Dumiso Dabengwa, the minister of home affairs, was promising to crack down on journalists. "Stringent measures will be put in place to ensure political stability in the country by protecting the military against bad press," he said. "I would like to warn the press that granting them the freedom of expression does not give them the right to publish lies, with the intention of creating public disorder."

Meanwhile, dozens of the nation's judges and lawyers staged a black-robed demonstration against the crackdown. A judge on the nation's high court, the equivalent of the U.S. Supreme Court, wrote to Mugabe, asking him to make a public statement affirming the rule of law. He was joined by his colleagues on that bench, and by three superior court judges as well, who added their own letter.

In the middle of that tumultuous week, as I was running to interviews and press conferences, we got a call from the Department of Social Welfare. Florence Sibanda, our case worker, left a cryptic message on my answering machine late on a Friday, saying we were to be in court next Tuesday for a "custody hearing." But she didn't say which court, which judge, or what time. It sounded like good news—our foster hearing at last—but what it all meant wasn't clear, particularly considering my job, the current environment, and Kaseke's charges of two months ago. Sibanda wasn't in her office that Friday afternoon or on Monday.

So at 7:30 Tuesday morning, we were in our Sunday best waiting outside the locked gates of the municipal court. This was a complex of tin-roofed buildings set inside a fenced-off yard downtown. There was a large crowd milling about the gate. Then it swung open and everyone ran, hustling to be the first in line for their particular courtroom. We didn't have any idea of where we were going, but we ran too, keeping up with the herd because, well, there didn't seem to be anything else to do. Then the crowd split up at the different buildings. None appeared to be marked. We wandered from building to building, from line to line, until we found the juvenile court. We sat down to wait. An hour later, the judge still wasn't there. He called in half an hour later to say he wasn't going to make it that day. A substitute magistrate was summoned, and about that time Sibanda, our social worker, appeared. But now no one had the key to the original judge's office, where all the files were. Half an hour later, somehow, they were produced.

Ours was missing.

Sibanda said, "Oh, shame. We must try again next week."

I said, as politely as possible, "Oh, *hell* no." Then I was sprinting back to our truck, a good quarter of a mile, a crazy white man in a double-breasted suit skipping through traffic, my tie flapping over my shoulder. I cranked the truck, swung by the court, and picked up Sibanda. We rushed across town to her office, the entrance to which was now jammed with people wanting her attention on other cases. She waded through them and retrieved our file, and we went back to court.

While we were gone, another case had gotten under way. It was a divorce with a nasty custody dispute. The father had taken the children and put them with his relatives in the rural areas. When the mother went to see her children, the relatives ran her off with hoes and axes. This was actually getting pretty interesting when the court interpreter got sick. He had stomach ulcers and had to leave. So they summoned a substitute.

Sibanda was tapping her foot by this point, politely muttering that she really had other things to do. Vita, trying to keep Chipo still in her new red dress, replied that she was glad we all had something in common. So Sibanda interrupted the judge, explained our case, and he agreed to recess the divorce case for ten minutes.

We sat down behind a table, and I was suddenly aware I could not take off my suit jacket because, particularly after my sprint through downtown traffic, my starched white shirt was now soaked through with sweat. My fingers were twitching. Vita looked to be just as tense. Meanwhile, Sibanda stood and addressed the court. She recited the case history. She pulled out a few documents. She pointed out how fat and happy Chipo now appeared to be. Chipo gave evidence of this by trying to eat a court-provided pencil. Sibanda said that she was recommending Chipo be placed with us as our foster child.

The judge never looked up. He said, "Okay."

Then the bailiff prodded me by tapping on the table, smiling and saying, "You can go now."

We didn't even know the hearing had really started, and it was over. "That was *it*?" Vita said. "Seven months of work for a three-minute hearing?" The judge had neither asked us a question nor acknowledged our presence.

We picked up Stella for a celebratory lunch, stopping at a popular Greek restaurant where I often met sources for lunch interviews. I parked the car and got Chipo out of her infant's seat while Vita and Stella went to get a table. When I walked in, something was wrong. Vita was glaring, and Stella looked embarrassed.

"They say there aren't any tables," Vita hissed, gesturing at two white waiters standing at the entrance to the dining room.

"Maybe we should go somewhere else," Stella said.

I looked. The restaurant wasn't even half full. It was 1:30 in the afternoon. There was no more lunch crowd coming at this hour. The maître d' saw me. His face blanched.

"Oh, Mr. *Tucker*," he said, as if I were Bill Gates appearing at his door. "Why didn't you make your usual reservation?" Now he looked as uncomfortable as Stella. He and his assistant studied the reservation list as if it were a missive from the oracle at Delphi. "Yes, yes," he said, tapping on the list, "it looks like there might be a table opening just now." We were seated immediately. No other customer came in while we were there.

It soured the enthusiasm of the day. A country 99 percent black, and two well-dressed black women couldn't get a table at one of the capital city's nicer restaurants. I left a two-cent tip.

WE WERE DELIGHTED to have the foster question settled, but in the ensuing weeks it began to seem as if I had blown some sort of gasket. I began to physically break down, as if the years of traveling and the past seven months of near-sleepless exhaustion started taking their toll all at once. I had always been slender, but now I was so strung out as to be bony. My knee was still in a brace. A large boil developed under my left arm. A specialist in Harare lanced it. The next morning, my upper arm was bright red and nearly double its usual size. It was rigid with cellulites. I could scarcely bend my elbow. A fever started burning behind my temples.

"Whoops," the doctor said when I returned to his office.

He lanced it again, then put me in a private clinic, which turned out to be a former psychiatric hospital that still drew some of its old clientele. For five days, I lay on a narrow bed with my left arm in a sling above my head, next to a flatulent Rhodesian farmer in his nineties and across the hall from a disturbed young man who roamed the corridors at night. The arm was so badly infected that if I pressed my left wrist with my right thumb, a brown and yellow gunk oozed out of the incision above my bicep. The nurse on the night shift could not bandage this properly, nor could she set the IV drip in my right arm. When it would rush eight hours of antibiotics into my system in forty-five minutes, she would scream that I was trying to kill myself.

At night, the crazy man walked the rooms. He'd stand at the end of my bed and stare.

"Give me your water," he'd say.

"Okay," I'd say, handing over the bottle.

"Bobby Charlton [the English soccer star] was a great man," he'd say, taking a swig.

"You know it," I replied.

Our friend Dionne Ferguson stopped by one day.

"How is it in here?" she asked.

"You see *One Flew Over the Cuckoo's Nest?*"

"Yeah?"

"Leave out the funny parts."

I staggered home to find that Vita was driving from store to store trying to find cornmeal for our workers and security guards. Known as mealie meal, or *sudza*, it was a starchy paste that looked like mashed potatoes but was much heavier. You rolled it in your hand, mixed it with meat or stew, and ate. It was the national dish.

It was sold in huge plastic bags, five pounds or ten pounds or twenty or more. Now the shelves were bare in store after store. It was unthinkable. Harare without *sudza* was like Beijing without rice. There had been no drought and harvests were fine. The Grain Marketing Board reported that the silos were full. Somehow, the country's networks of farmers, millers, grain merchants, and railroads couldn't coordinate services to keep the supply flowing.

Even the *Herald*, the government mouthpiece, seemed taken aback. "We fail to understand how Harare can go for three weeks without maize-meal while maize is available just around the corner and no one lifts a finger to do anything except to harangue over who is responsible for the shortage," noted an editorial.

The paper voiced suspicions that the millers were holding up production—which wouldn't have been surprising, since the government was ordering them to operate at a suicidal loss in order to keep prices artificially low—but whoever had been the problem, it took weeks before the shortage eased.

None of this slowed the government's attack on journalists, now the scapegoats for almost all of the country's ills. While I lay dazed in the hospital, the government had stepped up the campaign. Chen Chimutengwende, the information minister, was promising to overhaul the national law on how journalists operated. His ministry was rewriting the codes for defamation and libel and restructuring accreditation.

"We are not living in normal times," he told the *Herald* in a story reported in a heavy black box on the front page. "We have allowed the operation of independent media whose agenda is not to run a newspaper business but to destroy the country. We know that the owners of these papers are being funded by right-wing Rhodesians and other fascists internationally, so we cannot sit and watch while they destroy us." As for foreign correspondents, he said that international "neo-colonial" media campaigns were so virulent that the government was dispatching attachés to its foreign missions to help "lead the nation's defense against blackmail and intimidation."

He left no doubt where these right-wing forces were based. "Anti-Zimbabwe stories are allowed to pass unchallenged, especially in the United Kingdom, the United States, South Africa and Australia," he said.

I dismissed it as Chimutengwende venting his spleen. Mugabe was scheduled to make a national address on Saturday night. That would settle everything. He had remained above the fray since the journalists' arrest. Diplomats and policy experts assumed that he would now appear presidential: unflappable, unfazed, the veteran statesman of southern Africa.

Woozy from the antibiotics and painkillers, I slumped onto the couch to watch the Saturday night address. Mugabe did not aspire to the presidential look. He took the air of the schoolteacher he once had been, faced with a bunch of obstreperous sixth-graders. He told the nation that their national security was being undermined by judges, journalists, and white people (who were less than 1 percent of the population). He said the military's abduction of Mark and Ray was justified because the army had been insulted by a "blatantly untrue" newspaper story.

"[The story's] heinous objective was to plant the idea of a coup, thereby causing disaffection in the army and to instill alarm and despondency in the peace-loving people of Zimbabwe," Mugabe said. "Propelled by their unquestionable loyalty and commitment to the defense and security of the state, they went to the source of the falsehood and arrested those who had manufactured it."

He also turned his attention to the four judges who had asked him to affirm the rule of law.

"The judiciary has no constitutional right whatsoever to give instructions to the president on any matter as the four judges purported to do," he said. "Their having done so can clearly be interpreted as an action of utter indiscretion or as one of imprudence, or as I regard it, an outrageous and deliberate act of impudence."

After another broadside at the nation's comparatively wealthy white minority (who he said had "evil machinations" to overthrow the government), he went on to journalists.

"They think they have the freedom to disparage, deride, malign, libel, and viciously attack others with impunity," he said. "They mischievously interpret freedom of expression by extension to mean even the right to investigate and incite such arms of government as the army to mutiny or to turn against a properly elected government."

The president finished with a threat: "Any media organization which willfully suspends truth necessarily forfeits its right to inform and must not cry foul when extraordinary means visit them," he said.

The events of the past month left little doubt what "extraordinary means" entailed, and they left equally little doubt that the truth was whatever Robert Mugabe said it was.

After the speech, I called John Makumbe, an outspoken professor of political science at the University of Zimbabwe, for his reaction. He was a thickset, heavy man, an albino who had little fear of social ostracism, and his wit could be scathing.

"Well, in case you missed it, the president has just declared open season on the media," he said. "What we have now is a situation where the government and the military are on one side, and the people and the judiciary on the other. Things can drop rapidly into anarchy from here."

I liked Makumbe, as did most journalists who sought out his analysis. After a few minutes more, I ended our conversation as I always did, with thanks and a word to be careful.

He gave his slight, raspy laugh.

"I would think, Mr. Tucker, that you might need that advice more than I do."

The next week, four more local journalists were arrested.

The *Zimbabwe Mirror*, another independent paper, reported that a soldier's corpse had been returned from the battle in Congo. More to the point, only his head had been returned, the story said.

Reporter Grace Kwinjeh and editor Fernando Gonçalves were arrested and charged with filing a report intended to cause alarm or despondency—the same offense with which Mark and Ray were charged. During the course of making calls on this incident, I noticed that when I hung up the phone, it would ring back. When I picked up, there was no one there. It had been doing that sporadically for months. Now it was doing it on almost every call. Most journalists in Zimbabwe assumed their lines might be tapped, but this was getting ridiculous.

After another interview, I got the same ring back. But this time I didn't hang up. I just pressed a finger down over the button on the receiver. As soon as it rang, I lifted my finger and demanded, "Who's on the line?"

There was a pause. "Eh, is that two Rayl Road?"

"It is."

"Eh-eh. Do you still have those two big dogs, Mr. Tucker?"

We had two Rottweilers.

"Yes," I said. "But I can't afford to feed them so much anymore. They've taken to eating anybody who comes over the walls."

The man laughed, and the line went dead.

13

CHOOSING CHIPO

ZIMBABWE WAS NOT, at this stage, a country that struck fear into any foreign correspondent's heart. The incident with Mark and Ray and the journalists from the *Mirror* had been terrifying for them. But foreign reporters, at least at the moment, seemed to be regarded as a different kettle of fish. Most diplomats and analysts interpreted Mugabe's threats as local huff and puff, fodder to show the local faithful that he had powerful enemies and thus was an important man in world affairs. (This was surprisingly effective. With the government paper trumpeting stories about U.S. and U.K. "meddling" on a steady basis, many Zimbabweans thought that Americans were receiving the same diet of news. My friends were often incredulous when I would show them the international sections of the *New York Times* and the *Washington Post*, in which Zimbabwe was rarely mentioned, much less on the front page.)

Further, Zimbabwe was debating the rule of law. That put it on the upper fringes of most places I reported about. In the context of Rwanda, Burundi, Liberia, Sierra Leone, Congo, and southern Nigeria, Mugabe's tub thumping and a tapped phone line did not seem greatly alarming.

But these were not ordinary times, as Chimutengwende said, and I was not in any ordinary position. Mugabe's government was more than a little paranoid in its search for scapegoats. If I filed hard-nosed stories on the country's turbulence, as was my professional mandate, then those stories might anger the government. And if the general policy was to "actively discourage" foreign adoptions on principle, there was no need to wonder what the policy would be toward newfound "enemies of the state." If I angered the government for any reason at all, then Chipo would go back to the orphanage, an event she would likely not survive.

Neither was the adoption process formally started, despite our new foster parent status. The Department of Social Welfare had yet to allow us to file a formal adoption request, and it was becoming apparent that foster custody was no indicator that such an application would be approved. Worse, Florence Sibanda resigned from the agency. Now we would have to start all over with a new social worker, still in the foster section, and obtain all of Chipo's personal identity papers. Only when those were in hand could her file be turned over to an adoption officer. That person would have to conduct *another* home study and fill out and process yet another set of paperwork. Then the director of the department had to approve it. Then the provincial director had to approve it. Then it went to the national ministry for an application for an exemption that would allow foreigners to adopt. The minister, Florence Chitauro, had to personally sign the exemption. Then we would go back to a judge.

This could take years. Of course, that was presuming that each officer approved of the adoption. A "no" could come at any time.

It was about this time that my source in the Department of Social Welfare counseled me to back off for six or seven months. "Slow down," the source said. "They really don't like you guys. They think you're pushy Americans. Just let everything settle down for several months, and then come back and tell them you'd like to adopt."

But the longer I stayed in the country as a foreign correspondent—which my work permit, renewed annually, clearly identified me to be—the more risk I ran of running afoul of the government, particularly with such a tiny foreign press corps. After the fall of apartheid in neighboring South Africa, the full-time correspondents dispatched by Western media outlets to the region had moved from Harare to Johannesburg. Mine was the only American organization to still base a full-time staffer in Zimbabwe. Even the major wire agencies, Reuters and the Associated Press, staffed their Harare offices with talented local journalists instead of sending in career professionals from headquarters; Zimbabwe was just too small, too far off the beaten path. There was the BBC correspondent, a dedicated young reporter named Joseph Winter, and Andy Meldrum, an American national writing for the British paper *The Guardian*, but the other foreign journalists in town were stringers to one degree or another. If Mugabe's administration decided to go looking for an American correspondent to make an example out of, I counted noses and figured I was no lower than number two or three on a very short list.

I sent my editors a one-page memo, giving formal notice of Mugabe's speech and its possible implications for the company's assets in Zimbabwe. I recounted the series of arrests of journalists and told them that our phone was tapped. "Ordinarily, this would not cause much concern," the note read. "I would send Vita to Johannesburg in a difficult time, and follow only in the event of extraordinary violence directed at Western journalists. . . . But foster custody does not permit us to take Chipo out of the country. She has no birth certificate and no passport. If I get expelled or arrested, or if my work permit is canceled, she will be returned to the orphanage. I do not consider that an option."

I then told them I was invoking my contractual right to take three months of unpaid parental leave as soon as possible. I needed to lower my profile in the Information Ministry, while pushing as hard as possible on the adoption in the Social Welfare office, and hope the two didn't talk to one another.

I called editor Joyce Davis on the satellite telephone, the untapped line, a few minutes later. "What is this going to do to our coverage of Zimbabwe?" she asked.

"Pretty much kill it," I replied. "I don't see any other way. I get hauled in for one story and poof, that's it for Chipo. Then there's the conflict of interest—I'm going to be reporting on a failing administration in which I need a cabinet member to sign my adoption papers. It's just too dodgy. I've got forty-seven nations in my region. I'll be happy to file stories from any-place else on the continent—Angola, Nigeria, Sudan, Somalia, Rwanda, Congo, you name it—but I will file stories on Zim-babwe only at my discretion. If that's unacceptable, I under-stand, and we'll figure something out."

The desk was professionally dismayed, to put it mildly. A correspondent refusing to cover the country he is based in is extraordinary, if not unheard of. The editors were personally supportive—Joyce was an adoptive mother herself—and we agreed that I would finish my current round of assignments, about a month's worth of work, and then take my leave. Our understanding was that I would get the adoption completed and move the bureau to Nairobi as soon as possible.

I hung up feeling as though I was letting the pressure get to me, that I had lost my nerve. There was a lingering sense that I was allowing the emotional weight of reporting in more deadly countries to affect my judgment here, as if there were an over-lay making it difficult to distinguish between Bosnia and Zim-babwe, or Rwanda and Zimbabwe, or Congo and Zimbabwe. I would shake my head to try to focus on what was happening just in this country, stamping my foot on the ground to em-phasize that I was *here*. The problem was that the picture didn't look any better when I did that. I felt a hitch in my gut every time I looked at Chipo.

14

THE PAPER TRAIL

ESPITE MY FRIEND'S COUNSEL to spend several months away from the adoption process, there was really nothing to do but wade right in. If social workers got angry, then we'd just have to deal with being the ugly Americans. Besides, there was no guarantee social workers would do their work any more rapidly half a year hence, and what I had seen so far did not bolster my confidence.

So we got an official adoption application. It was four pages long. There were twenty-four questions and any number of subpoints. The form had blank spaces for our names, address, phone number, nationality, race, date of arrival in Zimbabwe, if we owned or rented, date and place of birth, religion, the name of any church attended regularly, employment, salary, if we had children, if we were physically able to produce more children, the particulars of a child we wanted to adopt, and information on our physical and mental health. Affidavits from a minister and a physician, testifying to our spiritual and physical health, were required. At least three professional and three personal references were also obligatory.

We completed the forms, got the letters, and took the batch of papers into Florence Kaseke's office. I knocked on the door, opening it halfway, and she motioned us inside. Vita and I sat in the chairs pulled up to her desk. All smiles, I told her that we wanted to file the official adoption paperwork. We had thought it over for the seven months Chipo had been living with us, and we had no doubt.

"Absolutely," Vita added.

"How wonderful," Kaseke said, looking less than over-joyed.

Then I pushed it.

"I know you think there is something improper about Chipo coming to live with us," I said. "So beginning next month, I am taking three months off from my job to work with you on this. I will answer any question at any time. I have a vehicle, so I can drive your workers on their rounds, if that will be helpful, on my case or any other. The department has no copy machine. I will be pleased to donate one. I'll be happy to work as a volunteer, a kind of support staff, for any or all of your social workers, because I can see how busy they are. I've got three months, and I'll be happy to assist the department in whatever way I can."

She smiled then, gave a slight laugh, and looked anywhere in the room but at me.

"That is so kind. We do not have that many vehicles here. It is very difficult for us. Our workers are not so well paid. But all our files are confidential. I could not let anyone but a worker handle them."

"I understand. It was just a friendly offer. As far as Chipo's paperwork goes, just let me know."

I left for Nigeria the next day, as that nation was holding democratic presidential elections after years of military dicta-torship, a monumental event in the world's most populous and potentially powerful black nation. For ten days, I trekked around the country, hopping plane flights and long taxi rides, talking to people thrilled to be emerging from years of a mili-tary dictatorship. It was swamp-hot in the delta, and pleas-antly cool in the inland capital of Abuja, but the hope in people's faces was a tangible thing that gave energy to the cam-paign trail. Meanwhile, the infection I had in Harare wasn't finished with me yet. By the time the ballots were counted, with former general Olesegun Obasanjo the victor, another abscess had developed—this one exquisitely located on the inside corner of my lip. It swelled with pus to such a painful degree that it pulled my lips away from my teeth. I couldn't close the left side of my mouth. I looked like Quasimodo with a hangover and felt worse. A doctor in Lagos did an expert job of lancing it in his clinic, but the medication and the painkillers were so strong that they left me hallucinating when I got back to my hotel room—which was located on the seventeenth floor. In the midst of lights flashing and visions that I was flying soaring through my head, I moved a desk and a chair in front of the balcony doorway to keep me from staggering onto the ledge. I was still dizzy two days later when I boarded a South African Airways jet for a flight to Johannesburg. A tropical thunderstorm blew in, leaving us stranded on the Lagos runway. The pilot announced that the crew was having an argument with the control tower. The pilots thought it was okay to take off. The control tower said the rain and winds were too high. "So we're going right now," the pilot said, and the plane jerked forward before anyone could protest. We rose into the storm, and the winds hit—the plane pitched from side to side and the wings bounced up and down. Several overhead cabinets clattered open. Things fell to the floor and rolled down the aisle. We wobbled, and the bottom seemed to fall out from under us, a dip so sudden that a book in my lap floated past my head, where I caught it. The woman next to me screamed, making me nearly jump out of my seat. "Lady," I growled in the jolting aftermath, "the nose of the plane is pointing up. When it starts to go down, *that's* when you scream."

I was ready to kiss the ground when I got back home to Harare, and then I pretty much literally did, leveled by a kidney stone attack. I lay on the bathroom floor for a week, out of my mind on more painkillers and antispasmodics, waiting for the damn stone to pass. My immune system was so ragged that now the doctors were testing me, not Chipo, for HIV. Dr.

Paruch, a Polish immigrant and our physician, said I didn't have that virus, but my body was worn out.

"Your immune system is beaten to little bitty pieces," he said. "You are only what, thirty-five years old? You look terrible." This was almost the verbatim assessment of my physical appearance the Italian physician had given in Nairobi. I thanked him for the confirming opinion.

"What did he say?" Vita asked when I got back home.

"That I look like hell."

"Did we have to pay for that?"

I couldn't help but laugh. She gave me a kiss, always good medicine, and I hobbled over to the couch. Chipo held her hands out and giggled, the sign she wanted me to pick her up, and I did. "And what did you do today, Miss Thing? Did you go to Harvard? Are you the new Brandy? Or Whitney? Could you please be a singing sensation at thirteen so your momma and daddy can take an early retirement?"

She leaned over and bumped her nose against mine, once, twice. She giggled.

There were only a few days until my leave started, and I was ready to sleep for three months. I padded out to the driveway early one morning in March to retrieve the daily *Herald*. Herbert, the security guard, was thumbing through it. He handed it to me and smiled. "Ah, you Americans are in trouble, sure."

I flapped open the front page. He wasn't kidding.

"Three Americans Held over Arms" was the headline stripped across the front page. The article, accompanied by a photograph of police looking over a flatbed truck with an array of rifles at the side, said that three unnamed U.S. nationals had been arrested at Harare International Airport attempting to board a Swissair flight to Zurich. One man had an empty pistol in his pocket, police said, and it set off metal detectors. Disassembled weapons were found in the luggage, and dozens more in false panels of their truck parked outside. The men claimed to be missionaries, but police recovered three AK-47 assault rifles, a light machine gun, two sniper rifles, five shotguns, six telescopic sights with infrared lenses, nineteen pistols, and more than seventy knives. Their truck bore license plates from the Shaba province of Congo. The main city there was Lubumbashi, a notorious hub for illegal diamond markets, gunrunning, and, during the Cold War, covert operations by the CIA.

The article's second paragraph said the men "appeared to be highly trained military personnel" and would be charged with espionage.

"You have absolutely got to be kidding me," I said out loud.

It was all too obvious what was coming—a burst of government-sponsored anti-American propaganda. The idea that, as an American journalist, I would not be under the same scrutiny as local reporters, or even expats from Britain, evaporated before I got back inside with the paper.

Mugabe's administration quickly said not only that the men were spies, but that they were a three-man hit squad, somehow out to assassinate Congolese president Laurent Kabila and then Mugabe himself. Security officers said the men had a map of State House, the Zimbabwean White House, to facilitate their assassination of Mugabe. I went to see Didymus Mutasa, a senior member of the Politburo, one of Mugabe's closest advisors, and probably the fourth or fifth most powerful man in the country. We had a good working relationship, as he thought the stories I filed had always been fair. But he was guarded about this matter, not even offering much off-the-record guidance. "We don't know what kind of game these men were playing," he said, "but believe me, we will."

This was not a story I could ignore—besides, this was one the government *wanted* reported—so on the final days before my leave, I was standing outside Harare's criminal court with a gaggle of other reporters when police brought in the three suspects. They were identified as Gary G. Blanchard, Joseph Wendell Pettijohn, and John D. Lamonte, all in their mid-thirties. They were a motley crew from Indiana, dressed in checked shirts and heavy trousers. They were charged with terrorism, espionage, and contravening the Law and Order Maintenance Act (the same offense as Mark and Ray), as well as unlawfully holding arms and attempting to load dangerous weapons onto an aircraft. They faced a possible life sentence if convicted.

"We're missionaries, a group called Harvest Field," whispered Blanchard. I called their director, a man named Jonathan Wallace, in Indianapolis. A deep voice came over the line. Wallace explained that they were a tiny group, no more than a dozen families, whom he said God had led to work in southern Congo beginning in late 1996. The mission had once had more people in the region, including women and children, but the others had gone home and the three arrested had been wrapping up their work. Congo had gotten too dangerous, he said. He denied the three had machine guns but readily admitted they had weapons for personal security and hunting.

This didn't seem too convincing, especially when Wallace didn't know what a 501(c)(3), a tax-exempt corporation, was or how it worked. But if they weren't men of the cloth, it was even more obvious they were not some CIA hit squad either. Their "highly sophisticated" weapons were outdated relics; there wasn't a modern, high-priced weapon in the lot. The "map of State House" turned out to be nothing more than a sketch of downtown streets, including State House as a landmark, sketched out for the trio by a local man who was giving them directions.

Out of public view, the serious charges against the men were quietly dropped. By the time the case came to court, they would be charged with nothing more than what they admitted from the beginning—that they had guns without permits.

Of course, this really wasn't the point. Their arrest was a godsend for Mugabe. He dramatically told his nation, over and over again, that the racist superpower was bent on exterminating him, the heroic defender of African independence, and he would defy them at every turn. This set off a carefully orchestrated campaign of anti-American propaganda, marches on the

U.S. embassy, and a roundup of foreign correspondents in Harare, who were mostly American, British, South African, or Australian nationals. One by one, the Information Ministry called us in "so that we can verify your information." After talking with several others who had been summoned, I went down to Liquenda House. I parked in the garage next door, showed my passport, and signed in at the sagging desk downstairs, then walked up to the Information Ministry office.

"You guys looking for me?" I said, showing my credentials.

The man behind the desk smiled broadly, laughing with a colleague.

"No, no, my friend, it is just that we like to see you," he said. "You journalists. So busy, sure. You never come to talk to us."

I forced a shared laugh, then put my work permit, passport, and press accreditation on the desk. He studiously wrote all these down. He asked for my phone number and address. Then he said I could go. "Our files are just old," he said. "Don't worry. It's just a paperwork task."

I didn't buy it—they were making sure they knew where to find us in a hurry. But despite Mugabe's constant attempts to whip up anti-American rancor, most people didn't seem interested. I can't remember a single case of an American being harassed or beaten, much less deported. Outside of the ZANU-PF-sponsored marches at the U.S. embassy, which never drew more than a couple of thousand, Zimbabweans were friendly, warm, and welcoming. And now that I wasn't traveling for the first time in six years, we spent afternoons with Bill and Dumi, or with Steve and Heather, soaking up the sun and the quiet. We went on picnics in national parks with Audra and Nevio, who ran a popular restaurant in town, chatting until dusk and the evening chill set in. Then we would drive back to town with the headlights on, Chipo sleeping in her car seat.

But I had a sinking feeling this peacefulness wasn't going to last, and Vita and I started looking for any help we could find to speed the adoption along. Surely other foreign nationals had adopted; those Germans had breezed through in eight months. We must be doing something wrong, we thought.

First, being Americans, we checked with the lawyers. There had to be a few who had handled international adoptions and thus could guide us through the process. We never found one.

I remembered that in Kenya, during the embassy bombing, an aid worker mentioned that a colleague in South Africa had adopted a Zimbabwean child. I now called the man back, got the name, and e-mailed Alisa, a New Zealander, who was then living in Cape Town. The same day the American missionaries/mercenaries appeared in court, I got a note back: "Yes, in 1994, I adopted a beautiful little girl named Chloe," she wrote, and I let out a whoop. Then enthusiasm sank with the next sentence. "She's from Lusaka [Zambia]. This was after a host of abortive attempts in Zimbabwe."

I picked up the satellite phone and called her at home.

"There were so many restrictions in Zimbabwe, so many bureaucrats who get in your way," she said. "They weren't very friendly, to be honest. They thought it was very strange that I was a white woman and wanted to adopt a black child. They took my paperwork, but it was clear it wasn't going anywhere."

She had given up and gone to Zambia, where the need was just as great but the process straightforward, she said. After officials cleared her paperwork, Chloe had been in her home within two months. But, Alisa said, she knew of an American couple in Harare who had adopted a Zambian child from the same home as Chloe. She couldn't remember if they had adopted a Zimbabwean child or not, and she passed along their phone number.

This turned into another dead end. Kelly and Diane too had tried to adopt in Zimbabwe but had also found the Department of Social Welfare to be a quagmire. They eventually gave up and went across the border to Zambia. Like Alisa, they quickly adopted there. "Zimbabwe was just impossible," Diane said over dinner. "They've got more orphans than they can keep up with, the conditions are terrible, and when you show up they act like you're the problem."

I went back to Alisa's first e-mail. She had mentioned a Canadian named Roger. He had worked at the High Commission in Harare but had now rotated back home. She was sure that he and his wife were adopting an older child, a teenager.

It took two days, but I tracked him down in Canada.

"It just didn't work out," he said. "The boy was fourteen or fifteen when we got involved with him. He was a street kid. He was getting into some trouble and didn't have anywhere else to go. We brought him into our home, and everything seemed to be working out. But Social Welfare just wouldn't process the paperwork. I would go by there and go by there, and nothing would happen. He finally got to be seventeen, which meant he couldn't be legally adopted, which I think the department knew, and then it all sort of collapsed."

"Did they ever tell you they just weren't going to approve it?"

"Oh, no. They just kept asking for this or that piece of paper, and then somebody who had to approve it who wasn't there, and so on."

"Do you know of anybody else who adopted?"

"No."

By now, Vita was working closely with Stella on a grant proposal that was aimed at lowering Chinyaradzo's infant mortality rate. There were long hours getting it ready for submission to the U.S. embassy's "self-help" funding program. Vita often used the time to ask Stella if there were any other couples like the Germans who had adopted from Chinyaradzo. She said she couldn't remember any. Then Vita tried a couple of faxes to something called Bethany Christian Services, an international adoption agency out of Michigan, our last legal residence in the United States. They listed their services in nineteen sites in thirteen countries, from India to Costa Rica. Not one was on the African continent. "I don't know that we've ever handled a case out of Africa," the head of the agency faxed us back.

I went back to my source in the Social Welfare office, who said there wasn't much to be said.

"Listen, we only do a handful of adoptions in our branch each year, even if the adoptive parents are both Zimbabweans," the source said. "It's always relatives who take in children for adoption, not what you might call strangers. It's just seen as odd here. And foreign adoptions? Maybe twice a year. I'm sure some Americans adopted at some point, but there's no way anybody is ever going to tell you about it. There's no record kept."

We turned to searching the Internet at night. *Africa* and *adoption* didn't bring a lot of hits on the search engines, except perhaps from Ethiopia, which had a somewhat established program. Then we hit on All as One, a California-based company that specialized in African adoptions. It was an oddity in the field. We had ordered several of those international-adoption books found in the specialty niches of bookstores, the how-to kind of book that lists regulations in country after country. For us, they were of no use. American couples fan out all over the globe to adopt children from Russia to India to China, but Africa is scarcely on the tour. There were only a handful of agencies that work on the continent. The All as One site showed them working in Sierra Leone, Ethiopia—and Zimbabwe.

"*Voilà!*" Vita shouted.

The site showed they had fifty-five children up for adoption in Sierra Leone, the world's poorest nation, which had been ripped apart by a vicious civil war. I clicked on the Zimbabwe page and, while waiting for an image to appear, figured we were home free. If they could work in Sierra Leone, then Zimbabwe was child's play.

"There are no children presently available for adoption in Zimbabwe," read their Web site. Vita and I let loose with the same expletive at the same time. I checked the time differences, then called Deanna Wallace Cox, the agency director, at her California office. It took a couple of days to hook up, but I finally got her on the line. She was the adoptive mother of several children, including some from Ethiopia, and she knew the ropes, all right. She'd traveled to Zimbabwe several times. She knew the players in the department, she knew Stella, she could recite the Zimbabwean legal statutes.

She also had given up and moved on to other countries.

"They just don't want it to happen in Zimbabwe," she said. "They will never tell you no. They smile. They tell you they like you. They never said they were rejecting my proposals. But they just lost my files, canceled meetings, and wouldn't show up when we did have them. They'd never return my phone calls. It's not a question of a bribe. It's not a question of race. They just want you to go away."

Such was the uneasy détente in which we found ourselves in the early months of 1999. We had Chipo and weren't giving her up. The department had the paperwork to make her ours. They weren't giving that up either. It was difficult to know what to do next.

"What happens if we just pick her up and go?" Vita said one night after we had put Chipo to bed. We were sitting in the dark of the patio, the lights in the house turned off, sharing a bottle of wine. It was at least the thousandth time we had done this—pictured scenarios for getting Chipo out of the country in an emergency, fought and argued and quibbled and planned all over again.

"We get across the border fine and then have problems getting in somewhere else," I said. "Ever try getting into the United States without a passport?"

"A lot of people do," she said.

"I just never pictured it that way."

"Yeah? Gimme your take of life on the lam."

"We get to Cape Town or Rio, live on a houseboat, and I write seedy novels under an assumed name."

"How attractive."

"Steamy stuff, bodice rippers. Heaving breasts, broad

shoulders, the smooth Panamanian who seems a little too well informed, the caustic Senegalese olive importer with the seductive Lebanese mistress."

"Wouldn't the Lebanese import the olives and the—"

"Rewrites, rewrites," I said, waving a hand.

"Do you have any serious idea of what we should do?"

I listened to the breeze come through the jacarandas. The dogs were wrestling in the grass, rolling over each other. The pool was still. It was quiet a long time.

"No."

Another pause.

"I'm going to bed," Vita said, and was gone.

I let her go. Day by day, our relationship was eroding. We had once hosted parties for dozens, even a hundred people at a time. But now, falling ever deeper into the adoption struggle, everything else seemed to fade away, as did our sense of humor and affection. Other than those occasional afternoons out with another couple, we didn't go out much, and when we did, it was mostly dinner alone, another of those endless strategy sessions. When we stayed at home, in front of a fire in the chill of late evenings in the dry season, the hours no longer seemed peaceful but nerve-racking. Sitting on the patio, I remembered an older female friend once counseling me that as long as there was laughter in the bedroom, then your relationship was probably doing fine. The problem was, outside of our delight in Chipo's steady growth, there wasn't much laughter anywhere in our house.

It was particularly frustrating because there was no clear obstacle. The department still would not give a checklist of all the documents it needed. The goal seemed to be to lead you into a thicket of petty bureaucratic entanglements so deep that you could never hack your way through to the other side. Further, investigations that constituted proper social work got lost in bureaucratic ineptitude, apathy, suspicion, and sullen hostility. I backed off the offer to provide the department with a copy machine, which they sorely needed, for fear Kaseke would twist it into "evidence" of some sort of a bribe. We were left to guess, and guess again, at what might work.

A couple of months earlier, with our citizenship appearing to be a major issue, we had gone on a three-week tour of the real estate market. We planned to use our life savings to buy a house because, as property owners, we could then apply for residency. With that in hand, we hoped it would show good faith of long-term plans to keep a residence for Chipo in Zimbabwe, and thus clear some of the resistance toward foreign nationals. We eventually negotiated a price on the house we were renting with the landlord, who was ready to close the deal right away. I called my brother and asked if he would loan me a few thousand to complete the deal. He said sure. While we were mulling it over before signing on the dotted line, I was hospitalized with that arm infection, and then Mugabe made his televised declaration about journalists being state enemies, and that plan went out the window.

We finally decided on a simple idea designed to push the process forward, to get the department to grant more paperwork while stopping short of adoption. The plan was based on a company perk called home leave—a return trip to the United States paid for by the company, that I was technically entitled to once every eighteen months. I was due for it now. We had no desire to go to the United States, but such a trip offered several benefits. First, we could portray it to the Social Welfare office as a professional obligation that required us to leave the country. Second, and far more importantly, we would just be asking to take Chipo on a trip, not to adopt her—but if they okayed the travel, it meant they would have to do the paperwork for her birth certificate, national identity number, and—the magic wand—a passport.

Finally, there was a bottom-line advantage: We would have copies of the state authorization needed to legally take Chipo out of the country. If need be, I could make a copy of that paperwork and change the date, and we could cross the border in an emergency with no hassle. I had never forged documents, but that didn't mean I didn't know *how*. I hadn't spent three months researching a story inside a Florida maximum-security prison, two days walking through the foothills of the Italian Alps with a couple of Romanian clandestines, and six years working in conflict zones without picking up a little *something*.

"At the end of the day, you're right," I told Vita. "There *are* a couple million illegal immigrants in the United States. I'd hate to think they're all smarter than us."

15

"SHORTCUTS"

EACH MORNING there would be a steady stream of people walking into the complex of buildings at the Social Welfare office, workers and citizens gathering outside the chain-link fence with vendors hawking peanuts, roasted corn, and soft drinks. I would park on the street out front in the early shade, where it never failed that a young man between the ages of twelve and twenty-five would materialize at my door before I could put the thing into park. The kid would tell me he would watch my car, then walk off before I could say yes or no. He'd go back up the street, sit down, and go to sleep in the shade of an overhanging tree until a friend woke him up to tell them that I was returning. I never really minded—at least they waited until you returned to an intact vehicle before collecting—so I always said okay. Then I would walk past the vendors and turn left to go past the drop-down gate at the entrance to the staff parking lot, which was on packed-dirt areas that ran alongside a narrow stretch of asphalt. Just inside the left-hand entrance to the building there was always a cluster of people sitting in an unlighted expanse of hallway, waiting, waiting, always waiting. I never knew for what. I would nod and say hello, which rarely garnered a response, turn left down the gloomy hallway, turn right into the next corridor, and rap on a door on the right-hand side. Most of the time Aaron Munautsi, our new social worker, kept the door ajar.

It was a small, open room with a concrete floor. Hundreds of files and papers cluttered his desk, the floor, the top of sagging file cabinets. There were one or two straight-back chairs facing his desk. A square window, with a heavy grate to block out the late-afternoon sun, was on the western wall. A fixture with a couple of fluorescent tubes was overhead. Sometimes it was on, sometimes it wasn't. As I sat down, I surveyed the wall behind him. Among other things, it bore a sign that rested just behind his head. Cast in heavy type, it read:

I'M BLACK— WHAT ABOUT IT?

I appreciated the attitude but wondered about its relevance. In the months I had been coming into the Social Welfare office, I had seen maybe two other white people. I mean, I couldn't help but wonder who he was telling.

He was in his mid-forties, I guessed, had a growing paunch, and wore a rumpled suit and tie. He had a husky voice, rarely smiled, at least at me, and accepted my paperwork with a harrumph. He said, "I have heard about you."

"Favorably, I hope," I said with a smile.

"Yeah, yeah," he said absently.

I paused, then quickly recapped our case, explaining our wish to adopt. It was in the early days of March 2000, and I explained that I was due for home leave in July. I asked if that would be possible.

"July?" he laughed. "Why are you telling me this now? That is many months away."

"Well, I know that you're busy, and I wanted to make sure it wasn't a problem. I didn't want to come to you at the last minute."

"That is no problem. We have plenty of time."

"Terrific. My company pays for the tickets, and they have many other correspondents to schedule as well, so if I can give them a specific time, it helps everybody's planning."

"You can leave my office now," he said.

Well. This wasn't going to be warm and fuzzy. I quickly repeated the offer I had made to Kaseke, that I would shortly be on leave and was around to be of any help on any case.

"I don't need any help," he said.

I came back a week later. He seemed surprised. I had a letter in hand from Joyce Davis, my editor, which I had requested she write. She informed him of the home leave and was kind enough to mention the dates I had chosen—my bosses didn't really have to see me in July—and he nodded. I told him it was simply written confirmation of my request, an American business habit. He said fine. Then he told me again that I could leave.

March turned into April, and I heard nothing. Another couple of weeks passed, and I was suddenly six weeks into my leave, halfway through, and hadn't gotten a damn thing done. We took Chipo on day safaris to see lions and hippos and giraffes, but my nerves jangled like a pocketful of nickels. I kept an eye on the charges against the three Americans, on Mugabe's increasing rhetoric, feeling as though a clock were ticking down while we were putzing around at Victoria Falls.

A week later, I stopped in Munautsi's office again. He stood up, not looking at me, and went to his door. He held it open. "You must leave my office. I do not want to see you anymore. I will call you when I have something to tell you."

"I appreciate that, Mr. Munautsi," I said, standing, "but it's been my experience that social workers are too busy to call us."

"I will call you when I have something to tell you."

I went home and told Vita that perhaps it was a race thing, particularly given that sign in his office. "Maybe it's his one chance in life to push a white guy around and he doesn't want to miss it," I concluded with a shrug. "Let's see how you do."

Vita went down there a few days later. He refused to let her in the door. "That son of a bitch," she came home fuming. "Acted like I was some little woman he couldn't be bothered with."

But ticking off Munautsi was not going to do us any good,

so we turned our attention elsewhere for a few days. There didn't seem to be any other option. I was idly taking care of paperwork in the office one morning when Vita shouted from the living room. There was an urgent tone to it, and I leaped from my chair and bolted into the living room, ready for anything. What I saw instead was Vita standing perfectly still, holding out a pencil. Halfway across the room, Chipo was wobbling on her hands and knees, a look of concentration on her face. Then she put her weight on her feet, bent her knees, and pushed back with her hands. Her upper body moved up, up— and somehow, she was standing upright, both hands out to her sides.

"Well, I'll be—"

"Hush!" Vita hissed. "Now watch this."

She leaned over and twitched the pencil, back and forth. "Come get the pencil, baby," she said.

Chipo was wobbling, a huge smile on her face. She was wearing a green pair of zip-up pajamas, complete with little footies. She held out both her hands, tilted her right shoulder forward, then swung her right foot a few inches in front of her. Then, teetering, she hunched her left shoulder and swung out that foot. Then the right. The left. She was walking, a kind of slow-motion Frankenstein stagger, but walking. She made it all the way to the pencil. Then she sat down with a plop on her bottom, giggling so hard she couldn't stand up.

We laughed and hooted and cheered so loudly that the two Rottweilers came running, thinking something was wrong.

"My little baby is a *biped*," Vita crowed, swooping her up in a hug.

We were delighted on days like this—I took an entire roll of film of Chipo walking six steps—but it was always muted when we went down to Chinyaradzo. Infants continued to die at the orphanage on a pace of one every three weeks. Both at the orphanage and in phone calls that stretched late into the evening, Vita and Stella talked for hours about how to slow this procession of deaths. Vita, from her contacts at the U.S.

embassy, knew that Ambassador Tom McDonald oversaw a program that offered funding for small projects. It was described as a self-help program, the sort of grants and loans that development agencies call microenterprise. It's designed for an enterprising farmer to get new tools, for women pooling their resources to open a small store, and so on. Vita and Stella, trying to identify the biggest threats to infant life at the orphanage, focused on little things that might eradicate the opportunistic germs and illnesses that triggered more serious health problems.

They put together a plan to refurbish the kitchen, including putting in a refrigerator and running hot water and modern cooking equipment, in order to make sure the children were getting safe and nutritious food. In the changing room, they wanted to install a new machine to clean diapers, provide a changing table, and bring in other amenities.

More importantly, they wanted to train workers in basic child-care issues, such as recognizing the onset of colds, viruses, and the flu so that they could be caught early. There were other simple proposals, such as staggering the feeding hours, so that three workers were not trying to feed fifteen infants at once. As it was, if the infants didn't eat rapidly, they didn't get a chance to eat at all, a factor contributing to sickness and malnutrition and, we thought, one reason why Chipo nearly starved to death. Finally, Vita went back to Dr. Paz's office. She explained the project, saying that she would like for him to visit the home for weekly lectures on health and hygiene. He could deliver these talks in Shona, increasing the comfort level for the young women asking questions.

There was no salary, Vita said. And there was no need, Dr. Paz replied—he would be happy to do it for free.

None of this sounds like a sweeping overhaul of the place, particularly in light of the mortality rate, but many of the health problems were either caused or intensified by simple human error. While some of the more mature women did backbreaking work, most of the younger workers were merely teenagers from the home. They had scant supplies, little training, and no experience in caring for special-needs children. They were sincere and they cared, but they were also desensitized to the orphanage's conditions to a degree that was almost beyond reach. Robert's death was a staggering example—how do you train a worker who will let a child die on her back because she's too timid, or too apathetic, to ask a doctor for help? These were far more serious and overlapping social issues, something a Nancy Reagan–esque "Just speak up" campaign was not going to cure. Nor was there anything Stella could do to upgrade her staffing, as the home's pauper status left no funding to hire professionals.

Once, shortly after my leave began, I happened to stop by on a day when the place was short-staffed. There were only one or two young workers around. They were busy feeding children at lunch. I went to pick up a crying child who, it turned out, was so soaked with urine that it seeped through the washcloth/diaper and gave me a handful of the stuff as well. I went to change him, but I had to clear an edge of a table in the changing room to do so. When unpinned, the triangle of rough cloth that served as his diaper spilled open with diarrhea. The child's hips were coated with it. I looked around for a cloth to clean up the mess. There was none. There were no paper towels. I finally held the wailing little boy beneath a stream of running water from the faucet, letting the excrement run down the drain. I grabbed an old rag out of a closet and used that to wipe him clean. Then there was no lotion. So I pinned him back up and looked for a pail to throw the soiled diaper into. There wasn't one. Not in this room, not in the next. I finally slung the soiled thing in a corner on the floor. There wasn't any soap to wash my hands, either.

I was fairly disgusted. We had donated pails, garbage cans, cases upon cases of lotion and baby cream, thousands of diapers—and no matter how much we bought, it all disappeared in weeks. The Australian nurse who sometimes visited had to lock away the vitamins we donated because they vanished at such an extraordinary rate. Some of the workers, or perhaps the older children, apparently were taking them either for themselves, for children in their homes, or to sell on street markets. I could understand their need, but it still didn't excuse the fact that the supplies were not being used for Chinyaradzo's children.

As I walked the little boy back to his crib, several infants were crying. The other worker was busy with one of them. So I set the first child down and went to get another. He howled the minute I set him down, so I turned around, picked him back up until he quieted down, then returned him to the crib. He howled again. This time, I kept going. The child in the next crib was soaked too. I cleaned her off in the same manner as the little boy. In fact, every child I picked up was soaked or soiled, no more workers were coming, and the din of so many children wailing was like fingernails on a chalkboard. All of them had diarrhea. The stench of it was so putrid, and the ventilation in the changing room so poor, that it almost made me gag.

This was what the proposal targeted—not just an infusion of supplies, but a better-trained staff to raise and maintain the level of care. Neither Vita nor Stella had any experience writing grant proposals, and the format of the thing was U.S. federal government bureaucracy—different from the Zimbabwean variety, but its own particular headache. When the day came to submit it, they were nervous, for the competition for grants was intense, and they had come to believe the project was a life-or-death matter for the orphanage's children.

Several weeks dragged by. Vita and Stella talked again and again about tiny details they should have included.

In the end, when the phone call came, they needn't have worried. The embassy staff approved the project for the maximum amount the program allowed—U.S. $7,000, or about 275,000 Zimbabwean dollars. Vita and Stella whooped and laughed on the phone for an hour, celebrating. When Ambassador McDonald signed on the dotted line, it became one of the largest grants in Chinyaradzo's history. At the awards ceremony, Vita and Stella signed their part of the contract, then talked excitedly with the three dozen other recipients, who were beaming just as much.

The next day, the Child Protection Society called Vita. They were the board that oversaw the home. The president and chief officer were quite excited.

When, they asked, would they get the money?

"Well, they don't exactly cut a check to anybody," Vita explained. The project worked on a voucher program. You presented bills for the supplies in your project, and the embassy paid the company or the contractor directly. There was no cash flow.

Oh, they said.

The new executive director called a couple of times, mainly about the need to include the CPS in future projects, but they quickly lost interest. After taking credit for the grant in a CPS newsletter (they said they had won the contract with an assist from Vita; actually, they were not mentioned in the grant at all), they seemed to disappear. No one ever looked in to see how it was going. No one said congratulations to Stella, who had worked so hard to make it happen.

For as long as we were in the country, Vita oversaw the implementation of the project. She picked up Dr. Paz and drove him down for sessions with the staff once a week. He was delighted with how eager the young women were, once they got over the nervousness of asking him questions. Vita haggled with contractors, most of whom were polite, professional, and happy to do work at the home. She also cracked heads with the few who tried to inflate prices or manipulate her into endorsements for more work at the embassy. Inflation was so severe that once she got a quote for a major appliance and the embassy approved it, the price had gone up, meaning the process had to start over. I had to get unpleasant once or twice with male contractors who had trouble being respectful toward a woman giving them orders. Stella did yeoman's work, overseeing the daily work at the orphanage, juggling the rehab work with the daily load of caring for all of her young charges, not just the infants.

When it was all done, the quality of care for the infants had improved and the facilities were upgraded. The place looked very fine. But the bottom line, at least in the short term, was dispiriting. The year we brought Chipo home, eighteen infants died. The next year, after more than $12,000 in supplies was brought in, the facilities modernized, and the staff trained by one of the best pediatricians in the country, seventeen infants died.

IT WAS ANOTHER gloomy morning in the Social Welfare office, and Munautsi was glowering at me. I had stopped in, once more, to check on the progress of Chipo's birth certificate. In an office with few typewriters, even fewer computers, almost no transportation, and bad phone lines, Munautsi had to fill out forms applying to Chipo's home region to get the document. Before he could do that, he had to explain the circumstances of her birth, prove that she was indeed found in that area, and provide police verification of all of the above. He also had to go through all of our paperwork to make sure that we qualified as parents. This was one of hundreds of cases on his desk. I really had every sympathy for the man. What I couldn't understand was why he viewed me as some sort of threat.

He was muttering something about shortcuts, me doing something wrong, papers not in order.

"You are trying to complete this process without all of your papers," he said. "You think you can take shortcuts."

"What shortcuts? What's not in order?"

"You have no references," he said. "You must have references from many people. But you have not submitted any."

"Not subm—Mr. Munautsi, I've given the department more than a dozen reference letters. From my bosses, from a priest, from long-term friends in America, from friends here in Zimbabwe."

"No, you haven't."

"Yes—" And then I caught myself. I didn't want to get into a third-grade did-not, did-too debate, which I was just about exasperated enough to do.

"You're saying the file has no reference letters?"

"That's right."

"Then I'll bring copies in tomorrow. But you're attributing motive that's not there, and I have to tell you I don't appreciate it. If you have a question about something, if there's a document that we haven't supplied, then it's from some sort of miscommunication, not deviousness."

This sort of Americanized formality approached the inane, I knew, but I couldn't see any alternative. I didn't have any threat to bully him with, and blowing up at him was only going to make things worse. Bottling up this anger, morning after morning, bounced my blood pressure into the stratosphere. There were many days, including that one, when I left his office as pleasant as you please, and by the time I got back into my truck I would be pounding the dashboard in anger, cursing out loud with what I had wanted to say. Which startled the street kid looking for his tip, but not much else. I still had to go home, make copies of the reference letters, and bring them back the next morning.

He wasn't there.

This game of catch-as-catch-can continued for two days, until I finally did what I had done with the previous social worker—I took a book, sat down in the hallway, and read. An hour or so later, Munautsi rounded the corner and I gave him the copies. He said thank you and opened his door. I started to follow him inside, but he quickly turned. "There is no need for you in here!" he almost shouted. "I am busy! You must leave!"

I apologized and left, shaking my head.

A few days later, it got worse. This time he was really worked up.

"*Shortcuts!*" he bellowed. "I knew it! I knew you! You are trying something!"

By now, he had thrown me out of his office so many times, like an umpire tossing a batter after a disputed third strike, that I scarcely paid attention. But this was different. He was shaking his finger, truly furious.

"You were never vetted by police! You did not do the criminal check! And yet you have a child! This is against the law! I knew it!"

I was startled. We *had* been checked by the police. We had been fingerprinted that day at the precinct with the prostitute. I tried to calm him down, assuring him that I would bring those copies in within the hour, for this was serious. If he pressed the matter, he could go to a judge to have our foster custody revoked.

I rushed home, got the copy of the fingerprint form—Vita kept on file five copies of each document related to Chipo's custody—and drove back. He wasn't there, of course, and didn't return for the rest of the day, but I caught him the next morning. I pointed out the date, the precinct stamp, and the signature of the officer. He was only slightly mollified. We had been printed, he agreed, but nobody from Social Welfare had verified with the police that we were not wanted criminals. Or, if they had, they had lost the paperwork. He handed me back the copy. The police couldn't run a check with that.

"You must be fingerprinted again," he said.

The next day, Vita and I were back at the precinct, once again rolling our fingers across the ink pad. This time, I drove the still-wet form to the police headquarters myself. The receptionist let me walk it back to the detectives. I begged the lady at that desk to investigate us, explaining the situation and the urgency. She was very nice and called back a week later. I drove down immediately. I picked up the form, complete with police sign-off in red ink, made six copies, had them notarized, then took them back to Munautsi.

He grunted.

Then, out of the blue, the birth certificate came through a few days later—but only, it turned out, because Stella happened to be traveling in the region where Chipo had been found and stopped in the local Social Welfare office on business. She saw several forms waiting to be mailed back to Harare, one of them with Chipo's name on it. She drove all of the forms in personally.

The next week, our entire file went missing, and we began to understand what the theory of "actively discourage" meant in practice.

"*Lost* it?" I said to Munautsi. This time I was the angry one. "How can you lose the entire file? Don't you keep a copy of *anything?*"

Munautsi said he had sent our case to the file room and now they couldn't find it. Without the file, there was nothing he could do. He didn't seem too upset about it.

When I asked him what I should do, he said, "Wait. Maybe we'll find it."

This was disaster, absolute pinwheeling disaster. Without a file, our case went back to square one. We had a notarized copy of our foster custody papers, and we had copies of the whole sheaf of papers we had submitted—marriage license, our birth certificates, proof of employment, work permit and so on— but the department was not bound to accept any of it. They had no copies of our home studies or of her birth certificate. Really, there wasn't any legal proof that Chipo even existed.

We had to get that damn file back. We put Chipo to bed, as she could sleep through the night now, and sat up for hours, yet another bottle of wine on the table between us. The situation in the country was getting worse. The U.S. embassy was of no use with something like this; their involvement would only make things worse. I couldn't ask friendly government officers in Zimbabwe to make a phone call for fear it would backfire. My source in the department couldn't intervene, at risk of being charged with taking some sort of bribe.

We discussed strategy, even argued about it heatedly. We considered personalities within the department. We discussed the names, races, and genders of the best lawyers in town, and how those might come into play for or against us, should we choose to retain them in a lawsuit.

In the end, we cut to the chase. We hit 'em with Vita.

She walked into the building the next day, avoiding Munautsi's office, and talked to the female clerical staff. It is a social stigma in Zimbabwean society for a woman not to be a mother. Vita, childless in her forties, was a figure of great pity. She wasn't Zimbabwean, but with her short physique, full figure, and dark skin, she could have passed for Shona. When we had first moved to Harare, women would ask her about her children, and she would reply that she didn't have any. They invariably sighed, dropped their eyes, and said, "Shame, shame." So when she went into the office that day, she played the last card we had.

"I can't have a baby," she told the women quietly. "I only have Chipo. But now her file is lost."

Moved, they took her behind the counter and down the aisle, where they threw open a door. The file room.

Some of it was organized. Most of it was not. Thousands of folders were dumped on the floor, strewn over shelves, stacked on counters. There were still file folders marked "Property of the Rhodesian Government." They located the most recent years, sat down, and handed a stack to Vita. Together, they all started sorting through files. Hundreds of folders went by, then thousands. Vita was in jeans, on her hands and knees, going over stack after stack of files. They searched all morning with no success. They picked it up in the afternoon, and again wound up with nothing. Late in the afternoon of the next day, a woman called out, "Eh-Eh! Mama Chipo! Eh-eh!" She was smiling, delighted. She held Chipo's file. Everyone let out a cheer. Vita hugged them all. Then she left.

One of the women waited to make sure Vita was gone, then took the file to Munautsi's office. She placed it on his desk, front and center. The next day, I stopped in and asked, with a furrowed brow, if that darn file had ever turned up.

"Yeah," he said.

He didn't appear to be particularly thrilled. I didn't particularly care.

I walked out of the office, turned the corner, and gave the air a double pump with a clenched fist. "Boom, baby!" I shouted.

It felt as though we were in some sort of tennis match, a duel of serve and volley, and we had just laced a cross-court winner. The bribery allegation, the delays in getting the emergency placement order, the lost references, the lost police clearance, the lost file—whop! bap! slice! We returned them all and were still in the match. Perhaps it sounds silly, but these sorts of battles consumed our lives, a roller coaster of political tension and bureaucratic drama. Getting that file back, whether Munautsi meant to lose it or just did, felt like we had just won a set point at center court. The resulting burst of energy sent us bouncing around town as though we were in some sort of pinball machine. Munautsi allowed me to make a copy of Chipo's birth certificate, of which I again made five copies and had each notarized as a "true copy," signed by the department head, Tony Mtero, himself. I returned one of those to Munautsi and kept the original. He didn't notice, and we had one more point in our favor. With the original birth certificate I could apply for Chipo's passport on my own. That office, in the same complex of buildings as the Social Welfare office, worked like a dream. If you paid the service fee of $75—a whopping amount in local terms—you could have your passport in forty-eight hours. Vita took Chipo to the photo studio, held her steady on a high stool, and ducked out of the way when the flash went off. I took that portrait of a startled Chipo, a completed application, and the cash to the passport office on a Friday morning. Monday afternoon, I was holding a green Zimbabwean passport, complete with a national identity number. Now we had the documents necessary to file a request over at the U.S. embassy, just a few blocks away, for her visa into the United States.

It was in the midst of this, when the Southern Hemisphere

brings the midwinter chill of June and July, when the air grows cold after dark and you need a sweater to keep warm, that we got our biggest break yet. We heard of a foreign national, a Canadian, who had just adopted. Somebody mentioned this to Vita at one gathering or another, but all they knew was her first name and that she worked at the Canadian embassy. Vita was on the phone the next morning, asking at the switchboard for anybody named Beth. A moment later a woman's voice came on the line and, after an apology for prying into her personal affairs, Vita asked if she was adopting a child. Yes, she said, a little startled to hear the question from a stranger. Vita explained our circumstance, and Beth agreed to meet her after work.

"You just wouldn't believe the hassles," Beth said when they sat down together. "They stonewall, stonewall, stonewall. They seemed to act like I was some sort of criminal. And then I just got sick of it. I told them my posting was coming to an end and that I was leaving. They got busy then, and actually started to do the paperwork. It just got approved. I'm out of here."

Beth had a couple of advantages we didn't—her status at the embassy gave her a diplomatic cachet we lacked, and she had not been declared to be an enemy of the state. Still, hers was the only success story we knew, and it greatly influenced us to push deadlines whenever possible.

The date for our scheduled home leave was within days, the one Munautsi had told us would be "no trouble" reaching, and we still had no approval letter from the department to make the trip. Morris Thompson, Knight Ridder's foreign editor, wrote a letter to the department assuring them of our return to the country. It landed with a thud. The date for departure came and went. We rebooked the tickets and I went to see the provincial magistrate, Mr. Mano (I never knew his first name). I offered him my assurances that Chipo would be returned, handing him copies of the letters from my editors. I even offered to put up a cash bond.

He was slightly puzzled by my appearance in his office—
the Social Welfare office had never put our request on his
desk—but he said it all seemed reasonable to him. He was a
man of his word. He signed the authorization letter within
days. I couldn't help but marvel when I saw it. We had spent
five months to get a plain sheet of paper with three lines typed
on it. It said we could take Chipo out of the country for a trip,
and it was signed, dated, and stamped. It wasn't even on let-
terhead. I could knock off a copy in fifteen minutes or less.

That wasn't going to be necessary, as it turned out. Vita
came home from another trek to the U.S. embassy a few days
later, honking the horn as she pulled in the driveway. She
jumped out of the car and came in the house.

"Lookit *this*," she said, tossing Chipo's passport on the
couch where I was sitting.

I flipped it open. There was Chipo's visa. "Great, great," I
said.

"No," she insisted, "*look* at it."

I opened it again, perplexed. I looked it over carefully, reading it aloud, and then I nearly dropped it.

It was a multiple-entry visa, with an expiration date of
2008. Chipo could go back and forth into the United States,
whenever she liked for as long as she liked, for the next nine
years.

It took me a minute to get a word out. "How did you do it?"
I finally managed.

Vita was laughing, dancing around the room.

"I didn't," she said. "I applied for a single entry. That's
what I got back."

I smiled, then thew up both hands. "Touchdown!"

Either someone at the consular offices had just made a mistake—and it seemed unlikely they would make a nine-year error for a two-foot-high toddler—or someone in there knew of
our situation and had just tossed us a valentine.

I never asked.

16

HOUSE OF ECHOES

I T WAS THREE days later that I called Peter Ndarowa, a taxi driver who had driven us around town so much that he was somewhere between a steady employee and a family friend, to give us a ride to the airport. There were heavy bags and packed suitcases, but none of them was mine. Vita and Chipo were going. I was staying behind. It wasn't exactly a bait-and-switch operation, but it was in our best interest for Vita and Chipo to be out of the country as long as possible. I was going on home leave, just as I told the Department of Social Welfare, but I never said we were all traveling together. The fact was, my leave was finished, and I had to get back to work. I would take the trip home in two or three months on regular vacation time, as I was calling in every chit I had earned over the past six years.

Meanwhile, Vita and Chipo would be at my parents' house in rural Mississippi, or at her sister Kathie's in Detroit. Their lengthy stay was not quite the risk it might seem, for we long had noticed that while social workers had been poring over our files and records for a year—or just ignoring them—they had never asked to see Chipo. It was odd. There was no document about Vita or me that was too arcane for inspection—for example, they had our marriage certificate but demanded that Vita produce evidence that her first husband had actually died. Persuading Health Department workers in the city of Detroit to issue a death certificate for a citizen who had died years before, via a satellite telephone call from sub-Saharan Africa, and then convincing them to mail a certified copy of the same to Harare, Zimbabwe is not a task for the faint of heart. But it can be done, and was, and the document was placed on the appropriate desk. But nobody—and I mean nobody—ever asked to see the object of this whole process. They never asked us to bring Chipo in for an evaluation; they never checked to see if she was bonding to us or even if she might have been abused in some way. They did not ask to see her health card, her schedule of immunizations, or any proof that we were taking her for checkups. After the foster hearing, they didn't ask to see her at all. How is Chipo? they would ask. Fine, we would say. Chipo could have been summering in St. Tropez for all anyone knew.

In fact, Chipo was summering on a farm near Starkville, Mississippi, not exactly what you would call tourist country. The series of plane flights was torturous for Vita and Chipo—Harare south to Johannesburg, then back north to London, then to Atlanta, then to Mississippi. By the time they boarded the transatlantic flight, Chipo was so sleepless and irritable, and Vita so visibly exhausted, that a couple of women in the row ahead of her insisted on holding Chipo for a few hours.

"You look exhausted, sister," one of them said. "And we're at thirty-five thousand feet. It's not like we're going anywhere with her."

Vita conceded this was so, and slept.

The last leg of the trip, from Atlanta to northeast Mississippi, is an hourlong hop on a prop plane. After a brief stint in the clouds heading west, the plane glides down over a series of lakes and pastures just outside of a town called Columbus, turns south to pass over a four-lane highway, and lands on a runway next to a field of soybeans. The plane had not yet taxied to a stop when Vita, Miss Big City Girl, found herself wondering how she was going to spend a couple of months out here with white people she barely knew. She tried to imagine how many black women, in the entire history of Detroit, had married white men from Mississippi and spent two months down on the family farm, complete with African child in tow. She looked at her hand and figured she had plenty of fingers to spare.

Duane and Betty were waiting inside the tiny airport building, perhaps a little nervous about the visit too but delighted to see Chipo and Vita again. Driving into Starkville, past the long row of gas stations and fast-food restaurants that lined the main drag, Vita's sense of unease returned. But by the time they got out to my parents' small, quiet farm—they had sold off the livestock years ago—she began to find it peaceful. She and my mother chatted easily, and my old man was so enchanted with Chipo that he had built her a swing on the back porch even before she got there. He had been a stern to terrorizing figure when I was growing up, maybe five foot six and two hundred pounds, all muscle, bone, and gristle, gruff and demanding. He was still a solidly built, barrel-chested man, though his hair was graying and his knees were giving out on him, and he was a buttercup with his only grandchild. He helped her into the special seat, buckled her in, tickled her under the chin, and then pushed her back and forth in the shade of the late afternoon. Vita wasn't sure who had the bigger smile, him or Chipo.

A couple of days after they arrived, Vita and my mother took Chipo to the doctor's office for a rigorous exam. Chipo wobbled into the clinic in downtown Starkville like a trouper. She stepped on the scales, stuck her tongue out when she was supposed to, and howled like a banshee when they drew a small sample of blood. The tests confirmed our wildest hopes—she was just fine. She was twenty-three pounds and twenty-nine inches long, which was small for American children, but she was walking now, climbing over everything in the house.

She didn't have much of a vocabulary, but one of her favorite things to say was "Hello," usually blared out like a little foghorn. She was delighted at a word that always drew an identical response. She would call it out during breakfast, playing on the back porch, or eating ice cream after dinner. It was during these evenings, with no one but family for miles around, that she and my old man began to form their own relationship. She couldn't say "Granddaddy," so she called him "Big Daddy," which came out sounding like one word, "Bidadn."

Chipo would give an "oof!" or "unfh!" going up and down steps or picking up something in the living room after dinner. Pop would repeat those grunts each time she made them. "Oof," Chipo would say, attempting to climb onto a chair. "Ooofff," my old man would mimic from his chair. She would turn her head and look at him, suspiciously at first, then give another grunt. He did it again. She did it louder. He did it louder. And then she was giggling, and they would do it back and forth, nose to nose.

"Oofff!"

"Oooofffff!"

"Duane," my exasperated mother called out from the kitchen, "don't you teach my grandbaby to grunt."

As the weeks passed, with Vita learning to watch rodeo on cable with my father after dinner ("It's not like there are viewing options," she would mutter over the phone), he noticed something odd about his daughter-in-law: She stayed awfully close to the house. With the livestock gone and the fences pulled down, there was now a large, well-kept backyard, huge shade trees, some open pasture, and miles of woods stretching beyond them. With this freedom at her disposal, Vita would scarcely go off the back porch. And when she discovered there were deer that would come into the yard at night, eating flowers or the feed my father left out for them in a bucket, she became resolute—she wasn't going anywhere out there.

My father thought this was a hoot, a grown-up who was frightened of deer. I confess I did too. "Honey," I'd say in a phone call, "articulate to me what it is you think the deer are going to do. What, you come out of the house and they rush you? Push you in a corner and take your lunch money?"

She wasn't moved, though she would laugh about it. "I'm not going out in those woods to mess around. They stay out there, I'll stay in here."

But she was also surprised to find how comfortable she felt in rural Mississippi. It was a different but familiar feel to black life, she said, sounding as though she couldn't quite believe what she was saying. "A lot of white people in Mississippi are a lot more like black people than they realize," she said. "Maybe it's just country southern culture and I'm not used to it. But did you know your mama made greens and corn bread for dinner the other night? And fried catfish? That's what *my* mother cooked. I didn't know white people ate like that. And church is a lot different, but it's still Baptist and everybody sits out front and talks and gossips afterward, and it seems to play the same sort of central role in everyone's life. The respect people have for their grandparents, their elders, is like black people too, in an old-school way."

"I don't know why you're so surprised. I used to tell you this in Detroit all the time," I said.

"Well, yeah, but this is *Mississippi*."

"Who you telling?"

"It's just not what I thought it would be. I wouldn't want to move down here, understand, but I'm actually enjoying this. The other day, I caught myself looking forward to going to Wal-Mart."

"Whoa."

"Scary, isn't it?"

ON THE OTHER SIDE OF THE WORLD, I went back to the other life I was married to, airplanes and two-bit hotels and a suitcase and a satellite phone set up next to the hotel window. I woke up one morning back in Sarajevo, covering President Clinton's trip to that city, where there were now stoplights and traffic jams. I had dinner with Aida Cerkez, who had taught herself journalism during the war and become the backbone of the Associated Press operation there. She put her toddler son on a bus out of the city with her mother when the war began, and she rarely saw him for years. When she was out of the city on assignment, she would loan me her apartment. I hauled water and took baths each morning during the war by squatting in the tub, then dumping a bucket of the stuff over my head, gasping and cursing in the cold.

Now the war was over, Aida's son was back, she was happily married, and we all had dinner in a nice place with tablecloths. The war days seemed another lifetime, something that had happened to someone else. Time blurred and I woke up in another hotel in Monrovia, a steady rain beating down on the Liberian shoreline, the waves rolling in on dirty sand while children in rags played in the shelled-out hulk of a building across the street. In Freetown, the capital of Sierra Leone, rebels whose modus operandi was chopping off the arms and ears of civilians who didn't support their cause had been granted a part of the government in a peace agreement that only the United Nations thought would work. To emphasize the bitterness of the agreement, President Ahmed Tejan Kabbah had taken a two-year-old orphan whose arm had been blown off to the signing of the cease-fire.

I worked out of my room at the Cape Sierra Hotel on the waterfront. They charged $125 per night, cash only, for a shabby room that reeked of bug spray, with dirty brown water spilling from the faucets. There was a rat paddling around in my toilet when I lifted the lid. I pulled the satellite phone and the computer into the open courtyard in the moonlight, the roar of the ocean on the other side of the hotel, and bounced a story about the orphan who accompanied the president, Memunatu Mansaray, off a satellite and back down to Washington. I closed down the computer and sat in the soft light for a moment, resting from the day's work, enjoying the quiet beauty of the shoreline. A moment passed, and I could make out the whisper of footsteps behind me. I swore, silently, as I was sitting alone in the dark with $5,000 worth of equipment.

But when I turned, it was only two prostitutes from the hotel bar, looking for a customer. I said no thanks, two, three, four times, and they finally left, sullen, hips in tight skirts turning back to the bar.

ON THE MORNINGS I awoke in Zimbabwe, I found it depressing beyond reason. Being alone in a hotel was fine. But alone in that house, rattling around the kitchen cooking dinner for no one but myself, building a fire to keep warm while I read late into the evenings, engendered a sense of loneliness that seemed to echo in my bones. I had lived alone for thirteen years as a single man, often moving to cities where I knew no one, and was no stranger to long periods of solitude. But this was different. The apartments I lived in during those years had been shells in which I invested little and from which I expected less. But this was a home filled with the smells and scents and voices of the women in my life. I kept waiting for Chipo to come tottering around the corner, or Vita to call out to me from the patio, and there was never anyone or anything there. I opened Vita's closet and could smell the perfume of her clothes; I saw the ghostly imprint of Chipo's hand on a window above her changing table. I found myself staring at it, startled back into the present only by one of the dogs licking my hand.

I let them outside, feeling the chill breeze across my skin, but couldn't place the feeling that was twitching beneath the surface. There was only a well of emptiness, in which I seemed to drown a little more day by day. Reuters photographer Corinne Dufka, a good friend, and I had met again during the Freetown trip. We wound up discussing such things in her apartment there. After almost a decade of photographing some of the most intense conflicts in South America, Africa, and the Balkans, Corinne had just left the media to work for Human Rights Watch. I was surprised, because I considered her to be one of the best—and toughest—conflict photographers working.

"Why did you stop?" I asked.

"Because I just couldn't feel anything anymore," she said. "I mean, what manner of human cruelty have I not witnessed at this point? How many people have I watched be killed in front of me? I can watch an execution, process my film, eat a good dinner, and get a good night's sleep. Which is fine. That's how it is. But you reach a point."

I did not realize it then, but when I was back in Harare in my house of echoes and voices that were not there, it began to dawn on me that I had passed that point myself. Everyone has a limit of how much violence he or she can stand—cops, criminals, firefighters, soldiers, even journalists—and although I had never had any intention of reaching such a point, I now realized I had crossed some barrier the day I picked up Chipo in Chinyaradzo. I never got over how fragile she was, and that fear had turned me into someone else, different, stronger, more resolute, and yet more vulnerable. Before she and Vita had left, I would let Chipo sleep between us, and I would lie awake, watching her sleep, with no desire to do anything else at all. Even in the daylight, I no longer wanted the constant travel, the risks. I no longer wanted to deal with heavily armed, drugged-out sixteen-year-olds at checkpoints in the middle of nowhere; I didn't want to drive out of a different Sarajevo over a different Mount Igman under a different siege with different people shooting at the truck. I didn't really care what I did anymore; I just wanted to wake up in a house where my daughter was safe. The tenuous nature of our position in the country was a corrosive acid, eating away at me, and it marked its progress in steady fashion. The possibility of going to sleep without a drink, then two, or three or more, became nonexistent. I would sit by the fire in the darkened house, sipping a whiskey over ice, watching the middle distance, and then the glass would be empty. I would get up, stir the fire, and pour another. I would awake several hours later, unrested and sweaty and apprehensive, walking through the house at four in the morning.

But as our first anniversary of bringing Chipo home came and went, there was no hope of leaving the country at all. Weeks passed with no word from Munautsi. When I finally tracked him down to check on our file, I got the familiar heave-ho out of his office.

With nothing else to do, I turned back to reporting. I tried to throw myself into it, and in most ways it was fascinating. Harare that winter was an odd mixture of political intrigue, rising prices, and, of all things, witchcraft trials and accusations. One self-proclaimed prophet was arrested in the town of Seke after exhuming the corpse of a two-year-old girl and chopping off her arms and legs. He was going to burn them to ashes, which would then be mixed in elixirs for evil powers, for there is no item more potent in the dark arts than human flesh, blood, or organs. There was such a spate of similar incidents that the *Herald* ran an editorial with this headline: "Let's Stop These Witchcraft Murders." Meanwhile, parliament was debating the possibility of lifting the Witchcraft Suppression Act of the colonial era, thus making it legal to call someone a witch, a charge that could result in the accused being stoned or killed on the spot. The use of *tokoloshis*, a near-invisible, ankle-high gremlin created by traditional healers, was believed to be rampant. Gordon Chavunduka, director of the fifty-thousand-strong National Traditional Healers Association, pointed out in an interview that most of the spirit world was a benign or comforting place, and almost all traditional healers used their work for solace, consolation, communicating with ancestral spirits for guidance, or medical healing. The increased use of menacing forces, he said, indicated an increase in social fear and desperation.

This manifested itself in many ways, and I could see none more tragic than the fear, and resulting waves of almost hysterical denial, triggered by AIDS deaths. The official number of deaths was a rough-hewn guess because so few people would have themselves tested. And while a number of prominent people in Harare worked hard on the issue, there was a larger body of society that often seemed eager to believe almost anything and everything about the disease except what the overwhelming body of medical evidence showed—that it was a disease carried in bodily fluids.

This skepticism drew on a good measure of historical fact, though few Westerners seemed to realize it. In fact, it made a certain amount of sense.

Colonial regimes in South Africa and Rhodesia apparently did try to develop some form of biological warfare against blacks. Zimbabwe's minister of health, Timothy Stamps (who is white), said in a 1998 BBC interview that there was "no doubt in my mind" that South African apartheid agents had "inoculated our population" with diseases such as anthrax, Ebola, and even bubonic plague during the 1970s liberation war. In South Africa, cardiologist Wouter Basson faced charges that he headed an apartheid-era biological warfare unit, before being eventually acquitted. Bioengineer Jan Lourens testified before government committees that the apartheid-era experiments included tests to inoculate blacks with poisons to reduce the birth rate. And the CIA had been up to all sorts of tricks in the Congo, once trying to poison nationalist leader Patrice Lumumba with tainted toothpaste.

Just as blacks in America remember the Tuskegee experiment, so too do Africans remember these events and regard the AIDS epidemic with skepticism. Political leaders, noting that the disease started flourishing in southern Africa during or shortly after the last stages of anticolonial struggles, thought that it was suspicious that blacks were harder hit than whites. This resulted in the beliefs that were voiced by Zimbabwe's vice president, Joshua Nkomo, who had said that AIDS was a disease white scientists had created to kill black people.

As interesting as these theories were, they did not address the raw facts that were not in dispute. Mary Bassett, a black American who was a senior lecturer in public health at the University of Zimbabwe, moved to Zimbabwe in 1986. The prevalence of HIV-positive blood donors in her surveys at the time was 2 percent. By 1999, it was 15 percent. She also assigned her students to keep track of the mortality rate in Harare, pulling figures from the city morgue each year. They paid closest attention to corpses between the ages of twenty-five to forty-four.

The death rate for that group was up 700 percent in a decade.

The government did try to combat the problem, at least on some level. There were AIDS awareness campaigns, and the government linked with Western nongovernmental organizations to provide condoms at subsidized price. The government also became the only one in the world to tax the populace to pay for AIDS health care costs. Finance Minister Herbert Murerwa announced that a 3 percent levy would be added to everyone's tax bill, and the Health and Child Welfare Ministry would create a fund for the revenue, expected to total some 26.6 million Zimbabwe dollars (about U.S. $760,000). That was more than double what the country had spent on AIDS the previous year.

"I know that this isn't as much as some people wanted, but I hope it shows we're trying," foreign minister Stan Mudenge said at Harare's African Diplomats Ball, an AIDS fund-raiser, to a hearty round of applause.

The problem was that the government didn't consult the population about to be taxed. Neither did they announce how the money would be used. Prevention? Treatment? More nurses and doctors? It was anybody's guess. There were no bold statements at press conferences and no returned calls from government officials.

I called any number of AIDS clinics, orphanages, and physicians to see what they'd heard. They hadn't been consulted either. Things were particularly difficult for Ernestine Wasterfall, the matron at Emerald Hills, the orphanage that had so many children with AIDS. The government was supposed to send her a monthly allocation for her charges, now down to an inflation-ravaged twelve cents per day per child.

They hadn't sent her a penny for five months. "We pray some of this tax money comes to us, but we don't know if it will," she said. "The government never contacted us about it. Even the money they are already supposed to send us, they don't. I don't see how this is going to be any different."

Her skepticism, which was widely shared, was based on historical precedent. In the early 1990s, a similar tax was imposed to compensate for a devastating drought. The drought came and went, but the tax went on for years. The government never explained how all the money had been spent.

Zimbabweans were no fools, and they now looked at their dilapidated hospitals and poorly paid physicians and were doubtful that the same government that allowed the health care system to atrophy was suddenly going to double AIDS spending. I asked Wasterfall if I might send a photographer, freelance shooter Rob Cooper, to illustrate the story. She said they didn't allow pictures of AIDS patients. But, she said, do you think Americans might send donations if they saw pictures?

I told her I had no idea, but if someone should send along donations, I would certainly relay them. But, I cautioned, this was a remote possibility.

"Send Mr. Cooper over anyway," she said, ever hopeful. "I don't see how it can hurt, and it might help."

Rob went over and took pictures, including shots of two terribly ill little boys. A decent man, he made prints of some of the nicer shots and took them back as small gifts for the boys, along with a donation to help. Wasterfall accepted the donation but not the pictures.

The little boys were already dead.

17

BETRAYED

L ATE IN THE DRY SEASON of 1999, the beginning of
the end made itself apparent to me in two ways, large
and small. The latter was a travel article a freelance
reporter had written from Zimbabwe and sold to the *Chicago
Tribune*. In it, she told of a bizarre flight on Air Zimbabwe, in
which the pilot first told passengers over the intercom that the
copilot had not shown up, but not to worry, he could handle
the jet for the short flight. Once airborne, he told them he was
going to the bathroom, but not to worry because the autopilot
was on, and so forth.

The only problem with this little bit of airborne legend is
that it was just that. The story wasn't true. The government
was unhappy, especially since tourism had been declining for
more than a year, and the *Tribune* ran a correction. The government was not mollified, as an editorial in the *Herald* made clear:
"American and South African newspapers, driven by a pathological hatred of the present Zimbabwean Government, fell for
this chicanery and ran the story . . . such mischievous reports
must be taken seriously and remedial action taken."

Pathological hatred? Remedial action? That had my attention, all right. The way this was going, one word from Kaseke
and I could be charged as a malicious hack who was abducting
a helpless Zimbabwean infant. "Wouldn't that make for a
cheery headline," I muttered.

The second item was far more serious.

Many Zimbabweans had tired of Mugabe's administration. Of course they admired his heroic past. But that was twenty years ago. The Poles had tired of Lech Walesa, the Nobel laureate who led them to freedom, in a single term. Now, in vast numbers, Zimbabweans were turning to an opposition political party that was taking shape. Morgan Tsvangirai and Gibson Sibanda, the leaders of the Zimbabwe Congress of Trade Unions, had resigned their labor posts to form the Movement for Democratic Change (MDC), a coalition that would draw on its leaders' high profile among the working class. It also drew immediate support from several international agencies who were alarmed by the nation's collapsing infrastructure under ZANU-PF. Tsvangirai, who had already been severely beaten by unknown assailants after he organized national strikes and stay-aways, announced that his nascent party would field candidates for all parliamentary seats when elections were held in eight months.

The government, accustomed to a badly fractured and tiny opposition, recognized the threat immediately. They lambasted and insulted the new party at almost every turn. Chimutengwende, the information minister, ridiculed the MDC as "fake . . . political upstarts . . . It is boys' work to think that just because they have succeeded in organizing a stay-away, then you can run the country."

Initially, I didn't give such statements much credence. But the more I thought about it, the more the government's reaction took on troubling overtones. The new party was going to be far more powerful than any electoral challenge Mugabe had ever faced. The elections would be sharply contested; Tsvangirai was clearly hoping to use success there as a platform to run for president in 2002. He had good reason to be optimistic. The power of labor movements to shake off unwanted regimes in developing nations had been demonstrated by Walesa in faraway Poland and by Frederick Chiluba in next-door Zambia. People in Harare and in towns across the country were bursting with optimism that Tsvangirai was well poised for a similar turn to elected office.

But to any interested observer, Mugabe had demonstrated that he was not going to campaign and lose. He had identified his pressure valves in the past twelve months—white farmers, journalists, the American and British governments. It seemed equally clear that he would intensify his punching of those buttons as the election approached. How? When? Who knew? Professionally, in another country, I would have regarded this as a compelling story to cover. But here, it spelled personal disaster. The anti-Western, antimedia climate would be certain to escalate. Anyone could see that foreign reporters were going to be one of the first targets. It was imperative, I realized, that we get out of the country before the elections.

That left us seven months.

I swore under my breath. We had planned to stay here at least five years, to buy a house. I had planned to write at least one book on African affairs, possibly even staying after my posting was finished.

All of that was in shambles now, as was a good chunk of my career—I was no longer ignoring a story in my own backyard, I was running from it. I had come to travel as little as possible, just forty days in 1999, about one-fifth of my usual work pace. This left us in something of a quandary. My paper's parent corporation, Knight Ridder, had taken over the Africa bureau after the *Detroit Free Press* had sent me here. They had no obligation to provide me with a job after my posting expired—and since I had been consumed with Chipo's adoption, they were less than impressed by my performance. In theory, I was to go back to the *Free Press*, but I had not worked in the city for seven years and had had little contact with anyone there since the corporate takeover of my foreign posting. The paper had been decimated by a strike in my absence, and I was now such a nonentity that the last time I'd gone into the building, the security guard at the front desk had no idea who I was—my name was no longer on the employee list—and would not let me pass. The editors upstairs made no mention of a job waiting for me.

The *Washington Post* had called about a job nine months earlier, offering a ticket from Harare to Washington to discuss the position. But we had not been approved as foster parents at that stage. Our prospects had seemed so bleak that I told them it would be misleading for me to even make the trip, as that might imply some possibility of us getting out of Zimbabwe. "I hope you won't think that the *Post* just calls once," the recruiting director said, in a tone that implied that my phone wouldn't be ringing anytime in the next decade.

Looking for something, anything, I had put together a book proposal while on leave. It fell flat. I wrote a couple of short stories while stuck in one airport or another and shipped them to three small magazines. Nice, the editors said, but not for us.

In short, as I boarded a plane for my trip back to the United States, my once bright career had deteriorated into a dead-end job in a Third World country with no prospect of another. Worse, I had been to the United States once in the past four years—and I now had twenty-one days to convince someone there to hire me within twenty-eight weeks.

It was not a happy flight across the Atlantic, and I was feeling pretty low by the time I made two connecting flights and was finally aboard a small prop plane descending into rural Mississippi. As the plane came in over the pastures, I could see my parents' car in the parking lot. Chipo and Vita came running down the corridor as soon as I walked into the tiny airport, and I dropped to my knees and let Chipo knock me over backward. I had not seen them in more than two months. Vita looked fabulous, rested and in great shape. Chipo had her hair in beautiful long braids. I swept her up into the air and spun her around, and she collapsed against my shoulder in a gigantic hug. "Dadn!" she kept saying, over and over. My father rounded us all into the car, and my mother had a table full of home-cooked food waiting at the house for what amounted to a family reunion.

After dinner, my father and I retired to the back porch rocking chairs to sip whiskey and talk about the prospects for Mississippi State's football season—an issue of paramount importance in that part of the world—while my mother and Vita chatted as though they had been best friends for years. Chipo went from group to group. She would crawl up into my father's lap and sit there while he rocked back and forth, her head against his chest. Then she would run into the house, banging on my mother's piano, just as I had done when little, and then scamper around the same yard I had grown up playing in. Later, I settled her into the swing my father had built, and pushed her back and forth, back and forth. It was that in-between time of year, late summer or early fall, and Vita and I listened to the soft evening breeze pass through the trees above, sharing a drink, content to soak up each other's presence and conversation. My home state had changed a great deal in my long absence, I was discovering, and while it wasn't perfect, no one hassled us either, even when we went into the local Wal-Mart, hand in hand, to buy ice cream for dessert.

But the next morning, our talk turned to our diminishing array of options, and things grew somber. I packed an overnight bag with two suits and a pair of white shirts. I kissed Vita and Chipo. And then I was gone again, bouncing from city to city, airport to airport. I talked with editors at major newspapers and book agents, looking for any kind of opening. Two weeks later, after tap-dancing for anyone who would have me, I was so worn out that I was nauseous most every morning. At a pay phone in Manhattan, just across from Central Park, I called the *Washington Post* on a lark, asking if they'd like for me to stop in when I came down to D.C., even though I had refused to come in to talk to them eight months earlier. To my surprise, they said sure. I was on a train the next morning. Vita and Chipo flew into Washington to meet me, as we would leave from there to go back to Harare. I went through the interview process at the *Post* the next day, but I wasn't optimistic, and kept my suit coat on because I was so nervous that I was sweating through my shirt.

Then I went back to my hotel room and waited two days for a phone call, from anyone, anywhere. None came. With nothing else to do, we began the long trek home. We loaded up the baggage, drove out to Dulles International Airport, and boarded an overnight flight to London. I was downright morose by the time we made the connection for the next leg of the flight, another overnighter to Harare. When we finally walked in the house, some thirty-six hours after we'd left Washington, the answering machine was beeping. It was my mother, and she was terribly upset.

The day we left, my father had been burning a pile of cut trees and branches, called "brush" in country parlance, in the small pasture behind the house. He was using a chain saw to cut up the larger limbs so that they could be tossed on the fire. He didn't notice the machine was dripping gas over his shirt, pants, and shoes.

After a while, he set the chainsaw down and dragged a few limbs over to the fire. He stood beside the blaze to throw them in. The gas on his clothes drew in the flame, then ignited with a whoosh. His skin went with it. He was sixty-six years old, he was alone in the pasture, and he was turning into a torch. He looked at himself aflame. He didn't panic. He didn't even say anything. He took off his glasses and set them down on a stump. Then he pulled off his burning clothes. He lay down on the ground and rolled over. The flesh on his legs was still burning. He scooped up loose dirt and packed it on the flames until they died. Then he stood up, still smoking, and walked to the back door.

"Betty," he called inside, "could you bring me a towel? I think we may need to go to the hospital for a minute."

He had second- and third-degree burns from his ankles to his hips. He had patches of equally severe burns on his arms. At the hospital, he never cried out. The emergency room staff was in awe. I learned of this over the phone, shaking my head at the old man's grit, but I wasn't at all sure that he would live. We had barely slept on the consecutive overnight flights, and I sat up again this night, making plane reservations in case I should have to turn around and go back. Somewhere around 3 A.M., I typed up a letter for the Department of Social Welfare.

We were in Kaseke's office six hours later. My temper was ragged and my patience finished. In our family, Vita is the one quickest to anger. She can turn on a rude store clerk in a heartbeat. When I finally go off, though, it's one for the ages. I got arrested in Warsaw for shoving a cop (who had insulted Vita), I had to be pulled away from a twenty-something white Zimbabwean kid in the bowling alley (same reason) and, when Vita once needed surgery, I read the riot act to a doctor in Detroit (um, see above) in such fashion that the hospital put Vita in a private post-op room that looked like a hotel suite. They sent her flowers every day.

I was now at a similar pitch. In fact, I was just damn through with the lot of them. Our application to adopt had not budged in nine months (so much for my source's advice to sit back and rest assured the department would process the application). It still sat in a brown folder, one of hundreds, if not thousands, of files stacked on desks around the department, mired in the foster section paperwork. I was so livid that morning that my foot was tapping the floor, my fingers were drumming on Kaseke's desk, and I was pretty sure I had lost the ability to blink.

Skipping the formalities, I told Kaseke of my father's accident, that his life was in danger—and then an idea came spinning down from the void. Keeping in mind Beth's winning example, I said this meant we would have to quit my posting and return to the United States as soon as possible. Family ties. Son needed. Surely she understood.

She expressed sympathy for my father. Then she sighed deeply and told me there was nothing she could do.

"There have been charges of bribery against you while you were gone," she said. "The matter is very serious. There was this matter last year, and now it has arisen again. It is very, ah, unseemly. If you have paid no one, as you say, it is curious that people keep telling us you have."

I bit the tip of my tongue, sharp enough to hurt.

"Mrs. Kaseke, I'm as tired of these allegations as you must be. As I told Mr. Munautsi, whom am I supposed to be bribing, and what am I supposed to be getting for it? You have seen Vita and me in the hallway here for hours on end, because your staff won't make appointments, won't return our calls, and won't keep regular office hours. It has been fifteen months since Chipo came to our house. Fifteen. We have had home studies by two different social workers. You yourself investigated this matter, and yet our case has not budged. This is not what happens when people are bribed. Things tend to happen then. Obviously, these charges are being made by someone who doesn't know us, or this case, at all."

"That is the problem, Mr. Tucker. It is actually someone who knows you quite well. Ah, it is your friends Heather and Steve. They have been in your home many times. I believe you have been to theirs. Heather has told me a great deal, and Steve was very clear about the bribes, I am sorry to say for you. There must be an investigation, one that is very thorough. I cannot advance any application that has these charges."

"Heather?" Vita nearly shouted. Kaseke had played her cards well.

Heather and Steve had indeed been to our house many times, and we in theirs. Heather had an adolescent daughter by a previous marriage. Steve was trying to formally adopt her. We knew that, of course, but it had not really registered. In fact, we had distanced ourselves from them after a series of incidents. There were a few unpleasantries, but the main event had been a reception I hosted for my editor, Joyce, when she had visited the year before. It was an evening affair, filled with an array of Zimbabweans and expatriates who worked at a wide variety of professions, from art gallery owners to political activists to architects. There were sixty or seventy people milling about, sipping wine and chatting. I thought the evening was going rather well when Nevio, my friend the cafe owner, mentioned that Steve was raising hell on the patio. I stepped outside, where the air was noticeably tense. Steve had been loudly proclaiming racist views of black Americans and Africans. It didn't seem to matter that his wife was Zambian and his audience entirely black. "I don't know who's worse," I was told he blared, "idiots who run these countries or black Americans who show up and think they know something. There's nothing more arrogant and ignorant than a black American in Africa."

Not surprisingly, people began leaving. By the time I had learned of the incident, it was pretty much over. "You're all right with me," said Jamar Evans, a friend from Texas who is black and was working in Harare, "but you need to look out for the white boys you run with."

Heather, meanwhile, had too much to drink and was holding court among a small group of women inside. At that time she was making clothes for Grace Mugabe, the country's new First Lady, who was half the age of her husband. She had arisen, amongst great scandal, from being one of the president's secretaries to being his wife. She was awkward in public and extravagantly overdressed for the simplest of occasions. She shopped in South Africa and the capitals of Europe. Her trademark large hats were parodied around town. She wasn't popular, to say the least. Heather—very attractive, always impeccably dressed, and with a walk that leaned toward a sashay—thought her high-profile client was a laughingstock.

"She's a simple country girl, a peasant," she told the women.

Then she went out to their car, an open bottle of wine in hand, and passed out in the front seat.

We had not seen them since that evening, politely declining invitations for dinner or get-togethers. We had no interest in being anywhere around Heather when her gossip got back to State House, and I didn't sip whiskey with men who held Steve's view of the world.

And now, we learned, we were targets of their anger.

"We haven't seen them in ages," Vita told Kaseke. "Heather doesn't know a damn thing about Chipo, much less our paperwork."

Kaseke smiled, looked down, held up her hands. "Ah, I am so sorry. But you must understand, we must investigate."

We got in the car. My hands were shaking as I put the key in the ignition. Heather would have been sure to oh-so-casually mention she made clothes for the First Lady to Kaseke, playing up her visits to State House. That would give her charges extra clout.

"This has to be some sort of bullshit," I said. "Kaseke is twisting something. Let me call Heather and see what's going on."

I walked in the house and dialed her number without slowing down to take off my jacket. She picked up the phone.

"Hey, Heather, I'm sorry to bother you, but you won't believe the nonsense I just heard," I said. "I just wanted to bounce it off you. Florence Kaseke told me just now that you and Steve were down there saying we paid people for Chipo. I know that can't be right, but I wanted to get it straight how she is under that impression."

There was a pause.

"I don't know that this is as untrue as you think," she said.

"I need you to tell me what that means," I said, struggling to keep the tremor out of my voice.

"We have been trying for Steve to adopt my daughter, as you know," she said. "It has been three years! Three years! I went to Kaseke's office, and she didn't even know where our file was. Can you imagine! I told her of your case and how you had no problems, you came and got a baby and that was that. It makes me mad, when we Africans are made to sit in the backseat to you Americans. Steve was furious, I tell you. He went to Margaret Tsiga and yelled at her for some time. You are paying her off—oh, we know. That is fine for you, but it pushes our case to the back."

"Heather," I said, snapping a pencil in two, "who is Margaret Tsiga?"

"The adoption officer, of course."

"Heather, goddammit, our file has never made it to adoptions. We are still in *foster care*. I don't know who this woman is. She could step on my toes and I—wait a minute. Three years? How many times have you been down there? To the department?"

"I told you. I went the other day."

"No, I mean before that. Like in the whole three years."

"I filled out the form and gave it to them. Then nothing happened. I had almost forgotten about it. I went by the other day to pick it up, and that's when they couldn't find it."

"Are you saying you've been down there two or three times in three years?"

"One or two times more than that. I don't count such things. I mean, one fills out the form and picks it up. It's very simple."

I was trying very hard to keep my temper in check. I kept telling myself silently *Make the smart play. Think two steps ahead. Picture a good outcome.* What kept coming to mind instead was an image of whopping Heather over the head with a baseball bat.

I lowered my voice and spoke as evenly as possible.

"Heather. We have been to that building more than thirty-five times. *This year.* More than sixty-five in all. I *do* count such things. I log them with fucking notations. They have lost our file, just like they lost yours. We got ours back because Vita crawled around on her hands and knees for two days. They don't do anything unless you make them do it, Heather. You put your file in a couple years ago and never called in? Of course it went missing."

She harrumphed into the phone.

The noise seemed like a shove in the chest.

"Do you know, woman, that you have just put my daughter's life at risk? That you just gave them ammunition to put her in an orphanage? That she will likely not survive if that happens? You know they hate Western journalists. You've seen the anti-American marches. If you thought we were doing something wrong, for chrissake, why didn't you complain to us? How does it help you to have Chipo taken away?"

"Don't be a fool," she said.

"*Me?* Did you just *fucking* say that *I* was the fool in this conversation? Jesus *Christ*. Put Steve on the phone. I want him to say to my face what he's been saying behind my back."

"He's not here."

"Fine. I'll call the motherfucker at the office."

"Steve will not take any call from you."

The line stopped me. It suddenly became clear, in a Zen-like moment of clarity, that they might have been among our enemies within the department all along. I suddenly remembered a day months earlier. We had seen Heather in Kaseke's office. She had stood up to go when we walked in, saying in passing that she was getting their adoption finished. Had she whispered in Kaseke's ear then? Was that why our file had been stuck for so long? Perhaps. Perhaps not. Whatever the case, there was no good outcome to be had. I was ready to give it to her in a double dose—but, I realized, I couldn't. The humiliating fact was that she had more pull than we did. Making her angry was only going to make the situation worse.

I slammed down the phone.

Vita and I roamed the house that night, all but breaking things. I threw book after book against the wall. I went in my office and shattered clipboards over my knee. We spit out every epithet, insult, expletive and threat known to either of us— and considering my southern roots and Vita's urban flair, this was a fairly colorful (and extensive) array of language. I think it fair to say that both of us were unbalanced for a period of several hours. One of the risks of reporting on so many conflicts, it seems to me, is that you deal with so much violence and so many unstable situations that the whole process begins to seem ordinary. You get on the plane in one violent spot, land back at your home base a few hours later, then go back, and return and go back and return and go back and return, and after it gets to be years of this sort of mental and moral Ping-Pong, sometimes you have to shake your head to remind yourself of what is "normal." I had interviewed enough people whose lives had been ruined to know better than to think disaster only happened to someone else, and the whole situation seemed askew, beyond reason. *This*, I thought, *is how your life blows up.*

Neither of us slept that night.

By nine the next morning, I had been for a ten-mile run in an effort to calm my nerves. Whatever benefit there had been to venting our anger the night before, ranting was no longer helpful. We needed something to break the logjam. There were no other flanking movements or misdirections or other pieces of documentation that we could obtain to nudge the process forward.

There was just the adoption order. Nothing else mattered now.

It was the last days of October. The parliamentary elections were in six months.

Other than the time Kaseke had come to our house, I had never seriously considered that we would lose Chipo. As I often told our friends, we wanted her more than the department did and, eventually, desire trumps bureaucracy. But with the political climate collapsing, our phone line tapped, the president naming individual journalists as enemies of the state, the law making foreign adoptions all but impossible—and now with the bizarre twist of the First Lady's dressmaker denouncing us—I had to concede we were about out of options. If this had felt like a tennis match a couple of months ago, I was no longer so jocular now that we were down to match point.

"We need a silver bullet," I said to Vita.

We were both in the office, drooped in our chairs, and she didn't say anything. Instead, she raised herself, cup of coffee in hand, and went to the filing cabinet. She began pulling notarized copies of every document that related to Chipo's birth, medical history, and our custody of her. I turned to the computer and, with a muttered curse, began to write a response to the bribery allegations.

The tactic we had decided to take was that Steve and Heather had done us a favor.

They had assumed we were much further along than we were. By accusing us of bribing Margaret Tsiga, whom the department managers had spent fifteen months preventing us from reaching, their own files would show the allegation to be false. If they said we bribed one of our foster-care officers, it might have been a body blow. Instead, we would treat it as a roundhouse that missed.

That was the plan, anyway.

I addressed the letter to Kaseke and, after pleasantries this time, it began: "Yesterday you informed us of allegations made by another client that we had taken 'shortcuts' during the fostering/adoption process. This letter is to clarify, I hope for the final time, the life-threatening situation that brought Chipo into our care. It appears the nature of Chipo's illness at the time has been frequently misunderstood within the department, giving rise to allegations of premature placement in our home."

I went on for three single-spaced pages, delineating every record in Chipo's medical history, the corresponding emergency custody orders, the times and dates of every substantial meeting we had with department officers (sometimes it helps to be a compulsive note-taker) and listed, by name and title, every person in the department who had signed off on our files.

The name Margaret Tsiga appeared nowhere.

Vita, meanwhile, was assembling copies and documents, down to the receipt for the oxygen Chipo had been given in intensive care. It was 2 A.M. by the time we finished. The table held two empty take-out pizza containers and two bottles of wine.

We pulled Chipo out of her crib to sleep between us that night. She sat up in the middle of the bed about an hour later, saw both of us, and was delighted. "Hellloooo!" she sang out. "Hellloooo!" she said again, louder, when that failed to draw a prompt response. I woke up and said, "Hey."

She went back to sleep. I couldn't.

At first light, I was in the front yard, throwing a ball for the dogs to chase. By 7:45, I was showered and dressed in the best suit I owned. Thirty minutes later, I was in Kaseke's office. I gave her the file, a brief assessment of its contents, and another one of my cards. "Call anytime," I said.

Then I pulled rank. The art of getting mad, after all, is getting even.

I went a few blocks over to her boss's office—that of Mr. Soko, the man who had signed off on our visit to the United States. I walked in without an appointment because I knew he wouldn't give me one if I called. I sat in the front room for an hour and a half before his secretary, after speaking on the phone, came over and said he would see me at 9 A.M. Monday. It was then Thursday. I said fine.

I could not sleep that night, nor the next. I became so sleep-deprived I couldn't concentrate on anything long enough to write a coherent sentence. I finally went to see Dr. Paruch, our friendly Polish doctor. He was a remarkable man. Raised in communist-era Poland, he had moved his family to Zimbabwe in the early 1980s, a country friendly to the Soviet bloc in the Cold War years. Somehow, on a state salary in an impoverished country, he had managed to put his two daughters through Ivy League colleges on scholarships. He counseled me not to worry so much, swallow the sleeping pills he gave me, and take the longer view of life. I promised to do the second and get back to him on the other two.

Monday morning, I was back in Soko's office. I handed him the file, told him of the bribery allegations, of my father's accident, and that I now had to return to the United States. I omitted my fears that foreign journalists were probably going to be deported within a year or two anyway.

He was very polite but firm.

"This is the second time you've been in my office, Mr. Tucker, and I must tell you I find this extraordinary. It is improper for parents to come to my office. This is the regional headquarters. Your concerns should be addressed to your caseworker, and they will take it to the head of the department. If there is a need, they should come here, not you."

"I know that, Mr. Soko, and I'm very sorry to disturb you. I hope you will forgive me if I seem to be a pushy American. It is not my intention. But I came to see you because the problem *is* your lower staff members. They seem to believe anything anybody tells them and to delight in believing it. The facts seem of no consequence to anyone; our work at Chinyaradzo seems forgotten; it seems every manner in which we try to get involved is twisted to have some evil purpose. Now with my father's injuries, I have obligations to two generations of my family on either side of the Atlantic, to my daughter here and my father there. I cannot fulfill one without the other, and I cannot do either without your help. I came to respectfully explain these things to you. I mean no disrespect by having done so."

There was a pause. I held my breath.

"You have spoken well, Mr. Tucker," he said finally. "I will see what I can do."

THE FOLLOWING DAYS were miserable. It was the end of the dry season; the ground was parched, tempers were edgy. My father seemed to stabilize, but I kept an open plane ticket booked to Mississippi. I had to get back to work, filing short dispatches, but delayed any travel because I could not budge from the bribery allegation. The work didn't add up to much, and what was left of my career seemed to be in freefall.

Then, late one afternoon, the phone rang.

It was a secretary from the Department of Social Welfare. She asked me to hold. There were a couple of clicks, and then a woman's voice came on the line.

"Is that Mr. Tucker?"

"It is."

"This is Margaret Tsiga," she said with a laugh. "You wouldn't believe what people are saying about you and me."

18

FRIENDS AND FOES

MARGARET TSIGA worked just across the hall from Aaron Munautsi, but it seemed like another world to me. When I walked in, she smiled, she laughed. Her voice had a warm, confident tone. She didn't seem bothered by the bribery allegations. If anything, she was amused.

"So this is the mysterious Mr. Tucker," she said, shaking my hand lightly. "Such things I have heard about you! My goodness. The director told me that Steve was saying you had given me money. 'How much did I get?' I asked. 'And who is this man who gives me money for nothing? Ah, this is the man all women are looking for.'"

"If only that were me," I said, trying to get adjusted to her pleasant demeanor. It was throwing me off. "I'm very sorry your name got dragged into this. I just don't know what to tell you about Steve."

"This is a rather unpleasant man," she said. "I believe he thinks Africans cannot hear so well. He seems to shout everything he says."

"Even hello?"

"He is not the type to say 'Hello, how are you?' Maybe he does to somebody. Not around here."

She rustled around some papers and folders on her desk, and I recognized the familiar edges of Chipo's file in her hands. She flipped it open and began to sort through the documents.

She started to ask the standard questions and took notes. I heard my voice going over the saga one more time. I looked around her office as I spoke. It was a small rectangle, with a concrete floor, a small window, and tired white paint on the walls. The space was cramped, filled with her desk, a couple of low-slung bookcases and filing cabinets, and the chair I was sitting in, pulled up tight to the desk. The surface of her desk was neatly kept, but the shelves and the space around it were filled with stacks of notes and files. The bookcases, along the wall next to the door, were filled to overflowing. I was overcome, once again, with what a tiny slot our case filled, at how many other children were in some need of assistance, and how poorly equipped the department's workers were to try to keep up. After a while she said she had what she needed for today and she told me I could go.

"The next time you come in," she said as I stood to go, "could you bring Miss Chipo? I would like to meet this young lady. And also your wife. I hear she is lovely."

I said yes, of course, and took a step toward the door. Then I thought for a moment and turned around.

"Does this mean you are actually considering our case?"

"Of course," she said with her slight laugh, as if I were a student a little slow on the uptake.

"So our file is now in the adoption section?"

"That's right."

"Which means it's not in the foster section?"

She laughed again. "Exactly so."

I opened my mouth again, to ask what had happened to the bribery mess and if it was all finished. And then I remembered my brother once telling me that my problem in life was that I just didn't know when to shut up. So I did, nodded goodbye, walked down the corridor to the exit, and then sprinted for the truck, grabbing the cell phone and calling Vita on a dead run.

"We're out of fostering! We got past Munautsi!" I shouted. A whoop on the other end was her response.

We were by no means home free; if the adoption process

took as long as fostering, we would never make it out of the country before the elections. We went on a charm offensive the next day. Vita, Chipo, and I went back to see Mrs. Tsiga, Chipo in a little denim dress, her braids pulled back in an upsweep. She walked in, holding Vita's finger for balance. Tsiga, looking up from her desk, burst into a laugh. She pushed back her chair, leaned down, and opened her arms.

"Come, little sister," she said.

Chipo walked into her arms as though she were a favorite auntie. She sat on her lap the entire time we talked.

"Boy, is *she* cool," Vita said when we were getting back in the truck. "She's more like Stella, or one of the women who work in the orphanage, than the social workers. Can you see Munautsi getting Chipo to sit in his lap?"

I came back in the building a couple of days later, bringing another sheaf of personal reference letters for adoption—the last batch had followed department regulations and just mentioned fostering—and I stopped as soon as I turned the corner into the hallway that led to her office. In the gloom of the unlit corridor, there was a line of seven or eight people outside her office. Some sat, some stood. One mother nursed an infant. A couple of other children scampered in and out. The door was halfway open, and I could hear Tsiga talking with a client already inside. I glanced at my watch. It was 3:30. I took my place at the end of the line, leaning against the wall and saying a quiet hello, getting nods in return. Clearly, these were not all adoption cases. Too many set faces, clenched jaws. Divorce and custody, deaths of parents, child support, allegations of abuse, charges of neglect, abject poverty—the somber laundry list of reasons people would be sitting in the Department of Social Welfare for hours on end. Tsiga was clearly involved in many areas of social work, not just adoption. I looked down the hallway, then walked back to the other corridor, where other social workers had their offices. No lines. No one else was in. I walked back to my spot at the end of the line and slumped onto the floor, back against the wall. I was already regretting not bringing a

book. The line inched forward as the clock moved toward the 5
P.M. closing time. Nobody in the line budged. Half an hour
passed, and then another. The rest of the department shut
down. Cars pulled out of the dusty parking lot outside. At a few
minutes before 6 P.M., it was finally my turn. And then a man
came walking down the hall, two children in tow. He started to
go in the office in front of me. I was about to protest when he
winked at me and said, "I'm the husband. I'll just be a minute."

She stood up, smiling to greet him and calling out a friendly
hello to me.

"This is my husband," she said. "He always comes to wonder when I'll be home." They laughed, talked briefly in Shona,
and then he was gone, giving me a handshake and walking to
the door, children swirling around him.

"Don't let me hold you up," I started, and she waved me
into the seat, dismissing the notion with another wave of her
hand. "I just have so much to do. Yours is a small part. My husband, he was stopping to see if I was going to cook dinner or if
he should make other arrangements."

"He doesn't mind you working late? You're the last one
here."

"He's used to it," she said, with that soft laugh I liked so
much.

"You have lovely children," I said. "You have those two?"

"We have several, actually. Sometimes I seem to lose
count."

"You've got four, five kids? And you're working late? And
I'm thinking I've got a lot to do with one? You're shaming me,
Mrs. Tsiga."

"You get used to it." She shrugged. "I think you have some
papers for me?"

I had almost forgotten the reference letters. I handed them
to her, continuing the conversation about families for a few
minutes. Over the next couple of weeks, as Vita or I brought
her one document or another, the pattern was the same. She often had a line outside her door—her office was never empty—

and to get to see her by 5 P.M., it was best to show up at least an hour earlier. I sat in the dim hallway next to the other clients and read one book after another. As always, there was no such thing as an appointment. She was in court, in interviews, or there was someone already in her office. In contrast to the workers I had experience with, she was there right on time each morning, or just a few minutes early, and she often worked past the close of the business day. She was so tired she often had bags under her eyes, and yet she was clearly committed to working with some of the city's most disadvantaged children. It was just plain inspiring, and our conversations often wound up drifting onto any number of subjects, not just Chipo's adoption.

In the midst of this, as we began to feel some small ray of optimism, the phone rang one night after dinner. Vita handed the receiver to me, mouthing that it sounded like an American woman on an international call. I said hello, and Jo-Ann Armao, the assistant managing editor for metropolitan news at the *Washington Post*, said hello back. Jo-Ann was not one to spend much time on small talk, and she asked if I still wanted to work at the *Post*.

"Sure," I said, trying to keep my voice steady. Vita looked up. "The *Post*," I mouthed silently, giving a thumbs-up.

Jo-Ann was talking about covering the city, about salary now, and I was waving to Vita in big country-cousin bye-byes, holding out my arms like I was an airplane, flying around the room, and she was shaking her head and laughing.

When Jo-Ann finished, I said of course I'd take the job. Then, using up my allotment for chutzpah, I asked for more money than she offered and asked how long they could wait before I actually showed up. We agreed on mid-February at the latest, nearly five months in the future and a month or so in front of the parliamentary elections. If the adoption didn't come through in time, Vita and I had already decided that she and Chipo would stay behind with friends while I moved to start the new job. It was an unpleasant prospect, but there was no way I could go on reporting in the country. If I had to go, Vita and Chipo would move across town, settling into a spare room in the home of our friends Bill and Dumisille. Bill was a senior officer for the U.S. Agency for International Development. Dumi was from Swaziland in next-door neighbor South Africa and knew the regional ropes. They lived in housing that was property of the U.S. embassy. The residence would give Vita and Chipo some measure of diplomatic protection if things got unpleasant, and Bill and Dumi were uniquely placed to help us out if it came to that.

It was in the midst of this planning, on a quiet Sunday morning in early November, as we all waited for the rainy season to descend upon us, that most expatriates and a good number of Zimbabweans woke up to wonder if the head of state had gone slightly out of his mind.

"Blair Using Gay-Gangster Tactics: Mugabe," screamed the headline stripped across the front page in the *Sunday Mail*, the government paper's Sunday edition. The proudly homophobic president was accusing the British prime minister of hiring homosexual thugs to force him to change his stance on Zimbabwean land reform. Britain's intelligence wing, MI-5, was said to be lending a secret, guiding hand.

This remarkable claim arose from an incident on the street outside the St. James Court Hotel in London, where Mugabe was staying. It hit on a popular refrain for him, as he had been saying for years that homosexuals were "lower than dogs and pigs," that they were not deserving of human rights, and so on. This vitriol had alarmed gay-rights activists the world over. So when he began to step into his limousine outside the St. James, four activists from a group called Outrage ran at him. Led by Peter Tatchell, they said they were going to "arrest" Mugabe for human rights violations. His bodyguards were inattentive or not present; Tatchell's crew got a hand on Mugabe before he was hustled into the limo.

Mugabe translated this publicity stunt to be a coordinated attack from the top echelons of Britain's new Labor government, orchestrated by Tony Blair himself.

Mugabe had scheduled a constitutional referendum for February. If passed, the new constitution would allow Mugabe to "take back" the land from white Zimbabwean farmers—most of them British descendants—at will, without paying anyone for it. Britain, like most everyone else, said this was unconstitutional and outside the rule of law. Mugabe said Blair was dispatching homosexuals to harass him into backing off the policy. He repeated the "gay gangster" allegations to reporters during the Commonwealth Heads of Government meeting in Durban, which grouped fifty-two national delegations from what had once been part of the British Empire.

The whole episode was so daft, so bizarre, that most diplomats and journalists in Zimbabwe—and a good number of citizens—simply threw back their heads and howled with laughter. It was the joke of every dinner party, every afternoon *braai*. The state-run paper printed an editorial telling citizens it wasn't patriotic to laugh at the president, but nobody cared. Tony Blair and his Gangster Gays! It sounded like a garage band in drag.

Edgar Langeveldt, Zimbabwe's first stand-up comic, picked up on the mood in his one-man show at Harare's Seven Arts Theatre later that month. He was colored, the regional term for mixed-race, and his often raunchy act encompassed song and dance, female impersonations, skits in which a bumbling black detective investigates the murder of an obnoxious Rhodesian housewife (she wore lime green bell-bottoms, made jokes about blacks, and danced around the kitchen to Abba; you felt she had it coming). In a taped monologue that played on a huge screen while he changed clothes during one skit, he appeared as Grace Mugabe—but all that could be seen on the screen was one of her trademark huge hats. It obliterated everything else. The audience gasped, then laughed so hard you couldn't hear the rest of the act. No one had done such in-your-face comedy in Zimbabwe, and certainly not about the president. I did a feature story about Langeveldt, interviewing him over a late lunch before the last show.

Not everyone was laughing.

Langeveldt went to a popular bar a few weeks later. Several men approached. They didn't say anything. They just beat him senseless. His jaw was grotesquely fractured. He could barely speak, much less perform, for weeks.

Needless to say, at this point in the story there were no arrests.

That wasn't all. On November 25, three local journalists received death threats. Ray Choto, one of the authors of the alleged coup story who was still awaiting trial, got a small package at his house. It contained a toy, two bullets, and a note: "See you in heaven before Y2K." Basildon Peta, news editor at the *Financial Gazette* and head of the Zimbabwe Union of Journalists, opened his mailbox to find three bullets and a note: "Watch out or you are dead." Ibbo Mandaza of the *Zimbabwe Mirror*, that had published the story about the soldier's head being returned from the Congo, got the threat by phone.

"Damn it," I told Vita. "I've got to go somewhere, get out of town. This could blow up any day. They could say they didn't like the story about Langeveldt. They could say anything they want. Sooner or later, they're going to come after foreign journalists, and they're not going to care about an excuse."

19

ON THE RECORD

I BEGAN setting up logistics for one last trip to Nigeria when Margaret Tsiga called. She asked me to come into her office the next day. Her voice sounded tense, and I could feel my pulse quicken to a steady throb.

"It's the police clearance," she said when I walked in the following morning. "Or the lack of it, perhaps. There's no record police ever investigated this case. There's no history of any search for the people who abandoned Chipo."

"But I talked to the officers who conducted the search," I said. "I spent almost an entire day with them. They told me about the investigation. There has to be a record. I mean, that's the only reason we could bring Chipo home. They had just completed their investigation and closed the file."

She shrugged. "Well, it isn't here now, and we must have it. It's really one of the most important documents in the whole package, you understand. Without it, Chipo is not legally an orphan, and therefore you have no right to adopt her. As far as the law is concerned, she could be kidnapped."

"I don't believe this. I know those guys filed that report. Mr. Mtero called out there himself to confirm the details. Chipo has been with us for sixteen months. They spent six months going over our case before approving us as foster parents. The judge approved it. Then Munautsi spent another ten months before he forwarded it to you. And *now* you're saying the department has never had any evidence that Chipo was abandoned?"

"Who knows? Perhaps the notice was there and slipped out of the file. Perhaps the police wrote it out but never mailed it in. In any event, it isn't in your file now, which is the only thing that matters."

She pulled out a piece of paper and began writing. When she finished, she pushed the piece of paper across the desk. The note, written in cursive on a sheet of pulp paper, was addressed to the police officer in charge of the district where Chipo had been found. It said there were "indications the case had been investigated," which I guessed I had just made, but it stated she had no official clearance to continue.

"Before we proceed with this application to adopt we would like to know if investigations have been completed to find the natural parents. We would like for you to kindly confirm in writing," it continued. After I read to the end, I handed it back to her. She stamped it with the department's official seal, folded it into an envelope, sealed it, and gave it back to me.

"I would like for you to take this to that police station," she said. "See if you can convince them to look it up. If I mail this, they might answer it promptly. Or it might get put on the bottom of a stack of papers and be lost. I don't know what they'll tell you when you go out there. But I can't do anything else without it."

I rolled out just after dawn the next day, clearing Harare's light traffic in half an hour. I turned onto a four-lane road that led out of town and kept going as it hit the outskirts and turned into a two-lane blacktop. Harare's urban sprawl quickly gives over to broad ranches, commercial farms, and open grasslands, and I was soon deep into the countryside. The truck had no working radio and I drove in silence, just the wind rushing past the open windows. It was a beautiful morning, the temperature in the mid-seventies, a light breeze and brilliant sunshine. I dangled my right arm out of the window, still bemused by driving on the "wrong" side of the road. Several

hours later, I turned off the highway onto a gravel road, putting up the window halfway to keep out the dust. The fields
were poorer now, more weeds, fewer crops. The trees came up
close on the road, the branches forming a canopy overhead.
The miles rolled by, slower, in thicker clouds of dust. There
was a turn to the right, where the road became more washed
out and rutted. There was a turn to the left across a narrow
bridge that spanned a dried-up creek bed. Then I was back on
a paved road in the tall, waving grasslands. The police station
lay just ahead in a grove of towering eucalyptus trees.

Several buildings were clustered together in the shade, as
the station provided living quarters for many of its officers.
The office itself was a one-story concrete block building
painted a watery blue. It was set on a concrete slab, which
formed a walkway around its perimeter. The roof, red and
rusty, was made of tin. I walked across the gravel parking lot to
the building at the front. There were perhaps a dozen people
milling about. Voices murmured; a manual typewriter clattered away in a side room. Everyone stared. A white American
with long white hair was, apparently, a rare sight. The electricity wasn't on. The illumination from the day spilled in through
open doors and windows, the interior holding a cool, gloomy
light. I walked up to a desk and asked for the officer in charge,
explaining that I was delivering a note from Harare's Department of Social Welfare. An officer asked me to wait. I sat on the
edge of the concrete sidewalk, plucking blades of grass.
Twenty minutes later, the officer returned and led me to a
room toward the end of the building. A thin, unsmiling man
sat behind a desk. He was on the telephone, idly tapping ash
from his cigarette into a tray as he listened. He looked up, saw
me, and waved me to a chair. He was the same officer I had seen
the previous year when I had come to investigate Chipo's case.

I sat down and looked around the room, trying to keep my
hopes up. The case had been closed more than eighteen months
ago. The commander's desk was wide, wooden, and old, covered with papers and two telephones. There were trays marked

O.I.C., Pending, Administrative, Crime, Out, and In. Each was stenciled in red ink. There was a picture of a pink rose, apparently clipped from a glossy magazine, glued to each one. A pair of huge maps were on the wall behind me. With the officer's conversation continuing, I made a gesture toward them, and he nodded. I got up to inspect them. The national map said Zimbabwe, but it still listed the capital as Salisbury, the colonial name for the place, meaning the map was at least twenty years old. It also showed the "Tribal Trust Areas," the colonial term for African-owned land. The other map was a street atlas of the main town in the district, with a series of different colored pins marking the location of each recent crime. The color of the pin indicated the type of offense, so that the officers could track robberies or assaults in a particular area.

The officer finished his phone call then, stood up, and shook my hand. "Ah, the man with the baby," he said, almost smiling. "How is our little sister?"

"Fat and happy," I said, and he laughed.

"What brings you back to me today?"

I explained the situation, trying to disguise the nervousness in my voice, and gave him the letter from Tsiga. He opened it, looked it over, and called out to a junior officer. He spoke quietly to him. "You may go with him," he said to me.

I followed the young officer back onto the concrete walkway, past what looked to be several defendants waiting to be booked, and into another room. Behind a desk, there was a wall of shelves. Each was sagging under rows of fat ledgers. The officer—he never said his name, and I never asked—went to the stack, ran his fingers over the edges of the leather-bound volumes, looking, looking, and then he pulled out one. He opened it and put it back. He pulled out the next one and brought it over to the table.

"We need to find the case number," he said.

He flipped open the book. I blinked back a migraine. On the front and back of each page were hand-drawn grids, lined out with an unsteady ruler, stretching across and up and down the two-page spread. Small blocks were listed for the date, site of the crime, the time, investigating officer and so on. The last block on the right-hand side, running down the page, was headed "Case Resolution." The binding formed an uneven bump in the middle, so that you had to count up or down on both sides to make sure you were following the same line, and thus the same case, across the page. The ink was in blue on the left, in red on the right.

Taken page after page, in volume after volume, in its differing shades of ink, the effect of the cramped writing was overwhelming. It looked and read like some sort of mysterious code, a vast library of secrets and passwords and multiple volumes. But the officer knew what he was looking for and, my apprehension aside, it did appear to be studious police work—so long as you could find the right book and the pages didn't rot and someone had remembered to enter the case on the right day.

So look up the date and there it is, you say. Cut the drama, man, and get on with it. Aye, but there was the problem. Neither he nor I knew the exact date Chipo had been discovered, nor did we know the precise date the case had been closed, and there appeared to be dozens of entries on most dates. I couldn't tell if the entries were just the loggings of each case into the system or whether updates, changes, and developments in preexisting cases were also noted. The officer might have entered it the day he got the case, or on the day he thought Chipo had been born. Or he might have entered it in end-of-the-month loggings. He was, after all, based in a precinct miles away. He only came into this office when needed. If he entered it when the case was closed, the single-line entry would be three months ahead or even later, at the end of that month. Further, although the log was chronologically ordered, it wasn't absolutely so. There were dozens of entries in the first few pages that seemed to have no date at all. Others had dates mixed in and out of sequence. I guessed that it added up to more than one thousand entries we might have to scan in several different types of handwriting, some clear, some convoluted, some in blue ink, some in black, or red, the colors apparently in random sequence.

Or, in the worst-case scenario, he might have forgotten to log it at all. Abandoned children, as he'd told me, were depressingly common. Maybe it just didn't rate.

I tried to force that last possibility from my mind as we flipped the ledger's pages to the days preceding the date on Chipo's birth certificate. There was a three-day window that seemed certain to be the correct date, and there were only a few dozen cases to scan. The officer ran his finger slowly down the rows of entries. Nothing. We expanded our search to the three-month period the case had been under investigation, pages and pages and pages of entries. Down the rows we went, looking for something that appeared familiar. I followed his finger down the page, both of our lips moving, whispering over this entry, now that one. We came across an abandoned child—no, no, it was a boy. Break-ins, burglaries, robberies, rapes; down the criminal history of the region we plowed, day after day, month after month.

Nothing.

"Let's look again," he said, and back we went, slower this time, the minutes peeling away into an hour. His finger was sliding down a page, slowly, and it came to a stop near the bottom. "Here," he said.

The ink was fading, the page beginning to tear away from the binding. But there was a scrawled-out case of an abandoned infant, female. There was a closure date and an original entry date that was so far to the right it was half in the wrong column, which was how we had missed it the first time. The binding in the middle had skewed the lines on the right from those on the left. We counted up from the bottom, three lines, on the left side of the binding, then on the right. And there was the date cleared, in fading red ink at the far right-hand side of the page. On a crumbling section of this page, rotting into nothingness, the notation read: "No arrest. Case closed."

The officer copied down the file number and the dates. He flipped the ledger shut and went to find the file. I walked around the room a couple of times, then wandered back to the front yard. There was still a sullen line of men in ragged clothes, sitting, not speaking, waiting to be booked or charged or to pay a fine. None was handcuffed. I looked at the grass-lands and the woods and figured if they all made a run for it, scattering in different directions, at least half of them would make it. Then I remembered that everybody knew everybody in the countryside. The cops would know their family members and where they stayed and who their friends were and they would get caught, eventually, because there really wasn't anywhere else to go. I suppose the resolute desperado could hitch a ride all the way to Harare, but what would he do there with no family and no contacts? I moved out into the sunshine, plucking more grass stems out of the yard and flicking them off the end of my finger, restless. The officer stepped to the door and called out.

I turned, walking out of the sunshine and back into the gloom, momentarily blinded.

"Your daughter's name," he said. "Is it . . ." He looked at a brown folder opened in front of him.

I held my breath and closed my eyes.

"Chipo?"

"*Yes!*" I shouted, startling him and the suspects outside, everybody seeming to jump into the air. "I mean, yes. It is. Chipo. Of course. Yes. My daughter."

He led me back into the head officer's room.

I sat back down in the chair, trying to keep still now. They spoke between themselves. Neither looked at me. The officer looked down at the paper, grimaced, and lit a cigarette. He reached for a pen and began to write. The young officer left. The phone rang and the old man took it, setting down the pen and cradling the receiver between his shoulder and his ear, lis-tening, then speaking rapidly in Shona.

It was growing late in the afternoon. Clouds passed in front

of the sun and the shadows rippled across the open fields of grass. The old man hung up the phone after a time. He looked back at the paper, set his cigarette on the edge of an ashtray, considered what he had written, and then resumed. I made a great study of the map on the wall. At length there was a rip of paper and the officer called out to his junior staff member. The young man returned, took the piece of paper and left. The officer took a drag on his cigarette and motioned to the yard outside his door. "You can go out there," he said.

The young officer had disappeared, and as I had pretty well plucked the front yard clear of grass, I roamed around the jacaranda trees, snapping off twigs, balancing them on a finger, then thumping them across the yard. Forty-five minutes later, the young officer emerged from the room with the noisy manual typewriter. He called to me and extended a single sheet of brown pulp paper.

It had the precinct address at the upper right, followed by the date. It was addressed to "The District Social Welfare Officer." The subject line read: "Re: Abandoned child Chipo."

"Madam," it began, and three short paragraphs followed. Each was numbered in the style of court documents.:

1. Please be advised that this matter was investigated by Police.
2. Efforts were made to locate and arrest the accused/ mother of the abandoned child with no leads.
3. Matter is now closed undetected.

It was signed by the member in charge.

I let out a long breath. I stopped back in the older officer's office. He was still on the phone. I clapped my hands softly three times, the Zimbabwean sign for gratitude. He nodded with a wave of his cigarette, still talking.

I sang out loud in the truck all the way back to Harare, an off-key celebration that matched my mood. Now we were getting somewhere, I thought.

I cheerfully took the file back to Tsiga the following Monday, but she seemed busy, distracted. Vita went down to her office; she was too busy to see her, too. This continued for a few days, and I resorted to the tried-and-true stakeout. I plunked down on the hallway floor outside her office early one afternoon, notebook and cell phone in hand, and settled into an afternoon of phone interviews and note-taking.

At 5:30 she finally called me in. The offices were all closed; she was again the last one there. Her eyes were tired, the skin on her face lined.

"This can be a very sad job on some days," she said. She opened a dusty manila folder on her desk. "Here is a nine-year-old girl. She is being sexually abused by her father and, I think, by her uncle. Here is a case"—she picked up another file—"of a child the mother and father are fighting over. Neither loves the child; they are trying to humiliate the other. Those"—now she pointed to a stack five or six inches high on an adjacent table—"are sex abuse cases. The ones next to that are orphans, or those that have lost one parent. Sometimes the father wants the child if the mother died, sometimes he does not. And here," she continued, picking up another brown file on her desk, "is Chipo's file."

I felt a wave of guilt coming on, as if I had been a well-heeled Westerner whining that his latte has grown cold. She was really very nice, doing a yeoman's work, and here I was, another obnoxious and demanding client. I was beginning to mouth some face-saving apology when she raised a hand. She pulled out a few pages that had been stapled together. She slid it across the desk toward me.

"And what I see in this file is a happy little girl with two happy parents. There are things that are complicated, and things that are not. You will excuse me for thinking I have better things to do."

I looked at the top of the stapled-together pages she had tossed me.

This was typed across the top:

APPLICATION TO THE MINISTER TO DISPENSE WITH
CITIZENSHIP REQUIREMENTS IN THE MATTER OF
AN APPLICATION BY NON ZIMBABWEAN CITIZENS
TO ADOPT A ZIMBABWEAN MINOR IN TERMS OF SEC-
TION 59(7) OF THE CHILDREN'S PROTECTION AND
ADOPTION ACT (CHAPTER 5:06).

The following six pages were facts, figures, a case summary
and chronology, and so on. I was reading every word when she
clicked her fingernails on the top of the desk, *tap-tap-tap*. I
looked up.

"This says I have approved your adoption," she said, smiling broadly. "If the minister agrees, you will be free to go."

I didn't quite know what to say. I looked at the file. I looked
back at her.

"Have I ever happened to mention what an absolutely gorgeous, scintillating, stunningly attractive woman you are, Mrs.
Tsiga?"

"No," she laughed. "But you can start."

20

WEST TOWARD HOME

THE DAY AFTER Margaret Tsiga approved our file, it was December 1, World AIDS Day, and the rest of the planet began to get an idea of the orphan crisis that was sweeping over the continent. In New York, the United Nations reported that in the eighteen years since the disease had been identified, more than eleven million children had lost one or both parents to AIDS. At least 95 percent of those children were in sub-Saharan Africa.

"The traditional African family is breaking down under the unprecedented burden of the pandemic," read the report. Dr. Peter Piot, head of the UN program on AIDS, acknowledged that the previous years' reports had emphasized the growing number of infections, not their social implications. In an interview with the *New York Times*, Piot said that orphans were "the most forgotten aspect of the AIDS epidemic."

In the odd way in which international journalism sometimes works, the report and Piot's press interviews crystallized what had been a sprawling morass of an issue spread over dozens of countries. AIDS in Africa wasn't a new story, but the full impact of the loss of millions of parents had not yet been fully understood—nor had the implications for the future been so stark. In some of the world's poorest countries, the social implications ten or fifteen years down the line when all these four-year-old orphans reached adulthood were unknown but troubling. As a number of studies had reported, these children would be left outside the all-important network of the African family. They would receive less schooling and fewer opportunities for work, and they would be far more vulnerable to social, economic, and sexual exploitation. In Harare, I knew the situation from the reports by aid organizations that outlined the country's orphan crisis, documents that had been forwarded to the UN to form part of their worldwide report. I knew the matrons of the orphanages and dozens of the children themselves. By my count, I had held at least three children who would die within days; Vita, in her work at the orphanage, had known many more. One of the last children I had helped care for was a toddler named Ferai, just like the infant we had lost. He was at Chinyaradzo when I took Joyce, my visiting editor, on a tour of the place. He was twelve or thirteen months old at the time and already had the shrunken frame and visible ribs of a body in the throes of full-blown AIDS. The skin on his face was pulled back so tightly you could see the shape of his skull. His lips were pulled away from his teeth, and his large brown eyes, the only things he moved with ease, glinted with a sharp focus. I wondered what I looked like through his eyes, what it felt like to be held, what the long hours in the crib held for him. I wondered if the shadows of darkness and impending death were anything that he could recognize. Joyce was shaken and wanted to know what she could do. I was holding Ferai in his shroud of blankets, rocking him back and forth, and I explained that this little guy was too far gone. She insisted, and I finally said that, short of trying to adopt him, the best thing would be to provide a steady supply of vitamins to boost his immune system. So she bought vitamins and I delivered them. Ferai somehow rallied. He really did get better. He perked up. He held my hand when I picked him up, gripping my fingers. I laughed, thinking I had underestimated a child's astonishing capacity for recovery, and then one day he died. Just like that. Fat folders sat in my filing cabinets, documenting the larger issue of

AIDS and abandoned children with statistics that went off the charts.

The UN report, filled with such data, put the issue before the Western world.

"10 Million Orphans," screamed the cover of *Newsweek*'s international edition a couple of weeks later, the words printed over the shrouded face of a Zambian child. "The AIDS epidemic in Africa is leaving a generation of children without parents," read the subhead. Inside were photographs of bodies in morgues and coffins being lowered into graves. There was one of an HIV-positive mother and child, lesions covering the infant's flesh. Another was of a wailing infant in an orphanage, so emaciated that the veins in his stomach were showing.

Time dispatched legendary conflict photographer James Nachtwey to shoot a photo essay on AIDS in Zimbabwe. The cover shot, in black and white, showed an older woman and a sad-faced child. It was run so large that the picture blocked out all but the last letter of the magazine's name across the masthead. "This is a story about AIDS in Africa. Look at the pictures. Read the words. And then try not to care." That was the headline.

On they came in the ensuing months, a phalanx of some of the best reporters and photographers in the American and European press corps, from newspapers and magazines and television stations and networks, all documenting the toll of AIDS on orphans in Africa, fanning out from South Africa all the way to Uganda. By late spring, even *Scientific American* had a lengthy story about it. "Care for a Dying Continent" ran the headline. The story was based almost entirely in Zimbabwe. The first full-page photograph was of the survivors of the Gombedza family in the eastern city of Marondera—six children. Both parents had died, as well as their grandmother. They were now all living with a thirty-year-old unmarried aunt, who had a child of her own, in a home with no water and no electricity. The magazine reported they were one of 107 families of orphaned children in Marondera's townships alone.

So it came to be that one of the most momentous stories of our time fell into my lap, there at the end of the world, the tale of an entire generation of abandoned and dying children, and I knew it to the bone. I had the sources, the data, the feel of daily life in an orphanage at the heart of the problem, exacting detail that none of my colleagues could ever match, and the record will show I never filed a single story. I took a dive. Punted.

The fact was that the millions of children on the continent did not have my heart. One of them did. I still needed the national minister of public service, labor, and social welfare, Florence Chitauro, to authorize Chipo's adoption. I could write no story about Zimbabwe's orphan crisis that did not implicitly or explicitly criticize Chitauro's ministry and the administration of which she was a part. Such a story would be a red flag to the same people who would consider our adoption request, and I was already well aware that any slight misstep could result in Chipo being taken back to the orphanage.

Perhaps I could have written stories that, by their detail and close reporting, might have led nongovernmental organizations or private individuals to designate lifesaving help for any number of children. I could have demonstrated how the government's decision to spend tens of millions of dollars to send troops to fight in another country's civil war affected its own orphaned children—that was the type of hard-nosed reporting on which I thrived. But there was no point if it endangered the life of *one* child, one who meant more to me than all the others. I had broken the first rule of Journalism Ethics 101: Never get personally involved in a story you are assigned to cover. I threw my notebook in the air. There was nothing to do about it now.

With the orphanages filled to overflowing and the country falling apart, I filed a story on elephant poaching.

Then I turned in my resignation, put four new tires on my truck and sold it for a song to my friend Nevio Prandini. I made plans to fly to Nigeria for one last story on a charismatic young Yoruba separatist leader who was wanted by police. I would drive around Lagos with him for a week, come back, and quit.

FOR A WHILE, the adoption paperwork seemed to fly along. It had taken the department six months to approve us as foster parents and another ten for them to forward it across the hall. By contrast, Tsiga completed her report in just twenty-three days. She sent it to Tony Mtero, the department director, who signed it in four days. He passed it along to Mr. Soko, the provincial magistrate, who signed it three days later.

Then it disappeared into the ether of the national ministry, headquartered in a charmless building downtown known as Compensation House. It was ten days before Christmas.

I drove down there each morning, crisply dressed in suit and tie, looking to talk to anyone who would listen. The problem was that the department was spread over several floors in different wings. I had no idea of what staffers worked in what divisions, of who actually set the paperwork in front of the minister. Mrs. Tsiga didn't know either, as foreign adoptions were not something she did often enough to be familiar with, and our roller coaster screeched to a halt.

It was a situation that would leave any Capitol Hill lobbyist reaching for the whiskey cabinet—deadline for a big bill to be signed and zero access. I did at least manage to learn that the person who handled adoption cases for the minister was a Mrs. Dhlembrewu. I once waited for six hours to see an aide to her chief aide. Nothing. Vita and I went back the next day and got a brief audience with a different aide. The man politely explained he was not aware of our case at all.

I had to leave for Nigeria then, and Vita went back a few days later. She avoided the aide to the aide and went straight to Mrs. Dhlembrewu's office. She was surprised to come across a parent in her reception area but agreed to see Vita for a moment. Vita explained the situation, tactfully omitting my status as an enemy of the state, but it still left Mrs. Dhlembrewu unamused.

"I've never seen your file, and I don't like it when social workers expect us to work miracles," she said. "Have one of them explain this to me."

Vita rushed home and tried to reach Tsiga, Soko, anybody. No one was in. She went to their offices two days running. No luck.

I wasn't getting much done in Nigeria, calling home twice a day for updates, and I was relieved to (a) not get shot or arrested with my young separatist friend and (b) knock out the story and head for home. I was nervous boarding the Kenya Air flight that night, though, as I had developed a case of the shakes about flying. My nerves were shot, and I had an unshakeable bad vibe, an intuition that I was going to be in a plane crash days before the end of my posting. I wouldn't mention such guff to anyone, of course, but it had been unnerving me for several months.

When freelance photographer Malcolm Linton and I had been in Sierra Leone, we were to fly on a tiny turboprop to Liberia. A heavy thunderstorm blew in. I stood on the tarmac, cursing my nerves, getting soaking wet, until Malcolm said, "You think *driving* there is going to be any better?" which prompted images of mud-track roads and machete-wielding rebels. I got on the plane.

But I still had the jitters, bad enough to cancel a flight Malcolm and I had scheduled within Nigeria. The tickets were $130 each and nonrefundable. I ate the expense rather than fly.

The overnight flight back to Nairobi, where I would catch my connection down to Harare, was uneventful. But when the landing gear came down and we emerged from the rain clouds above Jomo Kenyatta International Airport, I nearly jumped out of my seat. We were maybe two hundred feet above the tarmac and were flying *across* the runway. The pilot jerked us back up into the clouds. We were in a holding pattern for fifteen minutes, and then we were going down, down, until we broke free of the clouds and the runway loomed below us at the same cross-eyed angle. Back up, back down—by this time everybody was wide awake and staring out the windows—and now we all saw a third botched approach as we came out of the clouds.

The pilot jerked the plane up again. As we bounced through the turbulence, he announced we had just enough fuel to fly to Mombasa, on the Kenyan coast. An hour later, we touched down in bright sunshine. They refueled. By now, my feet were twitching. Then we were airborne, flying past Mount Kilamanjaro and then down, down through the clouds once more, finally gliding onto a very wet runway. The passengers broke into a spirited round of applause as we coasted to a stop.

The footnote to the story is this: Kenya Airways' tiny fleet only made that Nairobi-Lagos-Nairobi run twice a week. Two months later, the flight to Lagos crashed into the Atlantic Ocean, killing almost everyone on board. I do not know if it was the same craft and crew I flew with, but it had the same flight number, and it was likely. I watched the wreckage recovery on television, the shattered bits of the airplane bobbing in the waves, and wondered if my bad vibe had been so silly after all.

DOCTOR'S VISITS, more home studies, more fingerprints, visas, all for Chipo's U.S. adoption certification and citizenship. We did little else in the crazed first weeks of the new year. It actually seemed pretty easy.

"You know how bad it's been," Vita said, "when the Immigration and Naturalization Service looks good."

She was looking at a stack of paperwork from the U.S. embassy that explained what we would need. Most of the documents were in hand. But the consulate in Harare was small,

and they did not process applications for adoptions by U.S. nationals. That was at the regional headquarters in Nairobi—no, no, it turned out, that office was still in disarray after the bombing. A temporary office was operating in Johannesburg.

We flew there to be fingerprinted for a required FBI check of our backgrounds, filled out a stack of forms, turned around, and came back. Now Vita took Chipo to Dr. Paruch for the medical documentation of her health. (We already had this from Dr. Paz, but he wasn't on the list of doctors approved by the U.S. embassy, so we had to do it again.) Dr. Paruch plopped Chipo down on the examining table. He poked and prodded and listened. Her lungs were clear; her heart, sight, hearing, speech, and teeth were all fine.

He took a pen and began filling out the form. Under race, he wrote "A," which gave Vita pause until she figured out that it meant "African."

"Is the minor well nourished?" the form asked.

He playfully poked Chipo in the stomach, his finger disappearing into her Buddha belly, like she was the Pillsbury dough girl. She collapsed in giggles, leaning over his hand. Then she looked down, waiting for him to do it again.

"*Very* well nourished," he wrote.

By mid-January, the movers had come and turned the house upside-down. They were so slow it took them four days to pack up one house for two people. The last day, they brought in two extra crews to wrap up the job. It started at 7 A.M. and was nowhere close to finished at nightfall. We strung up lights in the driveway so we could see the package numbers as we loaded them onto the truck. The company made no provision to feed their workers. They were expected to work from daybreak until long after dark with only what they had brought for their lunch. I went to Nando's, a fast-food outlet, and returned with nineteen carry-out chicken dinners. We all sat down in the driveway, eating with our fingers, and then stood up and kept going. It was midnight when it was finally done.

We woke up the next morning in a house empty save for a

few pieces of furniture the landlord had left behind. There was nothing on the walls and nothing on the shelves. Our voices echoed.

The departure date on our plane tickets came and went. We pushed it back a week. That passed, too.

I was, at least until I arrived in Washington, unemployed. Vita had been barred from working by Zimbabwean customs protocols for three years, and I had been without a paycheck for three months during leave the previous year. We had no more pockets. We resigned ourselves to Chipo and Vita staying behind with Bill and Dumisille. There was no telling when, if ever, the adoption might be approved. The parliamentary elections were just two months away.

"We knew this might happen," I told Vita one night, trying to make it sound like a small detail. "If something goes wrong, they won't know where you are. If we get the adoption hearing, I'll be back on the next flight."

The next afternoon, four days before I was to leave the country, I was down to my last card to play. I drove down to see Margaret Tsiga one more time. We talked for an hour and a half, about families and children and some of her cases, about the rainy season and the problems in government. The hour grew late; everyone had left. I had always called her Mrs. Tsiga because she never told me not to.

"Margaret," I said at last, "we've got to leave Zimbabwe now. I have no job. I'm running out of money. I have to have my baby now."

"I know," she said with a sigh. "Meet me in the morning at eight o'clock."

I didn't have much hope. I went home and told Vita I was going to waste another day sitting around at Compensation House, and then I went to sleep.

The next morning, Margaret and I pulled into a parking space on the street outside the building. She was in a very nice dress, and I was again in a suit and tie. I started to get out. "No, no," she said. "You'll just be in the way."

I sat back down in the driver's seat. I left the door open, dangling a foot outside. I read the morning paper. I stood up and stretched, walked over, sat down in the shade of a tree on the sidewalk. Ten vendors tried to sell me fake gold watches at cut-rate prices. I went to get a Coke and sat back down in the car.

The sun rose in the sky. I pulled a novel from the backseat. Workers spilled from the office buildings; it was somehow lunch hour. I was dozing in the afternoon heat, sweating into my starched shirt, when the passenger door swung open and Margaret sat down. She did not smile.

"So how did we do?"

"Not good."

"No?"

"No."

She flipped open a folder.

"I believe," she said, looking down at the paper in front of her and working to keep the edges of her mouth turned down, "that we do not have a court appointment until tomorrow morning at eight o'clock. Or is it eight-thirty? Could you stay with us in Zimbabwe that long?" And then she was breaking into a smile, a schoolgirl's laugh, and she held out the ministerial dispensation. It was a single sheet of paper. It was signed, stamped, and approved.

I took it in hand as if it were the Holy Grail, found at last. With the minister's consent, the judicial hearing would be a fifteen-minute formality. I debated about the proper course of action at a time such as this. It was really an auspicious moment, not to be repeated in my lifetime. The record will show I hollered out loud and gave my social worker a big fat wet one, right on the cheek.

She didn't seem to mind.

THE NEXT DAY, we made it through the hearing in nothing flat. Then Margaret took us to the city registry to get a new birth certificate, walking past the throng of people lined up from the reception desk to the outside steps. She opened a door into the back room and we followed her through rows of tall shelves stuffed with files, around a corner, through another door, into an office, and there sat the registrar herself. This was the last step, and my palms were suddenly sweaty. Margaret spoke in Shona. The woman—I never knew her name—nodded kindly. She handed me a piece of paper, an application for a new birth certificate. I filled out the dates and so on, but stopped when it came to the line about filling in the child's name.

My handwriting looks like a fifth-grader's scrawl. I didn't want Chipo's name to look like that the first time it was written.

"You do it," I said, handing it to Vita.

She rolled her eyes. "There are times," she said, "when you can be the most ridiculous man."

She leaned over the table and wrote it quickly. She wrote "Chipo Katherine Tucker." The middle name was an amalgamation of Kathie, Vita's sister; and Catherine, the given name of my maternal grandmother, whose last name I carry as my first.

And so it was set down, stamped, and handed back to us. I took the paper in hand, kissed Vita, and looked down at Chipo.

She was asleep in her mother's arms, peacefully sucking on the same three fingers she had been on the day we first saw her.

IT'S FUNNY, the way your entire life can boil down to a moment nobody else in the world notices, and so it was with us that night. Vita sprayed champagne and we laughed and hugged and shouted and turned the boom box music up, Al Green and Barry White and Marvin Gaye old-school jam. We danced and shouted at the top of our lungs with a handful of friends in our empty house, because joy is a gift that should not be wasted, because our hearts had been touched with fire, and because when I took Chipo outside the stars seemed aflame and the night sky seemed to flow and shimmer with the secrets of the world, an invisible river of happiness that floated above and around us all.

"Look, baby," I said softly, as if in a trance, pointing to the sky. "Look at the stars."

EPILOGUE

In the end, stories are what's left of us,
we are no more than the few tales that persist.

SALMAN RUSHDIE
The Moor's Last Sigh

THE POLITICAL CRISIS that had been brewing in Zimbabwe erupted eight days after we flew out of the country.

Mugabe suffered a humiliating defeat at the polls, as his bid for a new constitution was rejected. He had asked his countrymen to give him the power to take land from white farmers at his will—completing the war for independence, as he put it.

But Zimbabweans, with fewer than twenty years of anything that resembled democracy, understood a thing or two about political maturity. The last thing they wanted to give an autocratic old man who took his young wife on shopping trips to cities they only read about was the power to take land from people he didn't like. They might very well be next.

So they went to the voting booth and told the father of the nation to get lost. They rejected the new constitution, 55 percent against to 45 percent for. The streets of Harare erupted in horn-honking celebrations.

Mugabe was furious.

Less than two weeks later, his followers began invading hundreds of farms, beating and killing their political opponents—some white, but most of them black. They ransacked factories, assaulting anyone who was not a ZANU-PF supporter. It didn't seem to work. Mugabe lost again in the parliamentary elections, as the upstart MDC claimed nearly half of all seats, a stunning result for a party that was eight months old. This time there was more violence—murder, assault, intimidation, and disenfranchisement. The next time that ZANU-PF counted ballots, in the presidential elections, they came up with a tally that showed Mugabe to be the winner.

Journalists were special targets of violence. The printing presses for the *Daily News*, a new independent paper, were fire-bombed shortly after we left. The government said that foreign journalists were the likely culprits, as they got to the scene "suspiciously quickly," and briefly arrested a photographer for the Associated Press. My erstwhile travel partner, Ann Simmons, called me from Harare the day after the bombing.

"You wouldn't believe how the police are cracking down," she said. "This place has changed so—" and the line went dead.

I looked at the receiver there in the *Post* building and remembered my tapped line back in Harare. *Nah*, I thought. I called her back at her hotel. The switchboard operator patched me through to her room. Ann came on the line, laughing.

"But it's really quite serious here," she said. "They are after journalists here like—" and the line went dead again.

Rob Cooper, my photographer friend, was attacked along with several other journalists while covering the farm invasions. Several men accosted them, ordered them onto the ground, broke their cameras, and beat them with steel phone cables. Rob sent me a picture of his back. His skin was slashed open in dozens of wounds from his neck to below his buttocks.

Joe Winter, the BBC correspondent in Harare, was awakened one night by a mob of men trying to break down his door. Thinking fast, with his wife and infant child huddled beside him, Joe called every photographer he knew. They arrived minutes later, standing at the gates of his yard and flooding the scene with flash after flash of pictures. The men fled, fearing identification, and Joe and his family were rushed to the safety of the British High Commission. They left the country the next morning.

By the first anniversary of our departure, the death toll of opposition figures had grown to forty-one, all but five of them black. In the same time frame, more than four hundred factories reportedly went out of business, more than ten thousand people lost industrial jobs, the unemployment rate soared above 50 percent, and inflation rose to more than 60 percent. Farm production collapsed so badly the country had to ask for international assistance to feed its population, and the World Food Program was warning of an impending famine.

And, almost one year to the day after we left, the nation's Information Minister began a policy to bar foreign correspondents from living or even working in Zimbabwe. Foreign reporters who wished to visit the country would have to file an application a month in advance. They might, or might not, be allowed in for five days.

I READ THESE reports from the other side of the world, and I sometimes wonder how close we came to everything collapsing on top of us. I think we probably had at least two more weeks. We certainly did not have twelve more months.

In the wake of a long story I wrote about Chipo's ordeal in the *Post*, more than two hundred people from five countries on three continents wrote or called or e-mailed Vita and me, wanting to know how to adopt other children, or to help Chinyaradzo, or to convey that they were moved by her experience. One minister in Baltimore even used it as the basis for a sermon. I found that somewhat amusing for someone like myself, long considered the religious black sheep of a family that includes a church pianist (my mother) and a seminarian with a degree in liberation theology (Vita). I probably liked the blunter messages, such as this note from a French television executive: "Bravo for Chipo!"

I laughed at that one, but I have rarely found solace in those letters from strangers, as kind as they are. I walk into Chipo's bedroom on some nights to listen to the magic of her breathing, soft and even in the darkness, and as she exhales I sometimes hear a sound that is not there, the silence of the dead children whom we might have saved, perhaps Robert or Ferai, had I not been so focused on my travels. We left the others to their fate.

The last alone is a staggering thought, but perhaps it was required triage. In fact, I believe it proved to be a necessity in the course of events. But I did not realize then the weight that action would carry over time. My daughter lived while so many around her died, and her beauty is the sharper now for the absence of those children who passed away at the orphanage, from the epidemic in Zimbabwe and beyond, in their tens of thousands, across the continent. There is the phantom weight of Ferai's soon-to-be-dead body in my arms and the sound of my foot in the child's rib cage in Rwanda, and the heat and dust of those days seem to be with me when I find myself lost in thought.

We now live on a pleasant, tree-lined street in the nation's capital. Upon our return, Vita tried to resume her profession as a paralegal and a research librarian. After nearly a year of trying one law firm and then another, she found it too empty in the wake of her experiences at the orphanage. At the age of forty-eight, she changed careers. She now works as the East Africa project coordinator for World Vision, the same charity that sent volunteers to Chinyaradzo. She specializes in children's issues.

Miss Chipo is a talkative, effervescent five-year-old with dreadlocks. She is happy to tell you, if you ask, that she is a big girl and a princess, or a pretty girl from Africa, depending on her mood. She visits her cousins in Detroit and Chicago, and likes the week she spends alone with her Mississippi grandparents each summer. My father eventually recovered from his burns and dotes on his grandchild.

I still work for the *Post*, currently at work on a series of stories about former prison inmates. I no longer travel abroad at all.

Back in the swirl of American life, the months have rushed past us, the days falling into the past as if into the pages of a faded scrapbook, to be recalled in a different time. We go to the mall, to church, to the park, just another family lost among the many. I had imagined that in these most American of surroundings, with cinemas and shops and well-lit restaurants, the disturbing images from those days might recede, but this is not always so. Sometimes, late at night, it seems there is some unsettled disturbance within me. I roam the house for two hours, aimless, restless, and then sit on our front step and watch cars go by. The images can be so clear, so achingly clear, as if time has stopped and I can examine each moment as if it were a still frame. I see John Mungai in his three-piece suit, waiting for the remains of his daughter to be pulled from the wreckage of Ufundi House. I see the young dead girl in Sarajevo, once again pulled from the car, this time as if in slow motion, the sunlight on her bare skin. I see an overcast afternoon later in that city at the end of the war. I was with Alija Hodzic, the bus driver who had volunteered to run the morgue during the war because no one else would do it, because his Islamic faith told him that human beings should be buried with dignity. He ran the morgue amid worms and formaldehyde and snipers for four years, and the reward for his faith was to come to work one afternoon and see his dead son lying on the floor, waiting for a coffin of his own, killed by a blast of shrapnel. One overcast winter day he took me into the Lion Cemetery, just down the hill from the hospital. We wound through the graves and then he stopped by a wooden slat of a marker, kneeling down beside it, running his fingers over the letters. Then he wept openly, great chest-heaving sobs that racked his whole body. I'd never seen a grown man in that kind of emotional agony before, and as the cold wind blew hard across the open field, I fidgeted with my hands and looked at the ground.

I see these images, frozen in memory if not in time, and I think I have finally come to understand John Mungai and Alija

Hodzic. It wasn't just the pain of their loss that tormented them. It was that the love for their children was still in them, and it had nowhere to go.

THESE IMAGES COME less often with the passing of time, I find, and the depressions that fall over me are almost all of the twilight variety now, an ebbing tide of darkness that can fall along with the night from the sky on a summer evening, when the world seems stilled and far away. At the end of it all, I consider myself the luckiest man I know.

I sometimes sit in church, listening to Vita and the rest of the choir blow through "Just a Closer Walk With Thee" or "It Was a Great Thing," and in the voices and organ and percussion I seem to drift away, lost in something that I would describe as a state of grace.

And that is why, on this particular Sunday, I am thrust out of my reverie by the sound of my daughter coming out of the back door into our small backyard. Her mother is in the kitchen and has just turned on the light over the sink, the one in front of the window, a small torchlight in the darkening air. She is cooking, I see, attuned to the stove next to her.

I stand and pick up Chipo, then fling her playfully into the air, a daddy-daughter game, listening to her laughter spill over me like warm summer rain. I toss her up, up above the shadows of the trees, her tiny body framed against the darkening sky, an image etched on my mind's eye, and then she is falling, falling back into my arms, happy and safe and warm, giggling against my chest.

The porch light comes on. We turn, her arm thrown around my neck. Her mother is watching us from the kitchen door, smiling, a glass of wine in her hand, and suddenly the resigned sadness of that place in that time seems something that happened long ago, far away, like a fairy tale I once knew but can no longer recall.

Acknowledgments

IN THE SUMMER OF 2000, I had lunch with Tom Shroder, then the editor of the Sunday Style section of the *Washington Post*, at the Red Sage restaurant in downtown Washington. Tom was a friend from when we both worked at the *Miami Herald*.

We had not seen each other in many years. Tom politely asked what Zimbabwe had been like. He was rewarded with a rambling summary of Chipo's adoption that lasted for most of the entrée. I finished up by saying that I was considering writing a lengthy, complicated book about race, family, and American society.

"That's nice," Tom said, his shoulders almost visibly weighed down by the idea of such a heavy-themed tome. "Meanwhile," he said, "why don't you write a piece for the Style section, just about the adoption? With maybe a little family history tossed in?" By the time the waiter brought the check, I agreed to write that story for him. The resulting 4,500-word article appeared later that summer.

Two years have passed, and I am now sitting in the same chair in my dining room where I wrote that story, this time writing the final words to the book that grew out of that article. I tell that story to make it clear the debt of gratitude that I owe Tom, now the editor of the *Post*'s Sunday magazine, on framing this project.

Vita and I also wish to recognize the large number of people in Zimbabwe whose professionalism, dedication, and devotion have saved any number of young lives both in and outside the state-run orphanage system, and improved the lives of countless more. Their work, either for free or for a pittance of a salary, was never less than inspiring. In Chipo's case alone, the daisy chain of people who kept her alive in the weeks after her birth includes the man and woman identified only as Herbert and Constance, Stella Mesikano, Helen Tanyanyiwa, and Isidore Pazvakavambwa. Later, of course, Margaret Tsiga was resolute in doing her job in the face of bureaucratic intimidation. May peace bless all of your days.

There are many people to thank for their assistance and insight in the writing of this book, but there is only so much space. I ask understanding from those whom I omit.

My parents, Duane and Elizabeth Tucker, allowed me a room to sleep and a room to write in their home for three months, a concentrated bit of time and solitude that made the rest possible.

At the *Post*, many, many thanks to Jo-Ann Armao, the assistant managing editor for metropolitan news, who was patient and supportive of our situation even before I worked at the paper, and who has remained so since. I also would like to say thanks to Tom Wilkinson, Gabriel Escobar, Bob Barnes, and Jackie Jones for their enthusiastic support during the writing of this book.

At the *Detroit Free Press*, I owe a lifelong debt of gratitude to foreign editor Nancy Laughlin for sending me abroad in the first place. I would also like to pay a special note of tribute to the late Bob McGruder, the former executive editor of that paper. Bob's editorial integrity, professionalism, interest in foreign affairs, and just plain decency were inspiring to so many people, myself included, for so many years. He is greatly missed.

At Knight Ridder, thanks to Joyce Davis, Morris Thompson, John Walcott, Kathleen Carroll, and the late Gary Blonston for their help to my family during an extraordinarily difficult time.

I owe a special, personal note of thanks to my friends and colleagues Corinne Dufka, Elmore Leonard, Tommy Miller, Dean Murphy, and Ann Simmons for reasons they all know, or should.

I have had the great good fortune to have Wendy Weil as my agent, who has provided help, guidance, and friendship, all with a sense of humor, and Doug Pepper and Juleyka Lantigua as my editors at Crown, who have done so much to put this into print. I also owe thanks to Glenn Frankel, Tom Lansworth, Malcolm Linton, Patricia Wicks, and Vita for reading early manuscripts. Any failings, shortcomings, errors, or omissions are mine alone.

I owe more than I can say to Vita, the girl next door, my best friend and that gorgeous Motown kind of a woman who has brought so much affection and laughter into my life. As I hope the preceding pages have made clear, I cannot imagine myself without your love, for you are, and always have been, the very best part of me.

And lastly, Chipo, light of my life, I wrote this book as a love letter for you to always have, and I am sorry it is not any better than it is. It is my hope that on some rainy afternoon many years and decades into the future, long after your mother and I are gone, you might pull this book from your shelf, flip through the pages, and know one thing: We loved you so. *"E chiara nella sera/tu serai la luna che non c'é."*

—WASHINGTON, AUTUMN 2002

About the Author

Neely Tucker, a reporter for the *Washington Post*, was born in Lexington, Mississippi. He has reported from more than fifty countries or territories in Africa, Europe, the Mideast, and the nations that compose the former Soviet Union, frequently covering war and violent conflict. He, Vita, and Chipo live in Washington, D.C.

Visit the author's website at www.neelytucker.com.